The
Headteacher's
Survival Guide

The Headteacher's Survival Guide

Marilyn Nathan

KOGAN PAGE

London • Philadelphia

The Management and Leadership in Education Series

Series Editor: Howard Green

Competences for School Managers Derek Esp
Educational Values for School Leadership Sylvia West
Essential School Leadership Gary Holmes
The Experience of Headteacher Appraisal Maura Healy
School Review and Inspection David Woods
The New School Governing Body Ann Holt and Tom Hinds
Managing Teachers as Professionals in Schools Hugh Busher and Rene Saran
The Headteacher's Survival Guide Marilyn Nathan

First published in 1996

Kogan Page Limited
120 Pentonville Road
London N1 9JN

British Library Cataloguing in Publication Data

A CIP record for this book is available from the British Library.

ISBN 0 7494 1707 2

Typeset by Photoprint, Torquay, Devon.
Printed and bound in Great Britain by Biddles Ltd., Guildford and King's Lynn

Contents

Series Editor's Foreword

The government's educational reforms have created an unprecedented rate of change in schools. They have also raised fundamental questions about the purpose of education and the nature of school management and leadership. Similar changes are occurring worldwide.

In this context, there is an urgent need for all of us with an interest in education to step back and reflect on recent educational reforms, to reaffirm old truths and successful practice where appropriate, to sift out and implement the best of new ideas, modifying or abandoning those which are a distraction from the central purpose of schools, to ensure that an education of high quality is a guaranteed opportunity for *all* our children and young people.

This series aims to satisfy the demand for short, readable books designed for busy people and with a focus on single issues at the forefront of school management and leadership. Written by reflective practitioners who are either working in schools or directly with those who do, the series celebrates the ideals, skills and experience of professionals in education who want to see further improvements in our schools.

A dictionary definition of 'survival' is to come safely through an experience. It is vital that new headteachers come safely through the early weeks and months of the job because, as Marilyn Nathan points out, 'headteachers have the most important role in managing change'. A failing head will almost certainly be linked to a troubled school. On the other hand, a person who survives the first stage of headship can usually look forward to ongoing success and even enjoyment in the later stages!

Early anxieties are often caused by apparently trivial matters and, if significant mistakes are to be made, they usually relate to people. The thoughtless comment can so easily become a shot in the foot, like the new head, appointed after the re-advertisement of the post, who said at his first staff meeting, 'Well, I wasn't even shortlisted the first time round, so you've got nothing to fear from me!' Not only do heads need reasonable confidence in their own ability to do the job but they must also inspire confidence and trust in others without fear or favour. That is why this book is an important addition to the Management and Leadership in Education series.

First, it focuses on people not on systems or organisation. Hence there are chapters on the senior management team, delegation, motivation, staff appointments, performance and working with governors and support staff. It is refreshing to see the author grasping some nettles in the field of interpersonal relationships, such as managing conflict and handling difficult people.

Secondly, the book combines helpful theoretical insights with advice about practical 'nuts and bolts' issues. The day-to-day concerns of headship are given realistic treatment through a series of case studies, some requiring reflection and others action. In this way the author underlines the dual role of heads. They have a function as leaders, with the emphasis on mission, longer term planning and reflection and as managers, with the purpose of getting teams of people motivated to achieve particular tasks.

At the outset, Marilyn Nathan turns the spotlight on the necessity for thorough preparation, an analysis of the skills required to the job successfully and the importance of heads being aware of their own need for professional development. A very wide body of research evidence now points to the conclusion that organisations of all sorts (including schools), which have managed to sustain very high levels of overall performance, are 'learning organisations'. If schools are to fall into this category, heads must be leading learners and act as role models for their colleagues who are then more likely to take their own staff development seriously.

Finally, I should add a health warning. The unprepared head will need more than this book to survive the pressures of the job. A task as demanding as school leadership takes time, training and appropriate experience. However, it will act as a touchstone for some of the key issues faced by heads and it covers territory less well explored in many similar books. As a head with some experience, but trying to remain in the learning mode, this book provided me with a rich source of ideas and helpful advice.

Howard Green
Eggbuckland
November 1995

Chapter 1

Preparing for Headship

You have recently been appointed to a headship or you aspire to one. You have been told that 'high quality leadership is vital to success', so how do you ensure that you deliver this essential commodity and just how do you set about preparing yourself for headship? This chapter provides advice for those taking up senior positions in schools, especially new headteachers. In their survey of new heads, Weindling and Earley (1987) highlighted the fact that most new headteachers felt that they need proper preparation for the post and that they would have liked more induction. The survey also revealed that it was often very difficult for new headteachers to visit the school while their predecessor was still in post and all too visibly didn't want them around.

CASE STUDY 1.1. FOR ACTION

She kept me out of the school until September 1st. I was only able to visit it once after I was appointed before I actually took up the post, and then she wouldn't let me talk to anyone on my own. It was impossible to get a clear impression or gather the information that I needed. It made preparing for the job very difficult indeed. (New headteacher describing his treatment by his predecessor.)

For action:

What advice would you give this new headteacher and why?

The above is an extreme example and you may not find it as difficult to gain access or information, but for a variety of reasons you may not be able to visit as often as you might wish and any information provided may not be precisely what you are seeking. Whatever you do, however, try not to create an unpleasant atmosphere by imposing yourself on anyone who is reluctant to see you or give the impression that you are trying to take over before the present head has left. Even if you take a softly softly approach there is still a lot you can do to prepare yourself.

What follows is a programme for preparing for headship. Of the five elements only the first is specific to those who have been appointed and are waiting to take up the post. The others can be used as a general programme by which to prepare yourself and as an ongoing self development programme once you are in post:

- finding out about the school
- analysing your role and the task ahead of you
- identifying the skills needed
- analysing your own skills, personal qualities and expertise
- creating your own self development programme.

Finding out about the school

Analyse the documents

A school's documents and brochures could be very useful in helping you analyse the state of the school. You will probably have been sent some of these when you were a candidate for the post and they will have given you an initial impression of how things stood and helped you to decide whether or not you wanted to proceed with your application. Now as the head designate you can ask for a complete set of the school's most important documents and you will certainly want to see the school development plan, which is often not given to candidates as they are expected to offer their own vision of the school's future. You can use the documents both to get an impression of how the school operates and to assess how well the school presents itself through its documents and brochures.

Meet the attached adviser

If you are new to the area and are joining a local education authority (LEA) school, it might be possible to arrange a session with the school's attached or link adviser at the education office. This would inform you about the school's relationship with the LEA and about LEA priorities and facilities and its attitude to current issues. If a meeting is impossible before you take up the post, arrange one early in the first term and in the meantime make use of LEA policy documents on current issues as a means of informing yourself. If you are to be the head of a grant maintained (GM) school, find out what form of consultancy is used by the school – does it buy a package from the local or another LEA, use a consultancy service or attempt to struggle through relying on the expertise of the governors?

Meet the chair of governors
If the opportunity arises for a session with the chair of governors, seize it. S/he is likely to want to spend some time with you even if the present head is less than welcoming and s/he will have an agenda of issues. The sooner you familiarise yourself with these the better. If the current head is operating blocking tactics you may have to visit the chair of governors at his/her business premises.

Gather information from the existing head
The person best placed to help you gen up on your new role is obviously the existing headteacher. You can expect a minimum of one visit, but you may need a number of sessions together, or s/he may arrange for you to meet a number of key people such as the bursar. Obviously the existing head will have his/her own gloss on things, and may want to see his/her system continue, but s/he cannot actually legislate for the future and while in post is the person with the most detailed knowledge of the way things operate. As one new headteacher recently commented, 'One of my main problems is that too much of the information was only in the previous headteacher's head, no one else knew what was going on and she didn't record it, or she shredded everything when she left. There is nothing in the file.'

Find out about mentoring arrangements
Most LEAs now have some sort of mentoring scheme for new headteachers. It might be useful for you to have an initial meeting with your mentor before you take up your post.

Meet the personnel
Don't worry if you can't meet the personnel before you actually start in post – you will have plenty of time for that once you have started the job. Make sure, however, that you don't give the impression that you have kept away because you are not interested in your new colleagues; make it clear to them that you don't won't to impose and that you are allowing your predecessor the space to depart gracefully.

In these ways you can gather information about the school, begin to analyse its current state of development and do a lot of thinking and planning before you start.

What kind of things do you need to think about?

- What state are the budget and the buildings in?
- What do the job descriptions and any meetings you have had so far with the senior management team (SMT) indicate about the tasks they undertake and their contribution (separately or as a team) to the running of the school? How does this fit into your vision of things?
- What seems to be the most urgent problem to tackle on your arrival?
- To what extent are you going to have to educate the governors into taking a greater or different role in school affairs?
- Do you need to arrive with a preset agenda or can you afford to be a gradualist?
- What are you going to do in your first week/term?

Analysing your role and the task ahead of you

Analysing your role as a head or senior manager could be a valuable exercise for a number of reasons:

- If you are a candidate for headship you must expect to be able to answer questions on what the job is about, so you need to understand it.
- If you are newly appointed to a post it will enhance your understanding of what is required of you and help you to prepare.
- Identifying what the essential components of the job are will help you decide what you can delegate and what you must do yourself.

What does it mean to manage a school under the complexities of LMS in the 'post ERA' period? The Education Act of 1988 significantly changed the role of the headteacher in that it greatly increased the autonomy of a school. Heads changed from being predominantly the administrators of LEA policies and handling a very limited budget to being the managers of the organisation, with much greater decision and policy making powers and being in charge of a totally delegated budget. It makes very little difference whether you are the head of a GM or an LEA school in terms of having to manage the budget – it is the amount you receive that may vary. In a GM school the governors are the employers, but this makes less difference than you might expect because the position of the LEA has declined in relation to the school and it is now the governing body which is the headteacher's main working partner. As a result of the legislation the volume and importance of heads' and deputies' management tasks are greatly enhanced and it is essential to their own success and that of the school that they carry them out well.

What does managing a school actually mean? Probably the best place to start defining the head's task is by looking at a headteacher's job description. Although these are produced individually for each school, and reflect to some extent the preoccupations of a particular governing body, many of the same key functions will appear. Your job description could therefore read like this:

CASE STUDY 1.2. FOR ACTION

A headteacher's job description
Besthampton Education Authority
School: Bestwick Park High School
Job Title: Headteacher

Relationships
Responsible to:
The headteacher is accountable to the school's governing body and, through the Director of Education, to the Local Education Authority.

Responsible for:
Pupils, teaching and non-teaching staff of the school.

Important relationships:

- pupils
- parents
- members of the teaching and non-teaching staff
- the governing body
- the school representatives of the teaching unions.

Important external relationships:

- officials of the LEA
- the school's attached adviser
- other headteachers
- external agencies
- members of the community.

Main purpose of the job
To be responsible for the internal organisation, management and control of the school, to ensure that the school is managed effectively so that it contributes fully to each pupil's intellectual, moral, physical and personal development.

Main responsibilities of the job

1. Formulating, in concert with the governing body and the teaching staff, the overall aims and objectives of the school and policies for their implementation.
2. Determining and implementing a curriculum that is in accordance with the National Curriculum, the needs, experience, interests, aptitudes and stage of development of the pupils and the resources of the school.
3. Evaluating the standards of teaching and learning in the school and ensuring that proper standards of professional performance are maintained.
4. Determining and implementing a policy for the pupils' pastoral care, behaviour and discipline.
5. Participating in the selection and appointment of teaching and non-teaching staff.
6. Deploying and managing the teaching and non-teaching staff and allocating particular duties to them in accordance with their conditions of employment.
7. Ensuring that all the staff have access to advice and training opportunities appropriate to their needs. This responsibility includes supervision of the school's appraisal arrangements.
8. Allocating, controlling and accounting for all the financial and material resources of the school, including the site and premises, which are under the control of the headteacher.
9. Promoting effective relationships and liaison with all the relevant persons and bodies outside the school.
10. Keeping under review the work and organisation of the school.

Overriding requirements
A headteacher shall carry out his/her professional duties in accordance with

- The provisions of the Education Acts and any relevant orders or regulations

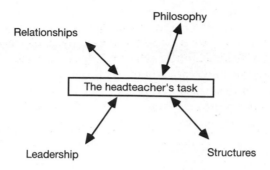

Figure 1.1 The management task

- the articles of government of the school
- any scheme of local management approved by the Secretary of State.

For action:

Compare this job description with the one you have been given.

What does this job description tell you about the nature of the management task of running a school?
The first thing it clarifies is the *purpose* of the job. It is your job to provide the pupils with the curriculum content and framework for learning which will give them the best opportunity for their overall development, and you will do this a lot better if you are an effective manager.

Using this job description it is possible to divide the list of duties and functions into four main areas.

Creating the philosophy
This aspect of the job is concerned with ideas. It is the manager's task to set the aims and objectives for the school and create its ethos or corporate identity. This is sometimes described as 'managing the mission'. There are two components to this task:

1. Creating the mission – by fashioning the goals
2. Moving the mission – this involves winning staff commitment to the aims and policies and actually making them happen and is closely related to the other three main management tasks.

7

Establishing the structures

It is the manager's task to formulate the policies and deploy the resources which will translate the aims and objectives into reality and provide the curriculum, the system of pastoral care and the administrative framework that the school needs in order to function. In practice much of this will be achieved by delegating responsibilities to deputies or task groups, but you remain responsible for the organisation and supervision and for ensuring that everything is actually done.

Managing and motivating the personnel

The job of running a school is all about people and relationships and most of this book is about managing people. You are responsible for the management and motivation of all members of the establishment – pupils, teaching staff, associate staff etc. You are responsible for the appointment, deployment and development of all members of staff. You liaise with parents, the LEA and its associated agencies, the community and industry, and you work in partnership with the school's governing body.

Providing leadership

It is the manager's job to provide leadership, direction and control. You are the director of the school, with a considerable amount of power and authority. How you choose to use that authority will depend on your management style, but you are expected to use it. You will also be expected to negotiate on behalf of the school or represent it in critical situations and, if you are the head, you will be the first line of contact for any outsider.

CASE STUDY 1.3. FOR ACTION

How does your job differ from the deputy's?

If you are being promoted from a post as deputy, take your current job description and compare it with your new one. Analyse whether your existing role includes tasks from each of the four areas identified in case study 1.2 or whether, as deputy, you have been given responsibility for one or more specific areas, eg providing the structures by managing the daily administration of the school. This analysis will help you decide how to tackle the job itself and focus your thoughts about your development needs. You may have had the opportunity to rotate posts as deputy but you may have spent several years concentrating on one area and need to firm up on areas of weakness.

Management and leadership

Of the four aspects of the manager's task described above by far the most complex and abstruse is providing leadership. Defining leadership and analysing its characteristics has long preoccupied writers on management and it would seem a sensible next step to review the debate and consider some of the main arguments and approaches. This section is intended to give a flavour of the debate rather than to be a comprehensive survey and its purpose is to encourage you to think about what leadership means and what kind of leadership you will want to offer.

Traits theory

One group of theorists concentrated on analysing leaders to see if it could identify distinct character traits. This resulted in labelling leaders as 'ambitious', 'charismatic' or 'decisive', but prolonged research failed to support the idea that there are sets of personality characteristics that recur in successful leaders. Setting historical personalities such as Joan of Arc or Alexander the Great, or industrial leaders who had 'made it to the top' against a grid, only served to highlight differences rather than similarities, and concentrating on personal characteristics of the leaders ignored the led and the situation.

Contingency theory

Contingency theory concentrated on the *situation*. The leader is not necessarily normally in charge, but when the crisis occurs s/he emerges to deal successfully with a difficult task or situation. Contingency theorists claim that it is the leader's capacity to understand the essential elements of a situation and provide the behaviour and paths out of that situation which distinguishes a good from a less good leader.

Another strand of this kind of approach is situation theory, where the situation has to fit the leader before s/he can work successfully. This approach covers only some aspects of leadership and is therefore regarded as unsatisfactory.

Styles theory

In styles theory the behaviour of managers is analysed in order to identify their predominant management style. Styles theorists claim that there are two sets of dominant behaviours in interpersonal relationships:

- Task oriented behaviour and maintenance
- People oriented behaviour.

A task oriented style of management is present when managers define and structure their own and co-workers' jobs towards achieving a goal. Direction, structuring ad defining ways and means are characteristics of this style and it is sometimes described as 'management by objectives'.

A people oriented approach involves the manager relying on trust, mutual support, avoidance of conflict and concern for the idea and feelings of others to achieve the organisation's goals.

Task oriented ◄──────► People oriented

Figure 1.2   The task—people axis

It was once thought that managers were either task or people oriented, but in fact most managers are not so clear-cut (though they usually have a bias one way or the other) and successful leaders are able to combine advanced behaviours in both styles.

Successful leadership is thus about managing both tasks *and* people. John Adair, working at Sandhurst Military Academy in the late 1960s, developed the following model with its interlocking circles, which he called 'Action Centred Leadership' (1973). This model became very popular with industry from the 1970 and 1980s onwards, particularly because it was adopted by the Industrial Society and became an integral part of its training programme. It does not, however, address the issue of whether leadership and management, which are often used interchangeably, are actually synonymous.

Is there a difference between management and leadership?
There are many definitions of what a manager does, eg Management is about getting things done with and through other people, or We see a manager as someone who:

- knows what he wants to happen and causes it to happen
- is responsible for the performance of the unit he/she is managing
- promotes effectiveness in work done and a search for continual improvement

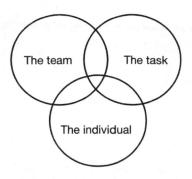

Figure 1.3 Action-centred leadership

- sets a climate or tone conducive to enabling people to give of their best. (Everard and Morris, 1985)

It is however much harder to find convincing explanations of the *differences* between management and leadership. Case study 1.4. which follows offers one view of how you can distinguish a leader from a manager:

CASE STUDY 1.4. FOR REFLECTION

Leader
- innovates
- develops
- challenges the status quo
- originates
- focuses on people
- takes the long-term view
- eyes the horizon
- inspires trust
- asks what and why
- is his/her own person
- does the right thing

Manager
- administers
- maintains
- accepts the status quo
- initiates
- focuses on systems
- takes the short-term view
- eyes the bottom line
- relies on control
- asks how and when
- is the classic good soldier
- does things right (Bennis, 1985)

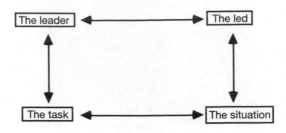

Figure 1.4   Components of leadership

This can be summarised as follows: 'The major difference between managing and leading is the leader's capacity to lift people up, to articulate purpose, to give reality to higher values, to resolve conflicting aims as a means to the fulfilment of the followers'. (Hunt, 1986).

Providing leadership is an essential part of the manager's task, and for the purposes of this book we intend to treat it as an aspect of management consisting of four components. Taking this view of leadership allows us to adopt the definition given by Hersey and Blanchard in 1982: 'Leadership is the process of influencing the activities of an individual or a group towards goal achievement in a given situation'.

Leadership styles
We must then address the issue of whether there is a particularly *effective* leadership style.

CASE STUDY 1.5. FOR REFLECTION

Jean is extremely direct in her dealings with people, the staff said approvingly. She is a good listener, gives you time to put your case and her decision is always fair. She is never influenced by preconceived ideas, isn't swayed by personalities and doesn't have favourites. It is her rule to think about something for a few days because she does not like being rushed and then to decide the issue on its merits, but then if she says 'No', there is no point arguing. You never have to worry that she will say something different to whoever next raises the same question, which is what they had found so irritating in the previous head. With Jean you always know precisely where you are. Most of the staff like this and think she is the best headteacher they have ever experienced; a minority, however, although they like her personally, feel that too much power is centred in the headteacher.

Nigel learnt his craft in an urban comprehensive when democratic management was in vogue and enjoys bringing teachers together in a collaborative management structure. He claims he manages through people, and from the front, back or sideways as appropriate. He would call himself a flexible manager. His staff, however, describe him as machiavellian, and he laughs with them and agrees. In Nigel's school to be called machiavellian is now almost a compliment. To gain support for his plans he relies heavily on his skill at interpersonal relationships. In his approach to change he does not give the impression of having a master plan, although some staff suspect that he might have one; rather that he is pragmatic and that he proceeds one step at a time, finding ways around obstacles. Instead of leading all the changes himself he often gets teachers who are trusted by colleagues to do so and they front the ideas or new initiatives. There is a lot of debate and discussion. Nigel always accepts the results philosophically, but usually the ideas are adopted and they seem to work. A great many of the staff like Nigel very much and enjoy working with him. They say it is never dull and that there are many opportunities for growth and development because he is so receptive to ideas and likes to encourage you to run with them. They also say he is supportive in the right ways if problems occur. A minority of staff, however, dislike the uncertainty.

The management styles, ie the working methods of these two teachers, could not be more different:

- Jean is direct and straightforward; Nigel is devious.
- It is clear throughout what attitude Jean is taking; it is unclear what Nigel really thinks or will do.
- Jean leads from the front; Nigel manoeuvres from the rear, often putting up other teachers to front his ideas.
- Nigel is more flexible than Jean. Once she has said 'No' there is no further debate.
- Jean is authoritarian; Nigel is collaborative.

Authoritarian managers are:
  High on
  + Telling

Democratic managers are:
  High on
  + Consulting

+ Instructing   + Involving
+ Deciding   + Accepting

Low on   Low on
- Consulting   - Directing
- Delegating   - Controlling
- Team building   - Setting structures

Nigel and Jean have very different management styles, but both are effective and successful managers. Jean is trusted and respected by her staff, who feel secure working for her. Nigel is popular with the majority of his staff, who enjoy the challenge of working with him.

The case study demonstrates that there is no one ideal management style or blueprint for good management. If it is to be effective your management style needs to be appropriate to the institution, its personnel and the given situation following the definition of leadership given on p. 12. Jean could face resentment in Nigel's school because his staff, who were used to and enjoyed his flexible approach, might consider her too authoritarian and feel that more of the staff should be involved in the decision making process. Similarly Nigel would face major problems in dealing with Jean's staff, who were used to her more direct approach. It is important that you know what the styles are, and are able to recognise your own dominant style, so that you can see how it is perceived by the people whom you manage and whether it is appropriate to the particular situation in which you find yourself. How to analyse your management skills is discussed next.

Figure 1.5 shows the range of possible styles and their associated characteristics.

A rule of thumb:

A new team, unused either to working with each other or with you, is likely to need a more structured approach than a well-established, confident team which knows you well.

Identifying the skills needed

If there is no ideal style, perhaps you should concentrate on firming up on the skills needed to be a successful headteacher. What are they, and

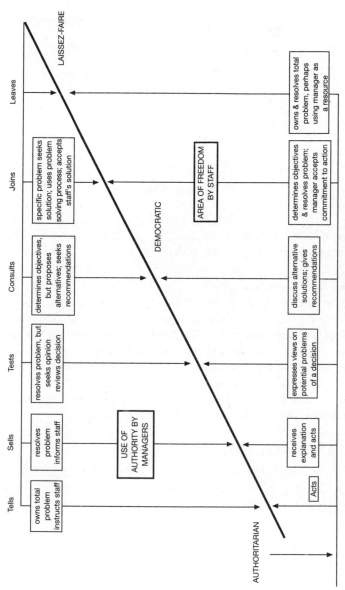

Figure 1.5 Continuum of leadership behaviour

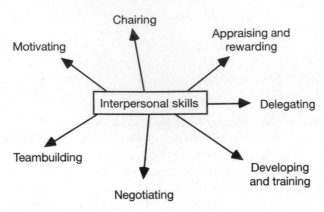

Figure 1.6 Interpersonal skills

can they be learnt? We can identify the skills used by successful managers under three headings.

Human – the interpersonal skills

If management is about getting things done with and through other people, highly developed interpersonal skills are essential. The most important interpersonal skills are listening, communicating and sensitivity to the needs of others and the organisation, and you will find that several chapters in this book emphasise that you need to make effective use of these skills.

Areas in which you will be expected to demonstrate strong interpersonal skills include those shown in Figure 1.6.

Technical – the knowledge and expertise skills

In educational management you need three kinds of technical skill:

1. Subject knowledge and expertise – you have to be a leading exponent of your own subject area in order to carry credibility in the staffroom.
2. Expertise in particular management areas, eg timetabling, finance or staff development. As a member of the SMT you may have been given responsibility for some specific management areas, eg resources or appraisal, but as headteacher you will have oversight of *all* areas. Your technical understanding must be good enough to

allow you to make informed judgements and decisions about what should be done.
3. You will need good knowledge of current educational issues, because the SMT will have to respond to consultative documents and take the planning and policy decisions about these issues as they arise.

Conceptual – the planning and visionary skills

This means the ability to assimilate and process information in order to reshape it into a new structure. It also means the ability to take an overview of a situation and form judgements about it. You will need good conceptual skills in order to:

- analyse and make judgements about a variety of data
- set aims and objectives
- formulate whole school policies
- articulate the school's corporate values and beliefs
- create an institutional development plan.

It is rare that any one manager is endowed with all those skills and abilities to an equal degree. But do not despair if you suspect that you lack some important skills, as there two ways in which you could improve matters.

First, you work in a team and not in isolation and, crucially, the SMT is composed of people with a variety of different abilities and strengths. The whole team does not need to be good timetablers or financial wizards. Indeed it would be a much greater problem for you if the team *was* too similar in its talents – resulting in tensions and conflicts over who does what. It is important to try to achieve a balance, to use the available talents most effectively and to think about the gaps whenever a vacancy in the team occurs.

Secondly, most of the skills you require in order to be an effective manager can be learnt. Peter White, when Associate Director of the Industrial Society, summed it up: 'The great majority of those involved in managing schools would greatly improve their performance if they received down to earth training in what a leader needs to be effective.' (White, 1984)

As the Industrial Society is a provider of training Peter White had a vested interest in promoting training, but we agree that it is quite possible for a manager to improve his or her performance in a particular area of weakness. Obviously some areas are easier to improve than others. Many new heads, for example, are inexperienced in financial management because the head in their previous school reserved this area for themselves. A lot of organizations run courses to help you improve your understanding of how to manage the budget and resources and practice will improve your performance and your confidence. Similarly, there are plenty of training courses available to help you improve the management areas which depend on interpersonal skills, eg team building. You do have to be realistic, however: you can certainly find a course which will help you improve how you produce your school development plan or your chairmanship skills, but creativity is much harder to develop.

Analysing your own skills, personal qualities and expertise

Your purpose in analysing your skills, personal qualities and expertise is to identify your strengths and the areas which need improvement. Further development should focus on the latter. You may want to do this exercise when you are applying for posts so that you can firm up in areas where you are weak, but you can usefully analyse and develop your skills while you are waiting to take up your new post. You will also want to do a needs analysis of what skills are essential to moving the school forward, although you will have to wait until after you have been in post a little while before analysing the SMT.

Psychometric testing

There are a range of tests available. Most were originally devised for industry, but can be used by educational managers. While none should be taken too seriously, they do deserve consideration. If used properly psychometric tests can help us work out our basic orientation or dominant approach to managing a group or situation. This could help you determine how appropriate your management style is and whether it needs any modification to be more effective. A common feature is use of a questionnaire (filled in by the individual, and sometimes by colleagues), the results of which are put on a grid and analysed to show your orientation.

Governing bodies now regularly use psychometric testing in headship assessment to complement formal interviewing. Whatever the criticisms, these tests provide an indication for the governors of your dominant style and the results can be set against their person specification for the post. Feedback on your results is usually provided by the consultancy firm used. If you have been through this process on the way to headship it could be useful to spend some time before taking up the post reflecting on the feedback and doing some relevant training. If you haven't done any of these tests you may be able to key into them through your contacts with industry.

Competency testing

A similar scheme, with perhaps a better reputation than psychometric testing, is a professional assessment unit of the kind that the National Education Assessment Centre (NEAC)/Secondary Heads' Assocation (SHA) have established. These have been developed to meet a specific gap in the management training market, ie to assess managers' competencies in a range of skills and to provide a development programme tailored to an individual's needs. Over the two or three days of testing detailed notes are made on your actions and interventions. You participate in a range of multi-purpose exercises, some on paper and some through simulations, and you are watched and recorded by observers, usually ex-headteachers. A headship testing package, usually one day, also exists and governing bodies are beginning to use it, especially in GM schools. This form of analysis is expensive if you have to fund it from your school's limited Inset budget, but it is very thorough, and the governors may find it a valuable way of supporting you as a new head. It is rarer for them to want to pay for it for deputies. Its main drawback is that it has set answers and you are graded according to whether you give those particular answers. But it does give you a good indication of how other professionals regard you, and you could use it as part of your appraisal process (see below).

Creating your own self development programme

Carrying out a needs appraisal

If you have followed the advice already given you will be well on the way to creating a personal development programme for yourself. By working out what the job was about and assessing your own skills and competencies against those needed to succeed you have carried out a needs appraisal, which should have given you a clear indication of where you would benefit from training and development.

Finding appropriate training

Training courses
Your needs appraisal may lead you to decide that initially you want a foundation course that focuses generally on the management issues in running a school rather than a more specialist course, or you may choose specialist training, eg in financial management or development planning.

You may find that the LEA provides an induction programme for new heads which you could use as the core of your personal programme, adding extra units as necessary. If it does not you will have to start from scratch using training courses, consultancy or industry as your key providers.

Learning from a manager

As a preparation for taking up my headship I did an industrial placement. The firm arranged three separate days for me during which I met managers at different levels in the company. I actually went to different plants, which also helped me appreciate differences in nuances in running the same kind of thing but with a different team. It was a fascinating experience and I learnt a great deal from it. It really made me think and focus on how I respond to my own responsibilities. I learnt from both the things that were similar and those that were very different in industry. Later I did some shadowing of their Managing Director which I also found very helpful. (New headteacher.)

Talking to managers in industry can be very worthwhile. Notice that this headteacher says that she learnt from both the similarities and differences, and found it valuable to see the same thing being done on more than one site. It is often very useful to meet a variety of managers, either in one firm or from several, especially when the sessions come fairly close together. Shadowing can also be beneficial.

Working with a mentor
Many LEAs provide their new headteachers with a mentor, a more experienced headteacher who acts as a guide and support for the less experienced colleague through the first year in post. Most new headteachers have found this form of support very useful. It provides them with someone to consult when faced with difficulties who can act

as a sounding board for ideas. It can also be therapeutic to have someone to talk to who is able to empathise with a problem.

Appraisal

Once you are in post, using appraisal to focus on strengths and weaknesses or specific skills could be the most effective way of analysing your development needs. Headteacher appraisal involves two appraisers, one of whom is another headteacher, the other an adviser or consultant. They will collect data from your colleagues, observe you in action and discuss the results with you. This is certainly the most cost effective method and could be very valuable. You may find that you want to link it to another method such as team analysis (see Chapter 2).

CASE STUDY 1.6. FOR ACTION

This exercise is probably most useful after you have been in post a term or two.

Choose a skill or competency, eg decisiveness. Mark yourself either on a bar chart or on a 1–5 scale. Choose five members of staff and get them to mark you in the same way. Compare the results to see if:

- you exhibit a consistent pattern
- you are perceived in the same way by all sections of staff
- you have flattered yourself.

Discuss the results and the development implications with your appraiser or mentor and, if necessary plan a training programme.

Chapter 2

Managing the Senior Management Team

The role of the Senior Management Team

The senior management team (SMT) is the executive group who give leadership to the school. They do the main planning, determine the policies and carry out the daily running of the school under the leadership and guidance of the headteacher. The SMT has evolved into its present pre-eminence since about the early 1970s with the development of large comprehensive schools in which the headteacher could no longer undertake personally all the tasks associated with managing the school: 'it is becoming increasingly impractical for any one person to encompass the diversity and work necessary to manage and organise a secondary school' (Torrington and Weightman, 1989).

'What has emerged markedly is the existence of a policy and management team, comprising deputy headteachers and occasionally other senior teachers, under the chairmanship of the headteacher' (Todd and Dennison, 1978). The SMT has thus become an important feature of educational management with a central role in running the school: 'Senior management's task is to review the effectiveness of the school in delivering programmes, to manage resource distribution and to propose and manage change' (Murgatroyd, 1986).

Although surveys of management in schools (eg Torrington and Weightman, 1989) agreed on the importance of the task to be carried out, they point to a clear discrepancy between how the team should function and what its members actually do, and they have been highly critical about 'the reality of school management'. The most frequent criticisms are:

- underutilization of team members – too much free time and not enough to do
- the work done by the senior teachers and deputies is not perceived as important by the staff
- the SMT is given trivial or administrative tasks which could be done by a clerical assistant
- they have no clear role
- many of their responsibilities are very nebulous eg 'liaison with . . .' or 'oversight of . . .' etc
- they fail to operate as a team.

The Secondary Heads' Association (SHA) survey of deputy heads (1989) reinforces this impression, as some deputies were carrying out as many as 50 or 60 miscellaneous tasks which included furniture moving and cleaning the graffiti off walls.

The deputies' acquisition of miscellaneous tasks seems to have happened for two reasons. One reason is historic, reflecting the way that the SMT has developed. As demands on the school have increased, new responsibilities have simply been added to the existing workload of the deputy, or a third or fourth deputy has been appointed to the SMT (occasionally in the wrong place) and this additional team member picks up a miscellaneous collection of jobs – normally the tasks no one else wants.

The other reason is more fundamental. The head decides what s/he delegates to the SMT, and in many cases the headteacher has retained the personal management of initiatives which could have been delegated to a deputy. This may reflect the head's lack of confidence in the abilities of his/her team members or a desire not to lose direct contact with staff. Sometimes it is simply the reluctance to share power. Whatever the reasons, the effect on the image of the SMT has been unfortunate, because in some schools it has led to the SMT being perceived as ineffectual and unnecessary, whose members do little and are being carried by other staff. 'Seldom did we find a situation in which the deputies had full jobs and never did we find a situation in which three deputies were actually needed' (Torrington and Weightman, 1989).

This survey slightly predates LMS, and things may have changed, nevertheless it is an utterly damning comment which obviously reflects adversely on the deputy heads and senior teachers described in the survey, because a job is what you make of it; but far more seriously it reflects on the headteacher as a team leader. It is essentially the role of the deputy head to undertake those tasks and responsibilities delegated to him/her by the head, and there are limits to how far a deputy can be expect to manage upwards. The head is the manager of the SMT and enough evidence has now emerged to suggest that some SMTs are being very poorly managed. 'When all decisions, procedures, communications and systems are focused on the head, serious weaknesses of management and organisation occur' (p. 143).

A good SMT can make all the difference to how well a school performs, but to be effective and to fulfil its functions it needs the right kind of leadership. Too many teams are poorly run, because the head keeps all the real power for him/herself, they lack any cohesion and do not function as a team at all or because the lack of proper leadership has resulted in the team losing its sense of purpose and direction. The team should be one of your most valuable assets, so try to make the best use of it that you can.

What then are the skills that you need and how should you set about creating a strong and effective senior management team?

For reflection:

Management skills/personal qualities needed to lead a team

- analytical ability – to identify team needs and characteristics. You could of course get a consultant to do this for you, or use Belbin's team roles analysis (see below)
- chairmanship skills – to co-ordinate activities, manage meetings, arbitrate, negotiate etc
- communication skills – the ability to share information clearly. Note that the team needs full information at all times.
- willingness to delegate power and demonstrate trust in others. This is linked to the ability to recognise and encourage talent or expertise in team members
- skill in developing or providing opportunities for the professional development of team members
- leadership skills – as head your task is to give a clear lead to the team and to be decisive when necessary.

Belbin's team roles analysis

In *Management Teams: Why They Succeed or Fail*, Belbin (1981) claims that one of the key determinants of a team's success is the nature of the interaction in terms of the qualities brought to carrying out a task. He argues that status, technical knowledge and experience are not necessarily the most significant determinants of an individual's contribution. In fact what he calls 'alpha teams' ie teams composed entirely of high achievers, may perform significantly less well than those made up according to his criteria for effective task achievement. Belbin identifies eight role types, which refer to the potential contribution of the individual in terms of behaviour or roles rather than knowledge or status. These are:

- **Chair:** controls and directs the team; is able to make best use of its diverse talents and balance contributions in order to secure the goals and objectives. *Characteristics:* stable and dominant.
- **Shaper:** pushes the team towards an action, sets objectives and looks for outcomes. *Characteristics:* dominant, extrovert, anxious.
- **Plant:** innovates, generates new ideas and approaches, problem solver. *Characteristics:* intelligent and introvert.
- **Resource investigator:** the team's contact with its environment, generates ideas and resources. *Characteristics:* intelligent, stable and introvert.
- **Monitor–evaluator:** analyses problems and evaluates contributions. *Characteristics:* stable and introvert.
- **Completer–finisher:** ensures attention to detail, maintains schedules. *Characteristics:* anxious and introvert.
- **Company worker:** capable of converting plans into action, working systematically and efficiently. *Characteristics:* stable and controlled.
- **Team worker:** supports and reinforces, improves communications, fosters team spirit. *Characteristics:* stable, extrovert and flexible.

Belbin's analysis is frequently used on management courses and is probably known to you. Briefly, each member of the team fills in an individual questionnaire which is then analysed to identify the dominant roles adopted by each member of the team. Members of the team then do the same exercise for each other as this will indicate perceptions. It is a useful management tool because it highlights whether a team has a complete range of roles or if there is an inbalance or overlap, eg if there are too many plant/ideas people or if an important role is missing entirely. In case study 2.1, which appears on p. 29 there are too many company workers and completer–finishers and not enough plants or shapers, so when a vacancy occurred in the management team the headteacher wanted to look for specific talents.

If you do use Belbin it is important to remember that people take on different roles in different teams or as the need arises, and that people rarely have only one dominant role.

Building the team

How teams develop will, by now, be well known to you and only the briefest resume is included here. The National Foundation for Education Research (NFER) survey of new heads, undertaken by Weindling and Earley (1987), has not dated significantly and informs the thinking in this chapter.

Organisational research has indicated that team development typically displays four stages: *Forming*; *Storming*; *Norming*; *Performing*.

Forming is the first stage, in which the team is put together. In order to achieve the best possible start industry has used a variety of aptitude and personality tests to select suitable team members so that they are compatible and effective. As a head you will inherit an existing team whose composition you may be able to alter over a period of time. This is not quite as bad as it sounds: the NFER survey (started in 1982) found that 51 per cent of the sample were able to appoint one new deputy within the two-year period. This is because a deputy often waits until a new head is in post, works through the first year to help the new head take over, and then retires.

Storming – a stage characterized by tensions and low morale as team members test each other out and jockey for position. The honeymoon period is over, but there has not been time to build up trust or confidence in you as leader, latent fears and anxieties come out into the open and co-operation and goodwill are at their lowest. You will eventually build a stronger team if the problems have been aired than if they remain submerged.

Norming – when the team begins to come together and to 'gel'. This is sometimes described as *welding* and it can be very rewarding – the members learn to work together and you test out and establish which are the most successful working procedures. It also means that you can delegate far more to the team than in the early stages. The NFER survey found that it took a year for most of their samples to begin to delegate much work. Earlier in the process they had been reluctant to trust deputies whose strengths and weaknesses were still unknown. Learning to know and to work with each other is an important stage in team building.

Performing – this is the target for the team's style of operating. The two most common cultures are *club culture*, in which the team revolves around its charismatic leader, and *task culture*, in which the team's commitment to the common task binds them together. Which you use will depend very much on your own leadership style. In both cultures this stage of team development is characterised by a high level of trust and support among team members, who are prepared to be open and honest with each other. The team is confident and able to build on the strengths of its members in order to achieve its objectives. Its self confidence makes it possible for it to be self critical and willing to accept outside advice when difficult issues arise.

The process described above clearly takes some time, though some teams come together more quickly than others. As head you are the team leader and your role in team building is crucial. How easy or difficult it will be will depend on how compatible you find your team and your own skills in welding incompatible or unwilling team members into a fully functioning unit. Although we cannot offer you a blueprint for team building, remember that skills can be learnt or improved and you should use what you feel are the most appropriate methods to weld together *your* particular team.

There can, however, be problems. The NFER survey made it clear that the heads in their sample rated coping with a weak member of the management team amongst the most serious of the difficulties they encountered in their first year. Some of the problems derive from the fact that the team was appointed by the previous incumbent and reflects his/her management style, which is often very different from that of the new head. If the deputies have been in post for a long time, and are not used to a participative management style, it can be very difficult and possibly inappropriate to try to get them to change their ways.

Most frequently encountered problems

- members who lack flexibility – sectionalism or can't adapt to new roles
- a deputy who has been promoted beyond his/her ability
- overlap of roles
- burn out

- historic appointments – eg the head of science is a senior teacher but does not take a senior management role
- personality clashes between members of the team
- loyalty
- jealousy – one of the deputies is a disappointed candidate for the headship.

The following quotation from the NFER survey encapsulates this situation: 'The senior management team is certainly not as I should want it. I would never have appointed the second and third deputies, as neither, I think, is really up to the job.'

What can you do about this? The most commonly applied strategies seem to be:

- redefine the responsibilities of the members of the team. Be careful if using this strategy as it can lead to more problems and there are examples of deputies taking out grievance procedures against a head who forced them to change duties against their will
- pressure – tough measures against individuals to force an incompatible member of the team either to co-operate or to opt for early retirement. This can be very divisive for a school – use with extreme care
- secondment – used particularly with jealous or incompatible deputies. Sending them on eg an MA course gets them out of your hair for at least a year and improves their promotion chances
- training – short courses to raise awareness. These are useful when the person lacks the right experience or technical knowledge but is developable
- consultancy – using advisers or industrial consultants as mediators and facilitators. Sometimes this involves residential team building sessions off-site.

There are no easy answers, but exploring ways in which you can get the best out of the team available and building up trust over a period of time is the method most likely to result in success.

For reflection:

1. 'I realised that you can't wait for people to leave, you have to work with what you've got'. (Headteacher in NFER survey.)
2. The manager selects a few members of his team . . . but tolerates the vulgarities of many others. One could almost say that picking one's own people is an abdication of management, a part of the art

of being able to organise and co-ordinate the contributions of different types of people, including those one does not get on with. This involves the manager adapting his style and approach to the various expectations and needs of others, rather than being able to work only with kindred spirits, hand picked for their compatibility. (Torrington and Weightman, 1985)

The extended case study which follows explores some of these issues more fully.

<hr>

CASE STUDY 2.1

<hr>

The SMT at Bestwick Park High School

Yvonne Perkins

Yvonne had been deputy head for five years, with responsibility for the daily administration of the school and for constructing the timetable. It had not been Mr Smythe's practice to take his deputies into his confidence or to consult them about decisions and Yvonne had not been expected to offer ideas, rather it was her task to ensure that things ran smoothly and she did this very well. Highly efficient and extremely conscientious, Yvonne performed meticulously every task that Mr Smythe asked of her. She enjoyed creating the appropriate procedures for each event or occasion with the minimum of fuss or paperwork. She was respected by the staff because of her competence and because she always treated them fairly. She had no favourites and could be relied upon to find a way to allow them to go on courses or to be helpful when they needed time off for personal reasons. Cheerful and unambitious, she was almost unflappable, even when faced with a major disaster such as the main boilers failing or a dropped chemical that put the entire science block out of action for a day. She was not greatly interested in educational theory and was largely unsympathetic to the innovations demanded by current educational legislation. She nevertheless felt it her duty to make innovations work, considering that if a job had to be done at all it should be done well. Yvonne held a central position in the life of the school and staff regularly dropped into her office for a chat or to consult her about a problem. She had no formal training as a counsellor, rarely going on courses herself, but she had a reputation amongst the staff as a sympathetic listener, who would respect a confidence and who could be relied upon to offer some useful advice.

Fred Brown

Fred had been deputy head in the school which had amalgamated with Bestwick Park to form the present High School. It would not be unfair to describe Fred as a martinet, whose autocratic regime was feared as much by the staff as by the pupils. He was in charge of the pastoral system and it was his custom to hold regular, short briefing sessions once a fortnight to instruct his team of year heads, otherwise he avoided meetings as he viewed them as a waste of time. The year heads tended not to tell Fred about problems unless absolutely necessary, as he was inclined to blame them for any incident and generally treated them as if they were naughty children. This resulted in Fred being largely unaware of what was happening in the school. His rigid approach originally meant that discipline was tight, but in recent years his very remoteness had resulted in a breakdown of uniformity, as the year heads tried to apply their own solutions to issues that arose; but, as they worked as individuals rather than as a team, their styles and standards varied. Under James Smythe Fred had had relatively little to do as Mr Smythe did not demand much of his deputies. Fred was determinedly ignorant of current educational trends, regarding most of the recent innovations as ruining a good system, and was utterly hostile to change. His general approach suited the ultra-conservative Mr Smythe, who regarded him as an excellent deputy. When James Smythe retired and Brenda Gatlin was appointed to the headship Fred had two or three years to serve before his own retirement.

Mike Wade

Under Mr Smythe Mike had been the senior teacher in charge of examinations and Inset arrangements. He had been in the school for a number of years and was in his early 30s. He was a bright, well-informed young man, who enjoyed a challenge and had plenty of ideas to offer, especially about developing Inset, which interested him enormously. He had received very little encouragement from Mr Smythe, who regarded Inset as a nuisance and was determined its growth should not lead to the introduction of a staff development policy, which he equated with appraisal – an initiative to which he was particularly hostile. Mike tended to be the member of the SMT with responsibility for introducing those new initiatives which the head could not avoid altogether. Mr Smythe was very wary of Mike, however, and reluctant to give him a free hand. Mike's facility for thinking on his feet, and his enthusiasm for new ideas, could sometimes make other staff feel threatened. He was also rather shy, which made him appear aloof. Mike had come to feel both frustrated and taken for granted. He felt the outsider on the management team, yet his position as a senior teacher isolated him from the majority of the staff. When James Smythe's retirement was announced Mike was seriously considering applying for posts elsewhere. When Mrs Gatlin was appointed Mike thought that he would wait and see which way the wind blew.

Sarah Holly

Sarah had been in post as senior teacher in charge of the sixth form for two years and was in her mid-30s. She enjoyed her elevated status and ruled the sixth form with a firm hand. She was confident and efficient, regarding herself as fully on top of a difficult job, but she worked within closely defined boundaries, interpreting her responsibilities narrowly. She rarely took a whole school perspective, supporting or opposing an initiative dependent upon how it would affect the sixth form or her own position. She was a night rather than a morning person, willing to stay after school ended for sixth form surgery, but never available before the register bell in the morning. This created problems for those people who needed to consult her, because she regarded herself as off duty during breaks and unavailable at those times. Pupils tended to leave immediately school ended as they had after-school jobs, which meant they rarely saw Sarah. In fact they did not often consult her about their problems because they felt that she was insensitive and her manner tended to be curt and unsympathetic. They worried too about the UCAS references that she wrote for them, fearing that she would not do them justice – but here they did her an injustice. She cared about her year group, and when a pupil had a problem, worked very hard to help, badgering the relevant authority until something was done. When faced with a real difficulty, she still tended to consult Mike Wade, as he had been head of sixth before her and had guided her through her first year. People unkindly, but not altogether unfairly, said that Mike had all Sarah's ideas for her. Methodical and clear thinking, Sarah was not a fast worker, but once she was on task she was extremely thorough. Her determination to get her own way and total conviction that she was always in the right, however, was sometimes expressed in the most aggressive manner, which could make her an unpleasant person to cross, as some staff soon learnt to their cost. But as long as you played to her rules she was a friendly and helpful colleague.

Lawrence Payne

Laurie had been appointed to the SMT some three years previously as a new senior teacher to introduce computerisation and manage some of the other innovations demanded of the team. He was highly qualified and it was said that he had interviewed outstandingly well, so many staff were hopeful that Laurie would provide the element of dynamism so conspicuously lacking in the SMT. Once Laurie arrived, however, these expectations were quickly dashed. Ponderous and slow moving, Laurie gave the impression that he found life and its attendant tasks a burden. He seemed preoccupied with his Mathematics teaching, grumbling that his change of schools had meant changing syllabuses. Certainly his teaching commitment seemed to leave him little time for his senior management responsibilities. He was a notoriously slow worker who was never on top of things and who found it difficult to meet deadlines. At senior management meetings he offered no constructive suggestions – indeed he seemed to have lost all spark. He looked to Mr Smythe to tell him what policy he ought to adopt in any situation, which suited James Smythe, but greatly disappointed many staff who had hoped for more from this appointment. After a few months they wrote Laurie off as a nice, conscientious chap, but hardly a whiz-kid, and they wished that, if he wasn't going to improve things at Bestwick Park, he wouldn't keep telling them how much better things were done at his last school. What puzzled and rather irritated Yvonne Perkins was Laurie's general attitude, which seemed to imply criticism of Bestwick Park's practices and some resentment of the weight of the tasks that he was being asked to undertake. After three years Laurie had finally stopped talking about his previous school and had integrated well into the staff, who liked him but laughed gently at his ponderous ways. Slowly but surely the Bestwick Park data was getting on to the computer, but it was clear that, although a loyal subordinate, Laurie lacked all leadership qualities.

This SMT had served James Smythe's purposes well. It was sound, reasonably effective and loyal, and he would not have wanted a more innovative team. For Brenda Gatlin, who wanted senior managers who could give leadership to the school in a period of change, this team presented a problem. She could not however dispense with it and start afresh with people of her own choosing, and she had to face the fact that the majority of the team could be with her for some years. She therefore needed to make the existing team perform as effectively as possible, so she analysed individual strengths and weaknesses to see how far they complemented each other and to work out how to make the best use of the talent available.

Analysing the team

In Yvonne Perkins, Mrs Gatlin had a deputy who was an experienced and capable administrator, liked and respected by the staff. Her ability to construct effective procedures and her desire that things should work well was an asset for the team. Unlike Mr Smythe, Brenda Gatlin expected to consult her deputies regularly. Yvonne was well informed about what was going on in the school; she knew what would work, how to make it work, what would be popular or unpopular with staff, and her advice to staff was always sensible, she could be a useful sounding board. Using Yvonne in this way could have the knock-on effect of raising her awareness of current issues and giving her a better understanding of why changes were being made, making her more sympathetic to the changes themselves. Brenda Gatlin was likely to be out of school much more frequently than Mr Smythe had been, both because her perception of her role was very different from his, and because the number of headteachers' meetings had increased. Mrs Perkins was very well fitted to deputise for the head on these occasions, and enhancing her role in this way could improve her job satisfaction. Mrs Gatlin could also give some thought to how she could build on Yvonne's counselling work with staff.

Fred Brown constituted a major problem for the new head, because he was totally hostile to everything that she stood for and was not developable. It was a short-term problem, however, because in two or three years he would retire. When Brenda began to analyse the problem she realised that there were two interrelated issues: Fred's position in the team and the pastoral system.

A number of options were open to her:

- redefine Fred's role – put someone else in charge of the pastoral system and find Fred other duties
- force Fred to change the system

- pressurise Fred into taking early retirement (forcing him to change the system could have this effect)
- sit it out.

Taking Fred off the pastoral system could allow her to make the changes that she wants, but could humiliate Fred and increase his hostility to her, but she might need to use this option if changing the pastoral system was her most urgent priority. Finding Fred other duties could itself constitute a problem, and funding such a change could be expensive.

Forcing Fred to introduce changes that he detests and does not understand is unlikely to work. Even if he does not deliberately sabotage things, he lacks the skills needed to be a successful manager of change. Pressurizing him into early retirement requires both toughness and perseverance. It would entail making constant demands upon Fred so that he felt so threatened by and uncomfortable in the situation that he chooses to go. There is no certainty that this strategy will work and it could have adverse effects, because treating Fred harshly will win him sympathy from other staff and could affect their attitude to Brenda. Others may decide that they do not wish to work for this kind of headteacher.

Sitting it out initially seems the weakest solution, and would be if it meant that she ignored the problem or pretended that it was not there. She would certainly have to discuss the situation with Fred, because the timing of his departure was crucial to her development planning. Her terms should be that she would not interfere with him provided that he went sooner rather than later. It would take some skill in negotiation, as most likely Fred would interpret it as weakness, especially because he was dealing with a woman headteacher. This option was only viable if she put reforming the pastoral system into year three of her five year development plan and published it so that the staff knew that changes were in the pipeline.

The real issue was thus how long could she afford to wait?

Michael Wade is potentially an extremely valuable member of the team and is certainly the most talented. He is a good teacher, well versed in current educational theory and capable of carrying through the development work that Mrs Gatlin believes is essential for the school if it is to hold its own against competition. Undervalued by Mr Smythe, Mike is considering leaving and clearly wants and deserves promotion. If she is to keep Mike, Brenda must address this situation, and should have a job appraisal review with him. She has a third deputyship in her gift, and although she may not be able to afford three deputies in the long term it could ease the situation until Fred retires. Promoting Mike would give him the status to lead the developments that she wants and could benefit them both. She may need to support him through some management training, especially in interpersonal skills, and help him overcome his shyness. She may also need to help him cope with the inevitable staff jealousies arising from internal promotion.

What do you do about a dud appointment? The good interviewee is not always the best choice when it comes to doing the job and Lawrence Payne constitutes a real problem for Brenda. He is a conscientious and methodical worker who will earnestly undertake anything he is given, and he does have computer skills. Mr Smythe invested in a third senior teacher rather than promote Mike to the post of third deputy largely because of the lack of computer skills in the existing team. Now Brenda must get value for money from Laurie. There is no point in putting him in charge of development work which needs leadership skills which he cannot offer; she has to concentrate on using and developing his strengths. Completing computerisation is clearly the first task. Because of Mr Smythe's lack of interest the school is backward in this respect. It could be a sensible move to have Laurie work closely with Yvonne Perkins. It would give him training in working on options, timetabling and daily administration, and give her much needed backup in a colleague with computer skills. Yvonne is a creative administrator, so she could set the parameters, while he could create and run the programmes and do much of the routine work for her. This would free her up to take on other tasks as they arose. One of the advantages of this strategy is that Yvonne is extremely efficient. She will set the deadlines and expect Laurie to meet them. She is a good manager of people – kind, but never soft . Laurie is less likely to become resentful of the pressure to increase his productivity if he works with Yvonne than if he has to work with any other member of the SMT. He can also contribute to financial planning, working the budget programme for Brenda and managing the bursar. Adopting this strategy could remove a time-consuming task from Brenda's workload.

Laurie is ripe for a job appraisal review delivered in the context of the changing demands of school management. The issues of the volume of work tackled and time management would have to be addressed and this would need sensitive handling, but she could offer him a time management course and the changes to his job could be put to Laurie as a way of raising his status.

Sarah Holly would have been surprised to learn that Brenda considered her to be her most difficult problem. Sarah's inflexibility and her narrow approach, combined with her outbursts of aggressive behaviour when things did not go as she wished, did not accord at all with Mrs Gatlin's own management style, and she foresaw clashes ahead. Brenda wanted a head of sixth who could take a whole school view and not only think about the interests of one section – her own. She also disapproved of a member of the SMT who was not available when the pupils needed her. Sarah would have to learn who was boss, and that Mrs Gatlin would be setting the terms of reference.

What also worried the head was the likelihood of a sixth form curriculum review and restructure in the near future. Mrs Gatlin suspected that Sarah would not be able to provide the kind of creative leadership which the development programme would need. Training could raise Sarah's awareness of the issues, but it was likely that the real planning would have to be done by a team which included Mike and some of the most promising sixth form tutors. If Mike was to sustain the brunt of the work, there was all the more reason to give him the status to put Sarah down when she became difficult. If the preliminary planning was done by a task group led by Mike, then Sarah should be able to cope, because her 'completer–finisher' skills should enable her to flesh out the proposals and implement them.

We have considered how Brenda Gatlin could develop the individuals in her team. The next step is to think about how she could weld her team together. At Bestwick Park the team know each other better than they know the new headteacher, so Mrs Gatlin needs to think of strategies to bind the team to her.

Some ideas for welding the team

Review how regularly and in what ways the team meets
A briefing/information sharing session every morning before school could be very useful. Superficially it keeps the team members informed of what is going on in the school and helps them understand how other members of the team spend their time, but its real value is that it creates for the head a short working session with her team every day. If this isn't possible she should think about other ways to bring the team together on a regular basis.

Make the meetings more participative
Under Mr Smythe senior management meetings had almost been briefing sessions, monologues by the head. Mrs Gatlin could use the agenda to ensure that each member contributes, either through a review of the week or by introducing items for which they are responsible. More on senior management meetings can be found in Chapter 7.

Involve the SMT in decision making
Mrs Gatlin is planning to share more of the planning and policy making with the team. This could help her weld them together as she shares her ideas and plans with them, asks them for their ideas and involves them in the decision making.

Have regular working sessions with individuals
Mrs Gatlin can do this either through dedicated time each week or by working on a particular task. This regular contact will help the new head get to know the team members and begin to build up a relationship with each of them. It is important however to beware developing a closer relationship with some members of the team than others as this leads to jealousies or friction, so a strategy could be to pair the team for some tasks so that they work in pairs with each other as well as with the head.

Avoid public disagreements
If Mrs Gatlin wants to build loyalty she must beware of criticising any member of the SMT in front of the others or, even worse, behind their backs to other members of the team. Public disagreements could affect both the morale and the image of the SMT and disaffected team members could retaliate by airing their disagreements with the head – she will not want this situation to develop.

Confront the problems
Working round a weak, disaffected or difficult member of the team can create its own problems. If, for example, Sarah Holly persists in taking a sectional view, and becomes aggressive or unco-operative if things don't go her way, Mrs Gatlin is going to have to deal with Sarah, and demonstrate to the team who is boss, otherwise Sarah will impose her views on the team and prevent progress.

Avoid criticism of the previous regime
If the new head is too critical of her predecessor's methods and practices she will find it harder to win the team's loyalty. These people were the old head's team and criticisms of the previous regime will implicitly be criticising the team who implemented his policies. She has the freedom to change things, but it would be wise to talk in terms of the needs of the future rather than the deficiencies of the past.

Review the accommodation
Mrs Gatlin should have a look at whereabouts in the school the various members of the team are located and think about what effect this has on how they function as a team. Deputies are often in charge of particular buildings, which helps maintain discipline and protect property but, unless regular meetings are built into the week, physical separation of this kind can lead to isolation of a member of the team or to difficulties in creating an effective team.

Programme a residential weekend for the SMT
A weekend away together could be beneficial for the SMT. It can speed up the process of team building because team members spend a lot of time together working on a task. Mrs Gatlin will however need to think carefully about when this would be of most use to her. Too soon and it may not achieve much, indeed it might heighten the storming stage if too much time together brings latent conflict out into the open. It would probably be most useful when the team has begun to accept that the new regime means different working methods or when there is a major task to tackle.

Make the time to take an interest in the team
Taking an interest in the team means more than just providing them with opportunities for professional development. It means remembering their birthdays and asking about their health or their families'. Listening to and remembering what they tell you indicates whether your interest is genuine or not. Occasional social events such as inviting the team to dinner at your house or a local restaurant can also pay dividends.

Make the team feel valued
Providing encouragement and tactful support when a team member experiences difficulties in leading changes that test his/her management

skills to the limit, giving praise for a job carried out well and remembering to say thank you for a task which has involved someone in a lot of work will help a new head build up loyalty, because above everything else if you want to create an effective management team it is essential to make the individual members, and the team as a whole, feel valued. Remember that praise must be specific and sincere if it is to work.

How do you know when you have arrived?

The following checklist of characteristics of a good team is reproduced from *Middle Management in Schools: A Survival Guide* (Nathan, 1989), because it applies as much to a school's SMT as to the department or tasks groups for which it was originally devised.

An effective team

Shares clear objectives and agreed goals

- It agrees on what the team is trying to do and its priorities for action.
- It agrees on what differences are tolerable within the team.
- It clarifies the roles of team members.
- It discusses values and reaches a general consensus on the underlying philosophy of the team.

Has clear procedures

- for holding meetings
- for making decisions
- for delegating responsibility.

Reviews its procedures regularly

- It reassesses its objectives.
- It evaluates the processes that the team is using.
- It does not spend too much time dissecting the past.

Has leadership appropriate to its membership

- The leader is visible and accessible.
- The leader utilises the strengths of all the team members.
- The leader sets the mission – models the philosophy of the team.

Has open lines of communication

- Team members talk to each other about issues and not just to the team leader.
- It recognizes each person's contribution.
- It gives positive and negative feedback.
- People are openminded to other people's arguments.
- It welcomes ideas and advice from outside.
- Members are skilled in sending and receiving messages in face to face communication.

Has a climate of support and trust

- People give and ask for support.
- Team members spend enough time together to function effectively.
- Team members' strengths are identified and built on.
- There is respect for other people's views.
- The team relates positively to other teams and groups.

Recognizes that conflict is inevitable and can be constructive

- Issues are dealt with immediately and openly.
- Members are assertive but not aggressive.
- Feelings are recognized and dealt with.
- Members are encouraged to contribute ideas.
- Conflicting viewpoints are seen as normal and dealt with constructively.

Is concerned with the personal and career development of its members

- Regular reviews are carried out with each team member.
- The leader looks for opportunities to develop each member.
- Members look for opportunities to develop each other.
- Members look for opportunities to develop their team leader.

If you want a shorter list, then there are two tests you could apply:

- The volume and quantity of work being done by the team will indicate how well it is functioning.
- How the team is perceived by the staff – the cherry on top of the cake attracts attention and there is always some mole who will be prepared to give you a progress report. It is safer to take soundings from more than one source.

CASE STUDY 2.2 FOR ACTION

Integrating a new deputy into the team

Making the choice

When Fred Brown retired Brenda Gatlin, the headteacher at Bestwick Park High School, appointed a new deputy to the SMT. She wanted someone who would give strong leadership, who was capable of giving the school's pastoral system a complete overhaul. She also wanted to strengthen her own management team. She felt that she had several plodders, who needed strategies worked out for them, and that this was occupying too much time. Now that she had the opportunity to make an appointment of her own she wanted a high flier who would add both drive and intellectual rigour to the team. Thus ability and potential were more important to her in making her selection than pastoral experience.

From a good field of applicants the selection committee chose Derek Farr, a young man in his mid-30s who had been head of science in his previous school. His subject qualifications were good – he had a doctorate in physics from a leading university. His previous head-teacher spoke highly of his innovative work as head of science and Mrs Gatlin liked his enthusiasm, the way he talked about the projects he had run for his pupils and she respected his desire to widen his experience through managing a school's system of pastoral care. She did not expect him to be an expert in pastoral matters, but she hoped he was a fast learner and a creative thinker who would have little difficulty in transferring his skills to a different sphere of management and a different school.

How to manage the induction

Over the past two years Brenda had spent a lot of time building her management team, and she appreciated that introducing a new member to an established team would have its difficulties. She was particularly concerned that the team members should not regard the new deputy as having a special relationship with her, as this could affect team spirit, yet she needed to provide induction for Derek through his first couple of terms.

Providing a mentor

Her solution was to make Mike Wade, who had recently been promoted to the vacant third deputyship, Derek's mentor. This would provide Derek with the guidance that he was likely to need without making him too dependent upon the head. Mike's general responsibility was to oversee staff and curriculum development in the school, and this could prove helpful for Derek who was to be the leader of a major development. Mike was also near in age to Derek and his own recent promotion was likely to make him sympathetic to Derek if difficulties occurred, and there could be advantages for Mike in giving him someone of ability to work with, as hitherto Mike had done almost all the creative planning for the management team. The head realised, however, that this move could create division in the team if, through working so closely together, Derek and Mike became isolated from the others. She would have to make sure that there was enough group activity or opportunity for change of partners to prevent this from happening, and she made it clear to the existing team what Mike's role was to be and that it fitted in with his responsibility for the induction of other senior staff she appointed.

The new deputy experiences difficulties

What she hadn't anticipated was that Derek would find the change of school and role very difficult to manage. He seemed much more hesitant than she had expected and gave her and others the impression that he was out of his depth. 'He looks as if he wants to retreat into a corner and have a quiet weep', the head said to Mike during a review of his work with Derek. 'He was much more assertive at interview. Could I have mistaken his character and ability so completely?'

Analyzing the problem

Mike, who was taking the brunt of supporting Derek and realizing that a great deal of support was needed, reflected on the problem. Derek was clearly finding the change of school and all the new demands very difficult to manage. Why was that? What could be done about it? Mike decided that much of the problem was probably to do with confidence. As head of Science Derek had been an expert in his field, totally on top of the technical aspect of his job. Here in a new school, where he had to prove himself, he was the least knowledgeable and experienced member of the pastoral team. At the same time he had been presented with a highly complex and extremely difficult management problem.

He had to carry out a complete overhaul and restructuring of the pastoral system with a team who were not yet welded together and had not accepted him as a leader. The size and complexity of the problem was clearly bothering the new deputy. Talking to Derek made it clear to Mike, who liked Derek, that the new deputy simply did not know where to start or what his priorities should be and was anxious not to make mistakes which could be damaging for him. Mrs Gatlin, who had waited patiently for Fred Brown to retire, was impatient for Derek to deliver results. He did not want to disappoint her but, because he did not know her very well, he was not sure what she wanted and her obvious irritation when he appeared hesitant was not helping. She was beginning to feel that in Derek she had another senior manager who wanted to be told what to do and, as this was the last thing she wanted, she kept telling him it was up to him. It was therefore becoming increasingly difficult for him to discuss things with her at all.

Managing upwards – dealing with the headteacher

Mike decided to tackle Brenda first, because he felt that the head's failure to establish a good working relationship with her new deputy was a major part of the problem. 'I think unintentionally you have created part of the problem yourself,' he said to Brenda, as tactfully as one can tell the headteacher that she is partly to blame.

Your desire to give him the space to be creative was good in itself, and something that later on he is likely to come to value, but perhaps it was too soon. He does not know you or the school well enough to be sure what is likely to be acceptable and he does need to know what is wanted, particularly when the proposed changes are extremely sensitive and will affect everyone in the school. He is entitled to some guidance, and it is hardly his fault that some of the others lean on you too much. Making me his mentor has a lot of advantages, and I am enjoying it. I like Derek very much and think he has a lot of potential, but you need to build up a relationship with him yourself. I also think he would appreciate the opportunity to acquire some of the technical expertise he is so conscious that he lacks. Can't we find him a 'Principles of Pastoral Care' course?

Managing sideways – reassuring Derek

Mike took a different approach with Derek, for whom he had a lot of sympathy.

All this worrying is getting you nowhere. What you need to do is use some basic management techniques to help you stand back from the problem and get it into perspective. Doing an analysis of the issues will help you distinguish the wood from the trees and decide what your priorities are. No one really expects you to solve it all in one fell swoop. What you have to do is decide what the main issues are and in what order you want to tackle them, then the problem won't look anything like so bad. Working on it together will help and creating a programme will itself show people that you have the matter in hand. They would prefer a realistic staged approach to change than an ill-thought-out rush.

After a few working sessions it became obvious that working together and using the problem solving approach had paid off. Derek tackled the pastoral system from first principles, working back from desired outcomes to possible routes to achieve them, and produced a well drafted paper suggesting a possible new structure together with a programme for implementation. This very much pleased the head, who had taken on board a lot of the criticism that Mike had levelled at her and now realised that she had been unrealistic in her expectations of Derek. She had wanted him to run before he could walk. She now understood that there had to be a learning period before he became a fully integrated member of the team and an effective senior manager. Derek thus found her more amenable, willing to help him and generally easier to talk to, and his own growing confidence in turn helped him in giving leadership to the year heads and to begin to enjoy the challenge of getting fractious and sometimes unruly horses to water. The head thought the more of Mike for being straight with her and wanted to reassure him that he had not offended her, so she sent for him and thanked him for his advice and for the time he had spent helping Derek. 'Now I know that you can manage upwards and sideways as well as leading the more conventional teams,' she said.

For action:

What issues in terms of team management and development are raised by this case study?
What had gone wrong?
What techniques had Mike applied in dealing with the problem?
What advice would you give the headteacher and why?
Devise an induction programme for a new deputy joining an established team.

Chapter 3
Delegation

Mary had always been a most conscientious deputy, who willingly undertook any task given to her by the headteacher, and generally handled it most effectively. Her relationships with staff had always been good, as she treated them fairly and they respected her competence. Now she seemed to snap at staff a lot and was often irritable. Work seemed to be taking her longer, and she complained about deadlines, which had never worried her in the past. Mistakes began to occur quite frequently in the arrangements that she made for daily cover and room changes, and when staff came to her to tell her of the error she was either very short with them or insistent that it hadn't been her fault.

This had been going on for some months when George, the headteacher, observed a particularly acrimonious incident. Electricians were in school, necessitating some room changes. Two members of staff were mistakenly allocated the same room, but when they went to report the mix-up, they were harangued by Mary for interrupting her when she was so busy, with the result that, when she failed to remedy the situation, they began to shout at each other. 'This can't go on,' thought George, 'I shall have to have a word with her. Her mistakes and her bad temper are beginning to have an adverse effect on other people.' But when he tried to introduce the subject she became very tense and seemed reluctant to admit that there was a problem. She kept saying that if there was nothing really important to discuss she should get back to work as there was so much to do. George probed as gently as he could. 'Was it the menopause causing the trouble or were there some home difficulties that he did not know about? She never used to be like this. I don't want to intrude, just to help if I can.' Tact had never been George's strong point, and it was the reference to the menopause that finally pierced Mary's front that nothing was wrong. She was utterly incensed.

It's just like a man to hit on the menopause as the reason why things are going wrong. If you really want to know what's wrong, I'll tell you. It's not my fault. Just because I was a willing and efficient worker, you loaded me with every new job that arrived on your desk. You don't think about what I'm doing already, or who might be appropriate to do the job. Oh, no! You just think, 'I'll give it to Mary, she won't grumble like John does.' And you are quite right. I wouldn't dream of refusing to do anything you ask me. My job description says, 'Assist the headteacher in any way required' and I've done my level best. It isn't that the jobs are so difficult in themselves. With time to think them through I could do each of them well, but I just don't have the time these days to concentrate on running the school as I used to. I'm making mistakes carrying out the basic tasks that I have always done well in the past because I'm trying to do all this extra work. It's not surprising that I make a few mistakes these days, it's more surprising that I get the work done at all.

For action:

What issues are raised by the case study?
What mistakes had George made in dealing with his deputy?
What hadn't he understood about delegation?
Why might he benefit from Equal Opportunities Inset?
What advice would you give George and why?

Mary's problem is that she has been given more work than she can cope with effectively, and this is having an adverse effect on her perform- ance and upon her relationships with other staff. It often occurs in schools that new tasks are simply added on to a deputy's workload as an additional responsibility, rather than the job description being reviewed and the tasks distributed fairly. George's method of delega- tion is to offload anything as it arrives on to his reliable and hitherto uncomplaining deputy. What is needed here is that some of Mary's current functions should be delegated to other people.

What is delegation?

The *Concise Oxford Dictionary* defines delegation as 'entrusting authority to a deputy', a definition with which Mary would totally agree. For you as a head or a school manager, in practice it means handing over tasks for which you carry ultimate responsibility to another teacher with that teacher's agreement.

The main reason for delegation is that the job of running a school is too big for any one person to manage alone. However many hours you work you still cannot do it all yourself. There are too many tasks and too many people to deal with, so the workload has to be shared out. For this reason, as schools expanded in size and tasks have multiplied and become more complex and diverse, a senior management structure has evolved, so that there are a group of experienced staff who can deal with all the work involved in managing and organising the school. There are other reasons, however, why some tasks and responsibilities should be delegated:

- It prevents job overload and leaves managers with more time for thinking, planning and evaluation.
- It makes it more likely that all the jobs are done effectively.
- It promotes initiative and creativity by giving someone the opportunity to undertake a new and demanding task.
- It extends the skills and experience of those who take part and contributes to professional development.
- It provides training opportunities.
- It motivates by providing opportunity and challenge.
- It gives people confidence, because they have to demonstrate their capability to undertake a difficult task, and helps provide a sense of personal worth.
- It encourages corporate loyalty by promoting a sense of common purpose.

Although delegation is central to the successful management of a school, surveys such as John Sutton's, carried out for the Secondary Heads' Association (1985) indicate that many heads are reluctant to delegate, or do it badly.

CASE STUDY 3.2. FOR ACTION

An example of the problem that I have with the new head occurred only last week. She was out of school for a couple of days. On the second day a problem arose. I sorted it out and announced the arrangements to the staff. The head returned the following morning. Her first reaction, publicly in the staffroom was, 'You can't possibly do that! It will have to be changed.' It's always the same, if I deal with an incident she can't bear not to interfere and she has to show everyone that she's the head and I am only the deputy. (Overheard at a deputy heads' conference.)

For action/ discussion:

What issues are raised by this case study?
What does it indicate about the head's attitude to delegation?
What advice would you give this new headteacher and why?

Reasons why managers are reluctant to delegate

■ Managers tend to think they are indispensable, and they often want to hold on to all sources of power.
■ Upbringing – we are educated into thinking we must do everything for ourselves.
■ Guilt – people feel guilty about delegating or that they have failed in some way if they delegate any of their responsibilities.
■ Fear of taking risks – there may be a lack of confidence in our subordinates/the senior management team.
■ New teachers particularly need time to settle in and get to know and trust the SMT.

'We usually tend to overrate rather than underrate our importance and to conclude that far too many things can only be done by ourselves. Even the very effective executives still do a great many unnecessary, unproductive things.' (Drucker, 1970)

The problem with delegation seems to be largely one of attitude, but it has to be understood that the prior condition for effective delegation is a positive attitude. This means starting from the idea that delegation is a good thing in itself and will benefit you, the delegatee and the school. You also have to want to delegate and be prepared to take the risks involved.

What is implied in delegation?

Delegation requires courage, judgement and faith in others, because we still remain accountable for what they do. In these circumstances, it is not always easy to give people the right to be wrong. However it is worth remembering that we shall be judged, not so much on what we do, but on what we inspire others to do. Our aim ought to be dispensability, not indispensability and we should not fear it.' (White, 1983)

Genuine delegation means:

- allocating responsible as well as routine tasks
- possibly surrendering things that you enjoy yourself
- accepting that a job will be done differently from how you would do it yourself
- trusting others to do what you are ultimately responsible for
- willingness to accept failure as well as success
- careful planning.

How should you decide what to delegate?

Deciding what to delegate could involve you in some considerable heart searching. In the end you will have to resolve two issues: the kind of tasks colleagues should undertake in order to widen their experience and promote their professional development, and whether there are categories of tasks that are totally unsuitable for delegation.

You could start by reviewing what you do – your responsibilities, activities and functions. You may want to refer to your job description or you could simply list your activities over a period of time so that you can get an indication of how you spend your time. Then divide the activities into categories; some examples are: routine (eg planning and organising regular events such as parents' meetings), supervisory jobs, liaison outside the school, strategic decision making. There are obviously many others.

Classifying your tasks in this way will help you to offer your colleagues a range of different kinds of activity, which is the fairest way to approach delegation. Delegation entails increasing your subordinates' workload, and to retain their goodwill you must not simply unload a lot of your more time-consuming and irritating jobs. Delegating a whole lot of clerical or administrative tasks may meet one of your objectives – it will provide you with more time to think and do other aspects of your job more effectively – but it will not help the development of your team, so it is important to provide them with some elements of choice.

You might also want to analyse where regular tasks come in the annual cycle, so that, for example, you don't load one person with several heavy tasks which all need a lot of work at the same time.

CASE STUDY 3.3. FOR ACTION

Using the job description given in Chapter 1 try applying these tests to see which of your responsibilities are the most suitable for delegation:

- Which of the tasks on my list could be done by someone else as well if not better?
- Would those tasks provide a good opportunity for the professional development of a colleague?
- Which tasks should be managed by the senior management team (SMT) acting as a team?
- Which tasks should remain my personal responsibility and not be delegated at all?

If you then decide not to delegate a task, it might be helpful to apply two further tests:

- Are you retaining a particular task merely because you enjoy it?
- Is it appropriate in this particular school to delegate this task?

CASE STUDY 3.4. FOR ACTION

Jenny, newly in post as a deputy head, found the customs and practices of her new school differed sharply from those of her last school. In her previous post, as a senior teacher and head of the sixth form, she had regularly dealt with the parents who wanted a consultation about the progress or welfare of their child. Only the most serious problems had been reserved for the headteacher, and even then Jenny had been very closely involved and was present whenever parents of her year group came in to see the head. She had also organised and taken the leading role in interviewing the prospective entrants to the sixth form and their parents. Now, in the more senior post of deputy head, she found herself excluded from seeing parents, and as the head's practice of interviewing every prospective student personally meant that Jenny barely saw him for three weeks (with a knock-on effect on his communications with her and the staff as a whole), she felt the need to protest. 'Surely interviewing prospective sixth formers is a task that can be shared among the members of the senior management team,' she suggested. 'Not here,' said the head. 'In this school the parents expect to see the head. Interviewing prospective sixth formers together with their parents is a task that I simply cannot share or delegate. It is a vital part of my public relations function. If I stopped doing it, we should lose so much goodwill.'

For action/discussion:

How valid do you think the head's case is that to delegate any part of this task would be inappropriate and counterproductive?
What might it indicate about this headteacher's attitude to delegation?
How should the head deal with his new deputy who feels strongly that it is a waste of her experience and highly developed interpersonal skills if she is denied access to parents?
What advice would you give this headteacher and why?

The case study highlights the point that in different institutions different areas of responsibility are considered inappropriate for delegation and it raises the further question – are there some areas of responsibility which should never be delegated?

Recent writers on delegation have all stressed the developmental view of delegation and the need to provide the delegatee with freedom of action. If delegation means 'giving people the right to be wrong' then the delegatees must be given tasks which allow them a full measure of responsibility and authority.

Advice on the thorny question of how much you can delegate is that you can delegate most senior management responsibilities successfully as long as you go about it the right way, but that there are three categories of task which it could be unwise to delegate:

- vital jobs that only you can do
- tasks requiring confidentiality or particular sensitivity

- new or ill-defined tasks which may prove very difficult or which have a much higher than average failure risk.

Can delegation be learnt?

A significant test of good management is the effectiveness of delegation. (Sutton, 1985)

You may not be a natural delegator, but it is not difficult to improve your skills as the following guidelines show.

Guidelines for effective delegation

- Negotiate about what is delegated, never impose it.
- Provide a variety of types of task or the opportunity to rotate tasks.
- Select the person most suited to carry out the task – you want him/her to succeed.
- Use delegation as an opportunity to widen someone's professional experience.
- Build on an existing enthusiasm or interest in a new development – delegation will get it off to a good start.
- Don't be selfish in your attitude to delegation – this means not unloading your least favourite jobs or difficult jobs you wish to avoid, but *do* be ruthless and delegate as much as you can.
- Do not simply relieve your own overload by transferring it to someone else – that person will either have a nervous breakdown or s/he will look for another job.
- Clearly define the task that you are delegating – work out a job description and ensure that the person receiving the task knows what is expected of him/her.
- Make the terms of reference clear – how much responsibility, freedom of action etc are you delegating? Clarifying the position could prevent ill feeling later.
- Provide the necessary resources, and guidance. You cannot expect someone to know instinctively what they should do.
- Decide what the deadline should be and make sure that too short a deadline does not make it impossible to complete the task.
- Make regular progress checks to provide opportunities for feedback and to maintain an appropriate level of control. Bear in mind that whereas regular appraisal will contribute to the success of the

job (and is not inconsistent with delegation), frequent interference will contribute to its failure.

■ Determine the objectives and the targets together with the delegatee, then leave the delegatee the freedom to carry out the task. How s/he does this is up to him/her. Your concern is for results, not for routes.

■ Do not take decisions or make changes that undermine the delegatee's authority or position.

■ Recognise success with public praise and provide sympathetic support for failure.

Effective delegation is about encouraging creativity – this means:

■ welcoming new ideas, however apparently unworkable
■ not telling the delegatee how to do everything
■ discouraging unthinking imitation of the previous postholder, or of you
■ supporting new ideas with resources and training
■ matching responsibility to creativity, ie by increasing the level of responsibility and scope to create in line with the delegatee's professional growth.

What should you do in case of failure?

Providing the procedures for reporting and monitoring and trying to ensure that the right person has been chosen for the job are your best safeguards, but even so trouble can arise. You want to give the delegatee freedom of action and to interfere as little as possible, but you don't want him/her to fail disastrously. Such a result would damage the delegatee personally and damage the school as well; it would also make future delegation more difficult. So what can you do when you sense that things are going wrong?

Your aim should be to help the person as unobtrusively as possible. The first thing to do is to try to assess how serious the problem really is. If it isn't too serious, a warning in time could avert disaster. The regular progress meetings will probably provide you with your best route through which to tackle the issue so, if you handle it tactfully, it shouldn't seem like interference. You will have to assess whether the problem is occurring because of the difficulty of the task itself or because of the method adopted by the delegatee. Sometimes you will find that additional resources or time will rectify the situation and improve morale. Often talking through and confronting the problem will help to resolve it. The really difficult situations tend to centre on personality clashes, and here you will need all the sensitivity at your disposal to retrieve the situation. Only if there is utter disaster and no alternative do you resort to taking over publicly. In the end the final responsibility is yours. If the delegatee succeeds, s/he deserves and should receive the credit. If s/he fails, the blame and the ultimate responsibility are yours.

Delegation issues

CASE STUDY 3.5. FOR ACTION

Bob had been responsible for the timetable in the school for at least ten years. A mathematician, he had always enjoyed the job, which built on his subject skills. He was careful to consult people about their needs and was thorough and systematic in his approach. Hitherto he had coped ably with even the most unreasonable demands made by some departments. Now the changes brought about by recent legislation and DFEE directives are putting his considerable skill as a timetabler to the test. He is also very reluctant to use the computer package suggested by the governors, one of whom is a director of the computer company concerned, prepared to supply the software free and to assist in training Bob or whoever the school nominates. Bob says that he has tried computer aided timetabling in the past and found such systems time consuming and too rigid, particularly in dealing with the large contingent of part timers. Other staff however suspect that it is Bob who is too rigid. Some of the younger staff have expressed an interest in learning to timetable and have offered to help Bob with his increasingly difficult task, but he prefers to work alone. He says that having someone else there affects his concentration, but really he doubts their ability to handle such complex tasks as the curriculum analysis or the school timetable. When he was recently asked to run an Inset session on how the timetable was constructed he refused, saying that he thought it was a complete waste of time. Now the head has said that Bob is failing in his role as a developer and Bob, who has never seen himself as a developer, feels very hurt and aggrieved about this criticism.

For action:

1. You are the headteacher. Bob has been your loyal deputy since you took up the post three years ago, supporting you loyally during a

difficult settling in period when you faced hostility from a number of staff, but he has always been very traditional in his view of management. How do you get him to review his approach to his task and to consider delegating some aspects of it? How do you persuade Bob of the advantages to the school of establishing a shadow structure or to undertake his role as a developer?

2. What issues arise from this case study? What advice would you give to this headteacher in dealing with the situation and why?

CASE STUDY 3.6. FOR ACTION

'What was the point of the head giving me this major initiative to implement, if he isn't prepared to let me do the job?' Peter, the deputy head, was letting off steam in the pub after work one night with a close friend.

I didn't ask for the job. He begged me to do it. He said that I was the only person he could trust to handle it because it was going to be difficult, but once I agreed and took on the job, it was as if he just couldn't bear to let it go. He calls me in, questions me closely about every action I have taken and then rejects or reverses everything, including things that he insisted on having last time round. I don't know where I am from one moment to the next. He keeps insisting that he has the school's best interests at heart, and that he has to monitor things so closely because of the sensitivity of the issue. I think that he is actually scared of the implications of the change and terrified of provoking the unions. I think that he has panicked and got it all out of proportion, and for me he is a much bigger problem than the unions. I'm sure I've got enough goodwill to get a pilot scheme going, if only he would get off my back. Every time I call a meeting of the working party I have to tell them that he's rejected everything again and that we are back to square one. We can't make even the smallest decision without reference to the head. It's an impossible position to be in. It makes me look utterly ridiculous. I'm not really in charge. I'm just some sort of stooge and they all know it.

For action/discussion:

What is going wrong with this piece of delegation?
What advice would you give Peter?
What advice would you give the head and why?

CASE STUDY 3.7. FOR ACTION

The headteacher of Uptown High School has been giving serious thought to the roles and responsibilities of the SMT. Some of the appointments were historic, and some very senior members of staff are receiving allowances for leading a subject area. The budget will not allow this kind of luxury, moreover the number of tasks to be undertaken has mushroomed with the flurry of DFEE directives which followed in the wake of recent legislation. She feels it unfair to expect the middle managers to take on greatly increased responsibilities if the senior managers do not also increase their load. She has therefore drafted a working paper putting forward a scheme in which she restructured the SMT responsibilities so that, although the deputies would still do considerably more than the senior teachers, each member of the team would take on responsibility for a strategic area. She presented this paper to the team and suggested that they consider her ideas, but that before they were discussed as a package the members of the team should come to see her on an individual basis to discuss how it affected each of them. Her deputies liked the proposed changes very much, because for some time now each new task had been added to their already lengthy list of duties and to them the new scheme gave a badly needed coherence. Her interview with one of the senior teachers, however, revealed a very different reaction to her proposal. 'No, dear,' said the senior teacher, 'I read your proposals, but I really can't see my way to doing any of the things on your list. I have thought about it, but I just can't do any more. It takes all my time to run the department. I'm sorry but I can't help you.'

For action:

Why do you think this senior teacher has refused the delegation and what do you think the headteacher should do about it? Suggest some strategies that the headteacher could adopt.

Chapter 4
Managing the Mission

One of the most important aspects of the senior management role is planning and policy making, sometimes described as 'promoting' or 'managing the mission'. It is an emotive image, suggesting that the headteacher is some kind of visionary dedicated to carrying out his/her educational mission. The concept of a headteacher as a missionary does have its own distinct charm, but after one has laughed a little there is some mileage in following the idea through.

Defining what is meant by 'mission'

If you are promoting the mission you are trying to establish a corporate philosophy or system of shared values for the school. There are three stages:

1. You *create* the mission by fashioning a set of goals for the school which are published as a mission statement. In practice this often means the school's statement of aims.
2. You *move* the mission by winning commitment to it and by motivating the staff to support its implementation.
3. You *manage* the mission by formulating the policies and deploying the resources which translate the aims and objectives into reality.

Mission statements are more commonly used in industry than in schools, and the case study which follows gives an example of a set of company values.

CASE STUDY 4.1. FOR REFLECTION

High Grade Stores expect all personnel to demonstrate their support to our two linked value statements:

Our values in relation to the customer

- treat service as a priority
- listen
- be open and honest
- understand his/her needs
- be supportive, caring, flexible, professional and dedicated
- build good, positive relationships
- value his or her satisfaction/happiness
- be fundamentally in tune with the business.

Our values in respect of each other

- to own and commit to our values
- use principles of teams (not tribes), openness and trust to resolve conflicting priorities
- combine responsibility with accountability, measure our output
- be supportive, caring, flexible and dedicated
- be open and honest – listen
- build good, positive relationships
- learn from mistakes – no one is perfect
- lead rather than be driven by events
- give each other feedback
- identify with overall High Grade goals.

It would not be difficult to translate this list of values into similar statements for a school, using our values in respect of the pupils, each other and the community.

You would probably find it more useful, however, to produce two complementary statements for the establishments: a code of conduct for all personnel and a set of aims and objectives for the school.

The purpose of undertaking this kind of exercise is to formulate a set of agreed principles which would underlie all future planning and policy making. It is a major exercise to undertake because it makes the school rethink its whole philosophy and ethos and involves much discussion. It tends to be a strategy employed by a new head within a year or so of taking up the post when she wants to refocus the school's thinking, so it could be an appropriate way for you to give the school a shake-up and remodel its philosophy.

CASE STUDY 4.2. FOR ACTION

Bestwick Park High School – Statement of Aims
The following aims are based on the belief that all pupils are of equal value and concern:

- to provide a secure and caring community where a multiplicity of needs and interests are catered for and where pupils are encouraged to aim for excellence in everything they undertake
- to ensure that all pupils reach their full potential
- to develop each pupil's talents to the full so that s/he can lead a life of personal satisfaction and fulfilment
- to promote self discipline and an understanding of the needs of others within the community
- to involve the parents and the community in its everyday life
- to encourage the ability of pupils to make reasoned decisions and to participate in those concerning their school community and society in general
- to assist the pupil to understand her/himself and relate to the world in which s/he lives
- to ensure that equal curricular opportunity is genuinely available to both boys and girls and is positively encouraged
- to eliminate sexism whenever it occurs and create an antisexist environment in which girls and boys have real equality of opportunity
- to equip each pupil with the basic skills needed to function in the complex society of today
- to ensure that since we are a multicultural, multiracial society, all children are educated towards an understanding of and commitment to that society
- regularly to monitor and evaluate our curriculum, results and development.

Bestwick Park High School – Code of Conduct
The one rule for all of us in this school is that everyone will act with courtesy and consideration to others at all times. This means that:

1. You should always try to understand other people's point of view.

2. In class you make it as easy as possible for everyone to learn and for the teacher to teach. (This means arriving on time with everything that you need for that lesson, beginning and ending the lesson in a courteous and orderly way, listening carefully, following instructions, helping each other when appropriate and being quiet and sensible at all times.)
3. You move quietly and sensibly about the school. (This means never running, barging or shouting, but being ready to help by opening doors or standing back to let people pass and helping to carry things.) In crowded areas please keep to the left.
4. You should always speak politely to everyone (even if you feel bad tempered!) and use a low voice. (Shouting is always discourteous.)
5. You should keep silent whenever you are required so to be.
6. You keep the school clean and tidy so that it is a welcoming place of which we can all be proud. (This means putting all litter in bins, keeping walls and furniture clean and unmarked and taking great care of displays, particularly of other people's work.)
7. Out of school, walking locally or with a school group, you always remember that the school's reputation depends on the way that you behave.

For action/discussion

Define this school's mission.
What were the main principles underlying the Statement of Aims and the Code of Conduct?

Strategic planning

Your role in managing the mission will involve you in a great deal of strategic planning, and you may prefer to use this term (rather than referring to what you do as managing the mission), because it implies a far more down to earth approach. Another reason for using the term strategic planning is that it is a much wider concept, as it brings together and integrates all the various management aspects and activities.

What does strategic planning involve?
Strategic planning means wide-ranging and long-term planning, seeking to establish appropriate objectives and matching these objectives to the available resources in the most efficient and effective way.

Figure 4.1   Strategic planning

Why do we need strategic planning?

Prior to the Education Reform Act of 1988 maintained schools had to operate entirely within the policies of LEAs, which determined their numerical size and future and, apart from capitation, schools could make no decisions about the deployment of their resources. Under LMS or GM a maintained school (like any independent school) is fully responsible for its own destiny, and explicit overall direction is essential.

Strategic planning consists of four processes:

- **analysis or audit** – when the school analyses its strengths and weaknesses and assesses its own needs
- **planning and decision making** – generation and evaluation of options
- **implementation** – putting the plan into action
- **evaluation** – checking the success of implementation and reviewing targets.

Analysis

Your first task is to carry out a needs analysis as the basis of your planning. It asks two questions, first, 'Where are we now?' (the answers to which should provide an audit of your current provision) and second, 'What do we expect to have to do next year/over three years and can we cope?' (this assess how far your current provision

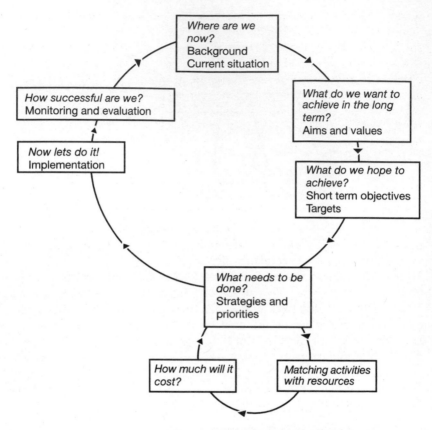

Figure 4.2 The processes of strategic planning

matches your expected requirements). You have to look *backwards* to check how far targets in last year's plan have been met and *forwards* to project likely pupil numbers and the demands that these will place on available resources. You will have to do this exercise quite precisely, otherwise you could be way out with costings and this could make nonsense of your plans. Your analysis of how things stand will help you assess what you can afford. Your development plan should be objectives, not budget led, but the budget cannot help but be influential.

You will also have to analyse some of the less tangible resources to assess the strengths of the school, which will also help you to deal with future demands. You will have to make some judgements about the school's value system and about how the school is valued by the 'consumer' – the local community, the pupils and parents. The case study below is an example of a questionnaire to parents to help a school assess whether parents thought the school was successful in what it was doing. Designing this type of questionnaire always presents problems and you may wish to compare this example with the one currently issued by the Office for Standards in Education (Ofsted) to parents before an inspection. Monitoring the extent of the response could also produce an indicator which could affect you planning.

CASE STUDY 4.3. FOR REFLECTION

Bestwick Park High School – parents' viewpoint questionnaire

Section A – Yourself and your children

1. How many children do you have at the school? (Please include both past and current.)
2. Journey to school – time and method of transport
3. Which local papers do you read?

Section B – About the school
Please comment on the following:

1. Receipt of information – newsletters, booklets etc
2. Visits to the school
3. Information about your child/ children's progress
4. Homework
5. Discipline in/out of lessons
6. Canteen facilities
7. Educational facilities – IT, sports, workshops etc
8. Pastoral care
9. Welcome and reception.

Section C – Your feelings about the school

1. Possibility of greater involvement with the school
2. Priority listing of the schools aims (list included)

3. Why did you choose this school?
4. Would you choose it again?
5. What changes would you most like to see?
6. What are the best things about this school?

Section D – Any other comments

Your analysis may also usefully include a trawl among pupils, teachers and parents for what they consider *special* about the school. This might sound a bit precious, but it can produce interesting results. Remember that if you do produce a list of this type, it must stand up to Oftsted inspection.

Planning and decision making

This stage starts with the generation and discussion of possible ideas and options as the senior management team (SMT) seeks answers to the question, 'What should go on the planning agenda for the long- and short-term future?' The needs analysis will have produced some of the ideas now under discussion, others will have come in as bids from departments or individuals, others again will arise from externally imposed changes. This last group of demands may not fit in easily to the school's plans, especially if the government has totally changed its mind about some important aspect of education, but will nevertheless have to be superimposed on the plans.

Not all the challenges facing the school can be responded to immediately, so the next task is to decide which issues should become priorities for the following year and which phased in over a longer period.

How should you go about determining priorities?

Determining priorities means making a decision about which issues are the most important and placing them in a time sequence.

Applying this formula means focusing your attention on what is absolutely essential for the survival, prosperity and effectiveness of the school. Criteria for evaluation could include suitability (how far does a possible course of action respond to what the analysis told you?); feasibility (how far can you resource what you propose? How many of the items can you afford to resource now, which could you afford next year and which are simply too expensive to envisage at all?); and acceptability (how far will the development be acceptable and to whom?)

The conflict between wanting to construct a long-term development plan for the school and the educational constraints, which were turning planning into a yearly operation, seems to have been resolved to some extent by schools constructing a three year management and development plan which is prioritised on a three year cycle of implementation.

Consultation about embryo plans can be helpful and, as there are various ways of doing this, there is no best method; rather it is a matter of what suits your school. However, if you want Ofsted or Investors in People approval you will need to show that you have consulted widely over the whole school community. In a maintained school the area education officer or the link adviser may discuss the plan with you; and there is also plenty of commercial consultancy available but, if you buy into this kind of package, you need to ensure that you receive value for money.

The school management plan is in reality the governors' management plan. In practice, however, much of the work of constructing it is done by the head and the SMT. Different task groups such as the governors' finance or curriculum committees will contribute to the plan by submitting ideas and recommendations or by imposing constraints, and it is wise to have some representatives from the governing body on the planning group.

Creating the school management/development plan

One of the results of LMS is that schools now construct a school management plan (also known as a strategic plan). It is a corporate planning document which has become the school's main policy and planning vehicle. Once the contents have been agreed the drafting of the document is usually delegated to one member of the group, either to you as the headteacher or to a deputy with expertise in drafting. You may have to amend the draft a number of times through the consultation process, as your knowledge of budgetary constraints becomes clearer and following a full governors' meeting. Once it has been adopted it becomes the school's main policy instrument for the time period it covers and will be central to any review of your school carried out by the LEA or by Ofsted.

CASE STUDY 4.4. FOR ACTION

Exemplar of a development plan

Bestwick Park High School – Development Plan
This plan follows on from the plan for last year. Most of our objectives for the previous year have been achieved and an interim evaluation is attached as Appendix 1. Fuller statements in support of our information form a series of Appendices to be found at the end of our development plan.

Aims
Our statement of aims is attached as Appendix 2.

Survey of the current situation
This year the school has 890 pupils on roll, which is an increase of 36 pupils over last year's figure of 854. There are 50.35 full time equivalent teaching staff of whom 44 are full time and 11 are part time. The staff also includes three language assistants, who are shared with another local school, and 14 ancillary staff, of whom only three are full time. Five members of the ancillary staff are funded by short-term contracts and there is a Site Manager and an Assistant Caretaker. Full details of our staffing structure may be found in Appendix 3.

The curriculum continues to provide broad and balanced courses leading to nine GCSEs at 16+. There has been no change to our complete menu of 18 A level subjects and we have maintained a variety of non-examined courses – see Appendix 4.

The buildings have been redecorated externally, but the backlog of internal redecoration and minor repairs remains a concern.

Objectives
- to raise standards in all areas
- to increase our knowledge base through various value-added schemes
- to work towards a greater variety of learning and teaching methods and to enable differentiation
- to seek ways of maintaining and where possible increasing pupil numbers at both 11+ and 16+
- to develop a marketing strategy which will enable us to achieve the above objective.

Curriculum development

- to provide discrete time for IT in years 7 and 8
- to introduce a new Technology GCSE syllabus
- to increase curriculum time for RE in accordance with DFEE requirements
- to introduce modular A levels into year 12
- to review provision for years 12 and 13 in the light of vocational developments.

Other initiatives

- expand our initial teacher training scheme to take eight students per year
- enter NQT competency scheme.

Resource requirements
Our curriculum forecasts show that we are largely able to service our National Curriculum requirements, but there will be a need to strengthen staffing in Technology and RE to meet increased demand. This may need to be done by retraining or by employing part time staff on short-term contracts. The increased use of a wide range of technological facilities has placed heavy demands upon our ancillary staff and we need to think how we can fund increased technician time.

Materials and equipment
We shall continue to need to resource the National Curriculum as it enters a new period of its development.

The increasing use of IT across the curriculum has placed a heavy demand upon our existing equipment. In the short term we shall purchase three more machines from our IT equipment fund. In the longer term we shall have to replace existing equipment and renew the network, which is fully extended and showing signs of the heavy use it receives. Developing a strategy for the future funding of IT is a priority.

Buildings and site
The growth of the school has meant that we urgently need additional laboratory space, especially to provide additional A level sets. Plans

have therefore been drawn up to convert a classroom in the new wing adjacent to the Science area. The conversion should take place in July and August of this year.

To compensate the Humanities faculty for the loss of a classroom, we have decided to partition the old dining hall, which is no longer used for school lunches, now that we have the new canteen. This will provide two additional classrooms for the use of the Humanities faculty.

The building needs to be redecorated in a planned systematic way and the buildings subcommittee has been asked to prepare a five year plan for redecoration. We have also begun a phased programme of furniture replacement which will be monitored by the buildings subcommittee.

In the longer term it is clear that the life of the huts is limited and plans are being prepared for six new, permanent classrooms.

Training needs

1. Inset will be needed to support the introduction of the new Technology GCSE.
2. Differentiation pilots will need development time.
3. Considerable Inset will be needed to support our proposed 16–19 developments.
4. Supporting changes to the National Curriculum over time remains a major Inset need.
5. Mentoring training for our subject mentors and professional tutor.
6. NQT training.
7. Management training for new/struggling middle managers – twilight course.
8. Technical updates and sessions on new developments/government directives for the SMT.

Financial plan

The improvement in our pupil numbers has led to a slight increase in our estimated income for next year, but this is more than counter-balanced by the sharply increased cost of staffing after the recent pay award. Although we contemplate being able to cover our costs in the coming year, if we maintain staffing at its present level, we have very little money to invest in badly needed resources.

Our priority therefore is to devise a strategy to raise substantial additional funding and in order to achieve this objective we have set up a governors' subcommittee.

A standstill budget using last year's prices has been prepared and is attached as Appendix 4. We can only provide a provisional budget as the revised LMS formula is not yet available.

Methods of evaluation

1. by outcome – evaluating whether our targets have been achieved
2. by process – to assess how far we have gone with each initiative
3. targeting one area each year for detailed evaluation. This year we intend to evaluate our Inset programme.

For action

What critical comments are the Ofsted inspectors likely to make about this development plan and for what reasons?

Bestwick Park High School's Development Plan is a rather discursive, chatty document which would benefit from revision in line with the Audit Commissioners' pertinent suggestion that management plans should become less wordy and align more closely with budgetary plans in their format.

The school's aims, rather than being listed as an appendix, should be numbered and cross referenced against initiatives, as Ofsted will want to know which initiative supports which school aim. Moreover, the school's aims are not the same thing as the aims of the development plan.

In Bestwick Park High School's plan there is some confusion between aims and objectives. 'To raise standards in all areas' is surely an aim rather than an objective, because objectives are the strategies which will help the school achieve its aims. 'To develop a strategy to fund IT' is a clear and urgent objective, yet it is to be found in the section on the financial plan.

This is a one year development plan, but schools are now expected to provide a three year plan, with projects prioritised according to urgency and importance and with the time span of the initiatives clearly stated. There is reference to a budget being attached, but the fact that it is a standstill budget is worrying and there are no costings anywhere in the development plan which is a major omission.

CASE STUDY 4.5. FOR ACTION

Headings for a three-year management and development plan for Bestwick Park High School

1. Numbered list of the school's aims (referenced throughout the plan).
2. Three main aims for the next stage in the school's development.
3. List of objectives (where do we want to be in three years' time?)
4. Our current position in relation to the objectives.
5. Action plan (to show how we plan to arrive at the objectives). Headings for this part of the plan could include: objectives; time required/deadline; key personnel; resource implications; Inset implications; outcome.
6. Evaluation procedures.
7. Appendix: Detailed Financial Plan/Budget (the Audit Commission highlighted the need for the budget to be included as part of the development plan).
8. Chart of the staffing structure.

Implementing the plan

Implementing the plan can be harder than constructing it and involves both moving and managing the mission. In order to carry out the management plan successfully, you have to get the details right and communicate them clearly, you have to delegate responsibilities and you have to win the commitment of all those involved. Implementation is a key management task and it is important to get each step right.

Ten steps to successful implementation

Allocate the responsibilities
The first step is to determine who should take responsibility for the various initiatives set out in the plan. You will not always have a choice, eg the introduction of a Science initiative will be co-ordinated by the head of Science, but you *can* choose which of your deputy heads oversees the management of appraisal or differentiation.

Win commitment to the plan
If you do not win commitment to the plan it has no chance of success. Winning commitment means that you have to 'sell' it to the staff, and convince them that this is the way to move forward. It becomes easier

to do this if people see that there are clear benefits for the school, its pupils and themselves; the task is manageable and likely to succeed and ownership is shared with the staff – a top down programme will be difficult to implement. You are most likely to win commitment for particularly difficult activities if you have delegated the task to a manager with the ability to enthuse others.

Make the task achievable
To make the plan succeed you need to create a *framework* for effective implementation. In addition breaking the task down into a series of stages, or 'bite sized chunks', each with its own target, makes the overall task less daunting and brings a taste of success each time a stage is accomplished.

Set realistic deadlines
'More haste less speed' is wise advice. If you carry through a major change too rapidly, without sufficient preparation and time to solve the problems that arise, you are likely to fail, so give yourself and your staff enough time to do the job properly. It is demoralising for them to have to keep trying to meet deadlines they know they can't achieve, and even more demoralising to keep having deadlines put back. Making the deadlines realistic helps you to succeed.

Establish clear lines of communication
Clear lines of communication are essential to effective implementation. Everyone needs to be aware of their own responsibilities and of reporting and demarcation lines.

Communicate the programme
It is important that the plan should not be a secret document known only to the SMT. Its contents need to be communicated to the staff as a whole and it is a sensible move to put a copy of the plan in the staffroom so that the staff can see the priorities for the year ahead and where their own activities fit into the scheme of things. Staff grumbles about not knowing what is going on in the school does not always go hand in hand with a real desire for information, however, and you may find that you will need to hold sessions to raise the profile of some major new initiatives.

Carry out regular progress checks
You design the programme, but then you have to rely on others to carry it out, so you need to know how well the various initiatives are

doing, and this means carrying out regular checks on their progress. A term sometimes used for this activity is 'taking stock'. One method of recording progress is shown in Figure 4.3. If the check reveals that the initiative is making slower progress than anticipated, or that it is experiencing difficulties, you will need to act swiftly to rectify matters.

Support and facilitate

An important aspect of your role as a senior manager is to support and facilitate change and development. The enthusiasm that often accompanies the launch of an initiative tends to wear off when the going gets tough. Inquiring sympathetically and informally about the progress of a development can both reveal the mood of a team and reassure a worried team leader that you haven't forgotten him/her. It can also provide an opportunity to discuss how an initiative is progressing.

You should also make time specifically for a formal session in which the progress of the initiative is discussed, and it can be helpful occasionally to attend part of a team meeting. Normally one of the deputies will be assigned to support the initiative, but some input from you indicates your personal commitment to the development.

If problems arise you, or the relevant deputy, are in a position where because of your experience and your senior position you can take an overview so that the problem is assessed and put into perspective, and you can offer advice or support (eg by providing the time for Inset, by improving the resources or reappraising the targets, deadlines or roles within the team).

Praise

You sustain motivation and commitment by making development possible, and you support progress by offering encouragement when things are difficult and praise where it is due. Never be fulsome or insincere – this is counterproductive. A warm and encouraging comment, which shows that you understand how much has actually been achieved, or some public support for the initiative, can make all the difference to morale and indicates to staff that their hard work is really appreciated.

Report progress

Feedback is an essential part of successful implementation. Reporting progress at least once a term ensures that there is no secrecy and helps to involve people outside the immediate team. There is no need for this to be a lengthy procedure. Its aim is to keep people in the picture and to make sure that the development programme remains high profile. A longer annual report will probably form part of the evaluation process and will be directed to a number of different audiences including the governors.

Implementing the plan – a checklist

- Have you clarified the responsibilities and lines of communication?
- Are the targets and deadlines realistic and achievable?
- Is the programme adequately resourced?
- What training/Inset has been provided?
- Are the benefits/advantages clear to all those involved?
- In what ways are the SMT supporting implementation?
- Who is responsible for the progress checks? What reporting procedures are used? Do they include all those involved?
- What problems are indicated as a result of the progress checks and what remedial action is being taken?
- In what ways do the progress checks influence the construction of next year's plan?
- What management lessons have been learnt from designing and implementing this plan?

Evaluating the plan

Evaluation is concerned with assessing the success of the plan and helping the school take stock of what has been achieved.

The progress check described in Figure 4.3 is a monitoring operation which makes an important contribution to the evaluation process. It is a mini-audit or formative evaluation, providing valuable data about your progress towards achieving the objectives described in your plan.

The indicators included in your action plan will also help you see whether you have reached your destination and, if some of them are process indicators, they may help you analyse where you are on your journey. The analogy of a journey is helpful here because evaluation is about assesssing to what extent you have arrived ie achieved the objectives set out in the plan.

You will need to carry out an annual evaluation, which involves more than simply checking off whether individual targets have been met or indeed how many of them have been achieved. You will have to

Priority title:

Member of staff responsible:

Other staff involved:

Governors involved:

Report on progress:

a) Frequency

b) Mode of report (written, verbal etc.)

c) By whom

Deadlines:

Details of staff Outcomes Inset required	Progress indicators What evidence will be sought? How, when, by whom?	Other action

Figure 4.3   A progress checking sheet

think about what overall effect carrying out this plan has had on the school, how far the school's aims have been furthered and what the impact was on the pupils' learning. How you do this will vary according to the evaluation procedures established in your school, but the results of the evaluation will probably form a written report presented to staff and governors.

Evaluation should always lead to action, and evaluating the extent to which the management/development plan has succeeded should influence the next three year planning and policy making cycle.

Chapter 5
Motivating the Staff

In the education system it is the human resources which consume the most investment. (Everard and Morris, 1985)

The task of the manager is to achieve results through people – you must become a successful *motivator* of people. Managing, motivating and developing staff occupy three chapters of this book, which indicates how much of your time will be spent dealing with the staff of the school. In the past, however, staff management has been something of a poor relation, as educational managers have focused on achieving the task of educating the pupil, and staff management would probably have consisted merely of 'the recruitment, administration and deployment of staff'. Now, effective staff management is seen as the key to quality education and an essential component of running a good school, and it is the job of the headteacher and the senior management team (SMT) to create and maintain the conditions and atmosphere in which people can work with a sense of purpose and give of their best.

The case study which follows illustrates what can happen if the SMT are not sensitive managers of people.

CASE STUDY 5.1. FOR REFLECTION

How not to succeed

For some years the staff at Cheerly High School had been shielded from Geoffrey's worst failings by Joyce, his very competent deputy head, but she had finally got a well-deserved promotion and Geoffrey promoted Ian, the head of boys' PE to the vacant deputyship. It was rumoured among the staff, because two apparently better qualified women candidates had been passed over, that Ian owed his promotion to his long service to the school, his assiduous cultivation of Geoffrey, Geoffrey's keen interest in sport and the fact that Ian, at 50, was fast becoming a liability to the PE department. Ian tended to rush headlong into things. He was impatient both with the theoretical (which he considered a complete waste of time) and with worrying about details which he thought people could work out for themselves. He prided himself on being decisive and on not changing his mind. The staff, on the other hand, considered many of his decisions arbitrary and irrational, and he was regarded as autocratic, insensitive and sexist. Events organised by Ian tended to be chaotic and came to be dreaded by any member of staff who had to participate. It rapidly became very difficult to get volunteers to help with anything, because the staff knew that the activity or function would be ill organised. Geoffrey would not be available to provide support or leadership, so they would have to pick up the pieces and afterwards Ian would blame them for the disaster. Staff meetings became contentious because Ian took comments so personally, and staff began to dread these sessions and to make excuses to avoid them.

Going directly to Geoffrey, however, didn't help the situation. Geoffrey was much less aggressive than Ian and said 'Yes' to everyone, but he wouldn't implement your scheme, and certainly wouldn't have any recollection of the conversation having taken place. His priority was a quiet life. It was no good resorting to memos or to putting your ideas in writing, because Ian had no patience with pieces of paper and Geoffrey simply lost them. Trying to implement the necessary changes needed to bring the school into line with current National Curriculum requirements was generally regarded as hopeless, and after three attempts to get the SMT to consider his scheme for Integrated Junior Science the head of Science began to look for another post. The *Times Educational Supplement* was in great demand in the staffroom and staff turnover increased dramatically. A senior teacher post became vacant and the two women passed over for the deputyship were urged by their colleagues to apply. But they saw no point in applying, believing the school only had jobs for the boys.

There were clear signs of teacher dissatisfaction at Cheerly High School, and the reasons for this dissatisfaction were also clear. A combination of administrative incompetence and unpleasant working conditions led to a rift in the staffroom, and many staff began to take a low profile in order to avoid being involved in unpleasantness. Neither Geoffrey nor Ian gave any serious attention to the ideas put forward by staff, with the result that people became very discouraged, with teachers feeling unappreciated and unsure of what decisions actually meant.

Everard (1986) commented that he found in education more examples of inhuman, downright incompetent management than in industry, and the example of Cheerly High School encapsulates this view. But most schools are nothing like as bad as Cheerly High School, and LMS has forced heads to become better managers of all their resources. It is probably true, however, that whereas a lot of attention has been focused on improving the quality of education for the pupils, far less attention has been paid to providing the supportive structures and improved working conditions for those who deliver it.

Motivating the staff

In most schools:

- some people work hard, others do the minimum amount
- some want freedom of action, others want a highly structured environment
- some work virtually alone, others almost always in groups
- some are satisfied, others perpetually discontented; yet they work in the same institution.

What is it that causes these discrepancies? To find the answer we shall review the main ideas and theories about motivation and consider the findings of research into current practice. This section is intended as a summary and a starting point from which to think about ways in which you could make your management of staff more effective. For a more detailed consideration of motivation you should use more theoretical books on organisational behaviour.

What do we mean by motivation?

The two quotations below provide a basic definition and starting point from which to consider motivation.

CASE STUDY 5.2. FOR REFLECTION

Definitions of motivation

Motivation is made up of a number of factors of which the most important are the perceived value of the outcome to the individual and the correlation between that outcome and the effort necessary to achieve it. Motivation is therefore about action and is the product of determination, ability and performance. (Davies *et al* 1991)

Motivation arises from arousal and choices in the individual – a desire to allocate time and energy to particular goals in exchange for some expected result or reward. More generally motivation is the degree to which an individual chooses to engage in certain behaviours (Hunt, 1986).

Motivation theories

The most popular motivation theories have been needs theories, which collect goals, aspirations, values and behaviours into motives which they call drives, needs and wants. They are based on the premise that motivation depends on the relationship between the potential drive of an individual and the nature of his/her needs.

One example of this kind of thinking is Maslow's theory of needs. Maslow (1954) suggested that we could make needs into a hierarchy and predict the order in which individuals could satisfy their needs. The strength of this model is based on one level becoming dominant as another is satisfied. Thus, according to Maslow only unsatisfied needs motivate. Maslow's hierarchy is traditionally represented as a pyramid, as shown in Figure 5.1. The hierarchy is explained as follows:

- **physiological** – hunger, thirst, sexual drive etc. Unless these are satisfied little progress can be made because these needs come to dominate one's whole existence
- **safety** – these drive out the baser instincts of an individual as s/he seeks shelter, warmth, clothing etc
- **social** – the desire for companionship, acceptance, the regard of others etc are less selfish needs than the physiological and security

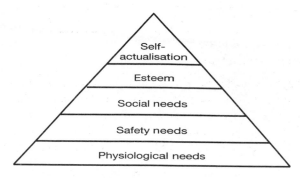

Figure 5.1   Maslow's heirarchy of needs

needs because they combine giving with receiving, and so they are regarded as being on a higher plane than the first two
- **esteem** – the drive to externalise one's inner feelings or creativity
- **self actualisation** – this forms the apex of Maslow's pyramid because only through self fulfilment can an individual realise his/her true humanity, and this cannot be achieved until all the other contributory and more partial needs have been met. Self fulfilment through work should thus be a key aim of any institution.

While most physiologists accept that people do find some goals so attractive that they will pursue them with considerable energy, many do not accept Maslow's theory of a rigid hierarchy because they consider it too simplistic.

Frederick Herzberg attempted to overcome the problems associated with Maslow's hierarchy of needs by developing a more sophisticated analysis of attitudes to motivation and work – a distinction between satisfiers and dissatisfiers which he called hygiene factors (Herzberg, 1974). Dissatisfiers could include:

- administration
- relationship with section head/supervisor/head of department/ senior manager
- working conditions
- salary
- relationship with colleagues
- status
- job security.

The problem with using hygiene factors is that dissatisfiers make people very disgruntled and demotivate, but removing them is not a motivator. This is reinforced by research into current practice: 'When teachers are satisfied with the management of their schools they do not mention it, because good management is not in itself under normal circumstances, a satisfier in its own right' (Nias, 1980).

Every deputy head who has ever handled cover for absence arrangements will identify with the findings from Jennifer Nias' research (1980). A crop of errors in cover or the overuse of any individual will quickly result in a rush of complaints. Success in dealing with cover may help to keep industrial action at bay, but it will not enthuse staff and it is rare for a deputy to receive any thanks for managing cover consistently well.

This does not mean that you should not remove the dissatisfiers, rather that when you have done so you will not have solved the problem of motivating your staff.

Following on from the work of Maslow and Herzberg a variety of motivation theories have emerged:

- **goals and expectancy theories** – providing staff with specified goals for them to work on will increase their motivation. This has led to an emphasis on management by objectives and much target setting
- **intrinsic motivation** – leaders can foster conditions within an organisation which build up intrinsic motivation, though it has been found that some extrinsic demotivators (such as poor pay) can affect this adversely
- **behaviour modification** – the use of positive reinforcement can substantially increase motivation
- **working in small groups or teams** – this can help teachers feel a sense of belonging and commitment.

No single motivating factor has been found to have a dominating effect and some behavioural psychologists now suggest that there are a number of factors which influence how people behave at work. For example J.W. Hunt (whose *Managing People at Work, a Manager's Guide to Behavior in Organizations* (1986) is a useful resource for headteachers who want to read some theory in an accessible format) researched some 10,600 cases, and identified abilities, experience, goals and values, energy and expected rewards as the most important factors in influencing how people behave at work.

His research led him to develop the opinion that our backgrounds provide us with themes or patterns which reappear in values, beliefs and goals, and he identified eight recurring goal categories: comfort, structures, relationships, recognition and status, power, authority, creativity, and growth.

Each individual has his/her goals which may shift over a period of time. Our goals tend to relate to the situations in which we find ourselves and the cues of the people around us – our subordinates, peers and managers are all important triggers. Research findings also indicate that people at different levels in an organisation seek different goal satisfactions and that, not surprisingly, the most motivated workers are those who identify with the organisation's own goals: 'If individuals have the necessary abilities and experience and their goals are the same as those of the organisation, then provided that they find the rewards attractive, and have the energy, they will work hard to achieve the goals.'

As managers we need to understand that there are a whole range of factors which affect motivation and, more importantly, we need to be able to respond appropriately to people's individual needs.

What are the implications for you as a manager and motivator of staff? One message which emerges very clearly from the research on motivation is just how important it is to have an effective and proactive approach to staff management. We now consider what this means for you. (The following examples serve as case study 5.3.)

Providing a supportive environment

This aspect of staff management addresses the comfort, support and security needs of your staff.

'Comfort' includes providing reasonable working conditions. Many teachers have to work under dire conditions – in many staffrooms there is room only for a social area, with nowhere for the teachers to prepare or mark, and very few schools are able to provide all their middle managers with offices.

> Staffrooms are typically too small, poorly furnished, untidy, badly laid out, with coffee making facilities which would disgrace a dosshouse . . . Yet the staffroom is the hub of the school community, where information is traded, working relationships are forged and innovation generated, as well as drooping spirits

revived, books marked, letters written and hosts of everyday tasks of teaching completed. (Torrington and Weightman, 1989a)

One of the most common demotivators is when teachers do not think they receive adequate support from senior staff in maintaining discipline or setting a standard.

The children are not motivated to work and are easily distracted. There's no help from the senior staff. If you send a pupil who has been difficult or disruptive to any member of our senior management team the pupil is back in your classroom a few minutes later, and this makes it much more difficult to control the class than before you sent the pupil out. So we try to cope, but it isn't easy. The management team here doesn't take a stand on anything. Even if they said that homework should be done, it would be a start. But we also need to demonstrate clearly to those children who failed to produce homework that some follow up action would be taken. If the pupils could see that the senior team were prepared to support us, it would be so much better. As it is some staff have given up trying to enforce a standard. (This extract from a teachers' discussion illustrates that a perceived lack of support can also deter staff from persevering with a difficult task.)

Job security is also a worry for staff in schools, both teaching and non-teaching.

Every so often one of the governors comes and talks to us and suggests that one of us should go. There are three of us and really they only want to keep two. They are not making us any offers, they just keep up the pressure, though if they did make a reasonable offer, Marjorie, who's in her late 50s, might take it. The head says that I should be safe, because I am his secretary, but I was the most recently appointed, and I'm worried about my position here. (Head's secretary discussing staffing issues.)

This extract illustrates that working in a school is no longer the safe and secure job it used to be. LMS, the competitive market place, depleted rolls and cost conscious institutional development can lead to redundancy and there is no longer the safety net of the LEA redeployment schemes.

Redundancy issues affect the morale of a wider group than those directly affected.

They told us that seven teachers had to go that year and we all knew that it was more than natural wastage could absorb. Of course I worried about it, even though I knew that I was relatively safe because I taught a shortage subject. There was a dreadful atmosphere in the staffroom. I think a lot of it came from the uncertainty. In the end enough people left and they did not have to make anyone redundant, but it affected morale badly and the whole relationship between the staff and the management team. (Teacher recalling falling rolls in an inner city school.)

Handling redundancy successfully while maintaining staff morale is an extremely difficult management exercise, requiring a great deal of sensitivity. It is explored more fully in Chapter 10.

Creating a feeling of belonging

The best organizations are run so that the staff as a whole regard themselves as part of a corporate team. Achieving this will draw on all your skills as a leader and your ability to create a corporate spirit. Chapter 4 discussed ways of creating a corporate philosophy that clearly articulated the values of the organisation. This philosophy needs to be understood, accepted and owned by staff if they are to be motivated. This will involve you in an ongoing planning dialogue involving the whole staff and regular restatement of the philosophy to hammer it home.

What is so different about working in this school, now that Philip is head, is that for the first time we really know where we are going and we're all pulling together. In the past it was like a lot of individuals who happened to work in the same building, now we are like one big team, and even the pupils seem to recognise that they can no longer play us off one against another.

If a survey of your staff can consistently produce that kind of comment, you are succeeding as a motivator.

Motivating through teams and task groups

Participating in group activities can also contribute to motivation, because it too creates a feeling of belonging. Both in industry and in education there has in recent years been a movement to management through teams. In schools subject departments have always existed, though it is only in the last decade or so, with its emphasis on change necessitating curriculum development, that the sheer volume of work has forced an increase in team activity, and schools have created co-ordinators to lead development work for new curriculum areas and for cross curricular activities. These teams, which have had to focus on working out solutions for the delivery of an aspect of the curriculum (eg Technology) are a form of task group, an organizational style which Handy and Aiken (1986) identified as 'the teachers' own preferred culture': 'Teachers with very few exceptions saw themselves as task culture aficionados.'

This kind of group has to undertake a demanding or challenging task, often with a tight deadline. It draws on the talents and abilities of its members and, although there is usually a group co-ordinator or team leader, it is not a hierarchical unit, more a team of colleagues co-operating on a project. It is the nature of the relationships formed through the team, the interaction of the personnel and the common task, goals or targets that provide the motivating force.

The task group formed for a specific purpose and chosen from volunteers or those with the relevant talents is the easiest team to enthuse or motivate. The ongoing department team, whose members may well be approaching new developments with much less enthusiasm, will need a lot more nursing and encouragement, and some training for your middle managers in managing change and personnel would probably equip them better to deal with this complex and difficult task. Effective, well motivated teams are the product of hard work and good leadership by their co-ordinator, who has to gain the commitment of the members.

A warning note:

Creating enthused task groups can sometimes be counterproductive to organisational unity as it sets the group apart from the rest of their colleagues, and this is something that senior management needs to monitor. While it may motivate small groups it could splinter an organisation as it focuses loyalty on the team and its task rather than on the organisation.

Making staff feel valued

This involves recognition of effort and valuable work, feedback and reward where appropriate, but most of all it involves *positive* feedback.

Our general observation is that most managers know very little about positive reinforcement. Many often appear not to value it at all, or consider it beneath them, undignified or very macho. The evidence from excellent companies strongly suggests that managers who feel this way are doing themselves a great disservice. The excellent company seems not only to know the value of positive reinforcement, but how to manage it well. (Peters and Waterman, 1982)

The case study which follows illustrates that some heads clearly understand the value of positive reinforcement and do know how to manage it in order to create a strong team spirit among their staff.

CASE STUDY 5.4. FOR ACTION

Open day

The open day means a lot of hard work for the staff. I always go round the rooms before the parents start to arrive so that I know what each department or unit has contributed. I have a word with as many teachers as possible at that time and comment positively on something in the display. The teachers and the ancillary staff have given up their time to support the school and this should be noted and their efforts appreciated. Even if technically it counts as directed time, their input is much more than the time factor – they make the displays very attractive and involve a lot of our current year 7 pupils. This has a positive knock on effect when our year 7 team goes round the primary schools in the summer term to meet the children who have selected us as their secondary school.

At the first staff briefing after the open day, I thank everyone and mention any positive feedback that we have received. I read out appreciative letters from parents and then display them on my section of the notice board in the staffroom. In this meeting I also take feedback from staff. We discuss how successful new ventures have been, and I ask for suggestions for the following year. It is important to do this when the event is still fresh in everyone's mind. The first year I was here I went on for far too long in my speech and they were a bit unsure how to tell me, but at last one of the senior teachers spoke up. I took the criticism on board, shortened my speech, and since then they have known that we can be honest with each other. Sometimes during the week I have a word with staff who have contributed a great deal to the success of the day, and I specifically mention what it is that I valued in their contribution. I follow this up with a short personal note of thanks so they can see that I valued their efforts sufficiently to put my appreciation in writing.

For action:

List the strategies adopted by this headteacher in order to make the members of his staff feel that their efforts are valued, comment on their effectiveness and suggest what else he could do. How do you convince your staff that this is not just a management ploy but that you are sincere?

Rewarding through pay and promotion

Pay and promotion of course are the most obvious ways of making an individual feel valued because it shows everyone that the recipient is regarded as worthy of reward and acts as a recognition of merit or effort.

Pay and promotion, however, are two edged swords. Choosing one person means rejecting many others. Pay is a particularly fraught area. For many years there was little room for manoeuvre because of national scales. To make matters worse falling rolls or a stable staff (who had reached the top of the scale, or who had already received any allowances that you had in your gift) blocked promotion opportunities for others and left you with nothing to offer staff who clearly deserved reward. Now pay arrangements which necessitate salaries being reviewed annually give you much more flexibility, and in theory you have much more opportunity to reward deserving staff and show them that you value their efforts. In practice you are restricted by the tightness of the budget and may find yourself having to deal with one of the worst possible scenarios – a climate of raised expectations which cannot be met. The criterion of classroom excellence is potentially extremely divisive, and not only do staff watch like hawks to see who are the lucky ones this year, but it is difficult to explain to teachers labelled excellent last year why someone else is excellent this year. Having a governors' pay policy with the criteria clearly established has become essential, but still does not solve all the problems in using pay to encourage staff. Rewarding a small number of individuals may motivate a few staff and encourage them to identify with the goals of the institution, but it is equally likely to antagonise and cause dissension and disenchantment among the majority. Indeed, where a teacher is not favoured or it is handled insensitively, pay can be a dissatisfier.

CASE STUDY 5.5. FOR ACTION

I don't understand why George is suddenly getting an incentive allowance. There are three other teachers in the Languages Department doing identical work to George. What has George got that the others haven't? They are pretty annoyed about it. (Teacher's comment on a colleague's good fortune.)

For action/discussion:

What does this comment indicate about how the pay policy is being applied in this school and what advice would you give the headteacher?

CASE STUDY 5.6. FOR ACTION

Bestwick Park High School: An extract from the governors' pay policy

General principle
The governing body will endeavour, within its budget, to use the national pay scales and discretion available to them as the 'relevant body to recruit, retain and motivate' teachers of quality to ensure the best possible delivery of the curriculum. Consideration will also be given to the non-teaching staff. The governors will be mindful of the need to create and maintain high morale among the staff in order to achieve the best response from pupils.

When considering the enhancement of the pay of any staff, the staffing committee should be aware of existing differentials and ensure that any proposed variation is based on relevant evidence and seen to be just and will ensure that all decisions are properly communicated to staff. The criteria will be as follows:

- responsibilities beyond those common to the majority of teachers
- outstanding classroom ability
- employment to teach a subject where there is a shortage of teachers
- employment in a post which is difficult to fill.

For action/discussion:

Comment on the Bestwick Park policy statement. What do you think should be the main principles of a school pay and conditions of service policy and what is the best way of setting one up so that it does not provide a dissatisfier?
Pay policies are discussed more fully in Chapter 10.

Job satisfaction

This strand of your staff management policy positively motivates because it addresses the needs of power, status, growth and creativity. It is the product of goodwill and an understanding of individual needs and opportunity. These are some of the ways in which you can provide staff with the opportunity for fulfilment through work:

- leadership opportunities – co-ordinator roles, chairing working parties, carrying out a specific task or leadership of a task group
- successful delegation, which gives the individual the freedom to interpret a role or task in his/her own way
- participation in a challenging or stimulating new development where there is opportunity for creativity
- participation in a team where the task is high priority, high status and well resourced (some Technical and Vocational Education Initiative (TVEI) pilot projects found themselves in this enviable position)
- promotion to a new post or the chance to undertake additional responsibilities.
- redesignation of an existing post, eg a change of responsibilities to prevent staleness and provide new challenges.

All of these examples provide the opportunity for individual growth and development either through new or enhanced responsibilities or through membership of a vibrant team. The two short case studies which follow illustrate how this could work in practice.

CASE STUDY 5.7. FOR REFLECTION

The first half term that we delivered the new Technology course we were really hyped up. We'd head for the staffroom at break or lunchtime after we had had a lesson with the group in order to compare notes and reactions with the other members of the team. The whole approach was new to us. It was very exciting, but also very demanding. None of us had done assignment based learning before. We had to learn to let go and allow the children to take control. We found that we really had to think on our feet, but it was exhilarating. What really surprised us was that whereas at the beginning some members of the team had not been totally convinced that all this effort was worthwhile, now the whole team really pulled together and these staff became as involved as those who had been committed from the start. They said that now that they could see how much the children were enjoying it and how much they were achieving, they suddenly saw the point of the whole enterprise. (Teacher describing the introduction of assignment based learning in her school.)

The example demonstrates how a growing belief in what they were doing motivated this team and brought in those who were initially unconvinced of the value of the initiative. It also helped create a sense of excitement and a strong group entity.

CASE STUDY 5.8. FOR ACTION

Who would have thought it of Janet? We all thought that she was just coasting through the twilight years of her career, then came this edict that we had to implement appraisal, and the head put her in charge of it, because she was experienced and sympathetic, but not a threat to anyone, because she wasn't in the senior management team. She really blossomed. It seemed to bring out all kinds of qualities we would never have guessed she had. In next to no time she had all the staff involved in some form of appraisal with no trouble at all. No other school in the county got off the mark as fast as we did. I wouldn't have believed it if I hadn't seen it for myself. How did the head know how to choose her? (Teacher describing how appraisal was introduced into his school.)

This example shows how finding someone a challenging task can unexpectedly motivate, but of course it has to be the right task and the right person. If Janet hadn't possessed the skills and personal qualities to do the job the results could have been very different.

For action:

What are the lessons of case studies 5.7 and 5.8 for you as a new headteacher?

CASE STUDY 5.9. FOR ACTION

When John, the head of year 9, had to have an operation, Nora offered to take over the management of his year group. She did the job unpaid for half a term and then was given an acting responsibility. She put a lot of time, thought and effort into the job, not only dealing with all the necessary aspects but introducing some ideas of her own, which seemed to go down very well with both the year team and the pupils. What was particularly noticeable was that although Nora had plenty of ideas she was sensitive about procedures and consultation, and extremely careful not to erode John's position as it was assumed he would return. When John did take up his post again he was far less sensitive to Nora's position than she had been about his, and every trace of Nora's tenure was immediately eradicated, regardless of whether the idea had any merit or not. At around the time of John's return another year head post became vacant and Nora applied for it. She was not among the shortlisted candidates and could not understand why her successful experience had not earned her an interview. From being a most willing volunteer within a few months she had become one of the school management's most vociferous and hostile critics.

For action:

How would you set about remotivating Nora?
What advice might you give the headteacher in Nora's school?

Key qualities

Openness

Regular and open communication should be part of your approach to management. A continuous dialogue between the senior management and the staff is essential. Always explain things as clearly as possible – if the staff feel that they are being kept in the dark about important things happening in the school it will be difficult to win their co-operation. Lines of communication and reporting should be clear to all concerned. Communication should include consultation, which needs to be genuine, and the results of the consultation should be communicated without delay so that the staff know that a decision has been taken, how it has been taken and what the decision is.

Concern and interest

It is more difficult for you to know a large staff as well as a middle manager can know his/her much smaller teams, but studying the staff files when you take up your post and learning something about each person, and what they are doing, will help to get you started. It is important to demonstrate your knowledge of and concern for the people you manage. A few well chosen words which indicate to a hard working member of staff that you have noticed the work they are doing, that you are interested in the progress of their current project, or that you are aware of a problem or of difficult home circumstances is likely to repay you a hundredfold in terms of goodwill. The qualities you really need here are a keen awareness of what is going on in your school and a sensitivity to vibes about people or contentious issues. Some headteachers rely on 'moles' in the staffroom for information, but this can be a dangerous practice.

Accessibility

Associated with concern and interest is accessibility. Having to book an appointment with the headteacher a week or so in advance to discuss a fairly minor matter, or having that appointment repeatedly postponed, does not promote goodwill. Some heads make a point of being in the staffroom for at least five or ten minutes each day to create an opportunity for informal contact. If someone wants to see you urgently then, if at all possible, make time on the same day at least for initial contact.

Willingness to listen

'She never really listens to what we say' or 'He's really only interested in what he wants to tell us' are all too frequent comments made about the senior managers in our schools, and they are quite damning indictments because they show a fundamental lack of interest in the affairs of the people being managed. All too often we only hear what we want to hear from a conversation or we are so determined to show that we are right that we dominate a conversation or meeting and fail to be attentive to others. The ability to listen carefully, showing interest in what other people are saying and with an awareness that makes you sensitive to the nuances of a situation, is an essential skill for any manager.

Consideration

Treating staff well leads to low staff turnover and encourages internal applications for vacant posts.

Treating people with consideration means not making unreasonable demands on them, eg by holding lengthy or unnecessary meetings or expecting them to do something at a moment's notice. It means providing good working conditions and consulting rather than imposing whenever possible. Treating people generously in respect of their personal requests helps to create a reservoir of goodwill.

Ability to counsel

As a senior manager you will have to deal with many situations which require counselling skills or the ability to resolve conflict. If your counselling skills are not naturally strong, you can work towards improving them through counselling courses. It is however important to remember that you are a manager, rather than a social worker or psychiatrist, and it is therefore your task to find solutions to problems.

Fairness

You have to be careful not to create 'haves' and 'have nots' by appearing to favour one individual over another. You have to demonstrate even-handedness, while managing to reward merit. Publishing the criteria you use to determine capitation, rather than a list of how much each department gets, is one way of avoiding interdepartmental jealousies. You should also be careful about becoming too dependent on any one member of the SMT – this can be very divisive.

Support and encouragement

So much development work is being undertaken these days that supporting change has become one of the senior managers' most important functions. It means that you have to give generously of your time and is linked to accessibility. Supporting and encouraging staff can entail acting as a sounding board or providing guidance and advice to a hard pressed middle manager trying to deal with a sensitive situation in his/her department.

Appreciation

Always give credit where it is due and make a point of giving praise when it is deserved. For example a member of staff, who may have spent hours preparing a display, will feel valued when the senior manager makes the effort to visit it and makes some positive comment to the teacher or technician concerned. Remembering to say 'Thank you' or 'You did that well' shows people that their efforts are appreciated. Making the praise specific – 'I really like that because . . .' – helps to convince people that you are sincere and have actually noticed what they are doing. Try not to be grudging, half hearted or too fulsome.

Decisiveness

If making decisions worries you you will not enjoy being a senior manager. Taking sufficient time to make a sound decision is one thing, indecisiveness quite another. Putting off making difficult or potentially unpopular decisions will soon lose you the respect of your staff. The meetings which most undermine morale are those that end without any decisions being taken. How democratically those decisions are arrived at is a matter of your own management style, but the point is that people want issues to be *resolved*.

Leadership

As a senior manager you are expected to set standards. If you spend a lot of your time at lunches, claiming that you are managing the school's external relations, you will quickly lose all credibility. Basically you have to lead by example. This means being first in and last out at an evening function that you have made compulsory for the rest of the staff. It means not delegating the really difficult things to your deputy or not conveying an unpleasant decision to someone through a note. It means offering to sit some lessons yourself when staff absence is high. And it *always* means being prepared to take the blame when things go wrong.

CASE STUDY 5.10. FOR ACTION

Most teachers feel undervalued by their fellow citizens. Partly they are sharing in the situation of other employed people, as there has been a general levelling out of status differentials, if not of pay differentials. But the particular situation of teachers' low self esteem has been aggravated by the acrimony of long running industrial action and widespread dissatisfaction with government policies on education. The feeling of low appreciation from outside makes it more important for teachers to feel valued by their colleagues and to be valued inside the school.

At the same time as teachers feel less appreciated by the world outside, the innovations to which schools are being asked to respond, generated largely by the same world outside, have multiplied in recent years. Bolam (1986) listed as many as 40 current changes (innovations, policy initiatives and developments) which have to be managed – and that was before the National Curriculum, LMS and more recent legislation. Seldom will all these apply simultaneously to a school, but never before have secondary schools had to cope with so many changes, many of them major. The fact that most of these changes are landing on schools from outside means that staff feel little or no 'ownership' of them. This not only reduces the likelihood of changes being implemented effectively, it also demoralises by creating a sense of being at the mercy of others. Many of the changes require staff to adjust their working practices, and nearly all of them are generating increased workloads. Most schools are suffering from innovation overload, just at a time when staff morale is – generally speaking – lower than it has been for some years.

Staff are responding to the situation in different ways; some by withholding commitment, some by withdrawing from out-of-school activities, some by increased militancy, some by reduced militancy, some simply bow their heads and resolve to work harder – again – like Boxer, the horse in *Animal Farm*. We encountered many staff who seemed stoically to have decided to concentrate on doing their best to tackle the major, inescapable tasks that face them. (Torrington and Weightman, 1989a)

For action:

Torrington and Weightman were writing in the1980s. If you were writing that extract today what changes would you have to make to bring it up to date? To what extent have the demands on teachers and their reactions to them altered?
What would be the main staff management issues for you as the head of a school? How would you address them?
Draft a staff management policy for your school.

CASE STUDY 5.11. FOR ACTION

Appraising yourself as a motivator
As motivation is a complex and difficult area to manage, it could be useful to focus an appraisal on it. Appraisal usually starts with the collection of data about performance. One way that you could approach this is to rate your own performance as a motivator in the key areas already discussed and then see how some of your colleagues rate you. You could use the findings as the basis of the appraisal discussion and to help you set targets. You will want to collect data from a number of colleagues at different levels in the organisation. As with any test of this kind, the first thing tested is your own self confidence are you brave enough to try it?

Chapter 6
Managing Appointments

As headteacher you need to attract and retain staff with the right qualifications, experience and personal qualities to enable the school to run as efficiently as possible. How well staff are recruited will have an overall effect on the quality of education provided. This chapter examines the procedures and issues involved in making appointments and provides some exemplar materials.

A member of staff has received a letter saying that his application for early retirement has been approved. You will have a staff vacancy for the following September. Your first move should be to consult your school management/development plan. Has it anticipated this development? How does this vacancy fit in with your staffing plans for next year? Will falling rolls or financial difficulties mean that you simply cannot afford to replace this member of staff, or does this resignation come as a longed for opportunity to restructure and replace overstaffing in this subject with someone teaching something much more popular? You can no longer consider any appointment on its own, you have to relate it to your overall staffing structure and to your budget.

Forming the selection panel

Once you have decided that there is a post to fill you will need to decide your method of selection, and this will necessitate involving the governors. They must deal with the selection of headteachers and deputies and may wish to be involved in the selection of other staff, so you should at least consult them. A change of head could lead to change in the way that appointments are managed, particularly if the old head clung to pre-LMS practices. There are three options available for appointments for all teacher posts other than deputies: selection by the headteacher, selection by a panel of governors and selection by a panel consisting of both governors and the headteacher.

It is unlikely that below deputy level you would need to raise the matter at a full governors' meeting. In most schools the vacancy would appear as an item on the agenda at the personnel subcommittee (which handles all the personnel/staffing issues) and be discussed there. This gives you the opportunity to advise the governors of the most sensible procedure. You will probably find that after a year or so a formula will have emerged. If it is a senior post, head of department and above, the governors will usually want a considerable degree of involvement. If it is a part time post, or a member of the support staff, they are likely to leave a decision to you. If it is a main grade teacher, they may or may not want a token presence.

For the purposes of this chapter let us imagine that it is a senior post eg a deputyship, and the personnel subcommittee decide to set up a separate selection committee consisting of three or four governors. What are the duties of this panel?

The duties of the selection committee

- drawing up a job description and a person specification
- deciding how the post should be advertised
- preparing details about the school
- deciding criteria for shortlisting
- making the shortlist
- dealing with references
- organising and conducting the interview
- deciding who is the best candidate for the post.

In practice a lot of the work, especially drafting and preparing the details about the school, is likely to be delegated to you as head, but the selection committee will want at least to approve the drafts (eg the job description) and must discuss the thorny issues such as the criteria for shortlisting.

Employment legislation

At this stage it is sensible to consult the relevant legislation. Nobody will expect you to know or remember it all, but the volume and complexity of recent legislation is such that you should take account of it. Remember that you must comply not only with education legislation, but also British and EU employment legislation. If you are an LEA school this could be a good time to have a chat with your LEA officer/adviser, for a reminder of likely pitfalls. It could also be a good idea to make one of the personnel subcommittee responsible for this aspect of staff selection and s/he could build up expertise and a file of information.

There are three main areas of potential discrimination in selection which are covered by employment law: disability, race and gender. We shall also look briefly at age and religious discrimination.

Disability

People with disabilities have the same rights under employment law as able bodied employees and employers of 20 people or more are required by law to employ 3 per cent registered people with disabilities. An employer unable to fill this quota may apply for an exemption permit and in practice prosecutions for non-compliance are rare, if not unknown. If you need additional information about employing people with disabilities you should consult the local Disablement Resettlement Centre through the local Job Centre. You would also get information there about grants and services to assist people with disabilities obtaining and retaining employment.

Race discrimination

The term 'race' includes race, colour, nationality, ethnic or national origins. It is illegal to discriminate on grounds of race at any stage of selection, and appeals against an employer for racial discrimination are quite frequently taken to industrial tribunal, so this is an area in which you should tread very carefully indeed.

Direct discrimination

This means treating a candidate less favourably than others because of his/her racial group, eg asking an Asian or Afro-Caribbean candidate a question about when she came to England, or his/her ability to produce the standard of written English required for the post, when no other candidate is asked these questions. This could lead to a claim of racial discrimination. It is likely that such a claim would be upheld by an industrial tribunal and lead to the awarding of damages. For this reason you have to be very careful about the way you ask questions at interview.

Indirect discrimination

This means creating conditions or requirements for the post which implicitly restrict the kind of applicant. 'Applications invited from UK graduates' is one example of a condition with which a far smaller proportion of applicants from one racial group can comply than another. Unless a justifiable reason for the condition could be found a claim of indirect racial discrimination would be upheld by a tribunal.

In limited and specific circumstances, however, discrimination on grounds of race is permissible, ie where it is essential to select candidates of one particular race, but you will have to prove the need. For example a Chinese restaurant may be allowed to select only Chinese waiters on grounds of authenticity, or Asian social workers appointed to assist Asian families. This need is described as a genuine occupational qualification (GOQ).

Gender discrimination

It is illegal to discriminate on grounds of gender or marital status in filling posts, the conditions on which the employment is offered and the non-offer of employment. Like race discrimination the ability to claim sex discrimination against an employer at industrial tribunal is quite wide.

Direct discrimination

This means unfavourable treatment which is directly linked to the sex or marital status of the person concerned, and applies whether or not there was the intention on the part of the employer and even if there was some justification. It is often tied to assumptions about gender or stereotypes. For example it is unwise to ask questions about a woman's marriage plans, when she is planning to start a family or child care arrangements if you don't ask the same or very similar questions of male candidates. Discrimination is about singling one person or group out from others and disadvantaging them by the questions you ask or the arrangements you make, so although it is important to your perception of how the candidate can cope with the demands of the post, in spite of being a one parent family with a small child, you may not single her out by asking direct questions at interview.

Indirect discrimination
This form of discrimination is about imposing a requirement or condition to the detriment of applicants of one particular sex, and this applies even if it means that a smaller proportion of the applicants of one sex can comply. An example of this form of discrimination will ask for, say, ten years' experience for a promoted post, while also requiring the candidate to be under 35. This requirement would disqualify many women who had taken time out for family reasons and would count as indirect discrimination.

Justifiable discrimination is permissible on limited and specific grounds, ie where special care, supervision or attention is needed for members of one sex. It will justify women teachers for girls' PE and a GOQ is used in the same way as for racial discrimination. A GOQ should not simply be assumed so do make sure you have got it right, discuss the perceived GOQ first with your LEA officer or adviser or, if you are a grant maintained school, refer the matter to any consultant you are using to help with the appointment. Voluntary schools may consult the Diocesan Board of Education or its equivalent.

Age discrimination
It is not illegal to discriminate on grounds of age, though as illustrated above it can easily become linked to gender discrimination. It is usually unwise to be too precise about age in the advertisement as it could adversely affect the field.

Religious discrimination
There should be no reference to religious belief when selecting for county schools, but the position in voluntary aided and special agreement schools is quite different and it is common practice to refer in some way to religious beliefs when seeking staff for posts in these schools. Even here however you must ensure that the need to appoint an applicant of a particular religious belief or outlook is genuine and necessary. For some posts, especially the headteacher of a 'church' school, there is a strong argument for the applicants being communicant members of that particular faith. When this occurs it should be clearly stated in both the advertisement and the particulars of the post.

To safeguard yourself you should show clear evidence of intent to operate a fair selection policy, ie by drawing up procedures of how all appointments in the school will be made and including in this a firm statement that you are an equal opportunities employer. An example might be: 'There shall be no discrimination against any applicant for any post in Bestwick Park High School on the grounds of race, sex, age or religion.'

Job descriptions

You can use a job description to outline the responsibilities and main duties of the post. It gives the prospective candidate information about the post and you can use it later for appraisal or regrading.

A job description is likely to contain many of the features given in case study 1.2 (p. 5) as well as the teaching and other duties, contract details and salary applicable to the post. In other words, it tells the applicants in broad terms what the post involves. It will help them to decide if the job is attractive, so it is important to get it right.

When a post becomes vacant you do not of course need to use the existing job description. This may be the opportunity to review the functions of the post, because demands change over a period of time but the job description may not have kept up with what was actually being done. So check to see to what extent it matches the job as it is now. You may want something slightly different this time round and this is your opportunity to include new components or change the balance of the responsibilities.

Make sure that you have included the flexibility to make changes to the duties/teaching commitment later on if necessary without affecting the grading of the post. All job descriptions should include a saving clause, eg 'These duties will be reviewed and revised as necessary.'

You will need to get the right balance between being too general and too detailed. A simple example is being too specific about the *kind* of equipment a technician will be expected to operate, when what matters is that she will need the expertise to operate a *range* of equipment.

A clear job description will help you attract the kind of candidate you want. An example of a job description is given later in this chapter as case study 6.9. You will also find a bursar's job description in Chapter 11.

Person specifications

The person specification is a supplement to the job description and should give you a pen picture of the ideal candidate by providing a statement of what personal attributes, characteristics, qualities and abilities are required for the job. The person specification is not usually sent out to the candidates but is used by the members of the selection panel to help them choose the most suitable candidates for the shortlist.

A person specification is likely to answer the following questions:

- **qualifications** – is a graduate essential for this post? What particular knowledge, skills and abilities are needed?
- **experience** – does the candidate need experience of A level teaching? Is it important that s/he has taught in a school similar to yours in organisation or ethos? Is this post suitable for an NQT?
- **broad age range** – is it a good idea to specify an age range, or will this create problems?
- **special requirements** – must the postholder offer a subsidiary subject, definite commitment to a multicultural approach or willingness to help with extra curricular activities?

CASE STUDY 6.1. FOR ACTION

The selection panel is considering the advertisement for a teaching post. They have written 'Applicants will preferably be between 25 and 45.' You are horrified, not only because this is a shortage subject, but because you suspect it could be challenged. A governor protests, 'We don't want an NQT if we can avoid it, but we need someone with a bit of experience, who can help move this department into the twentieth century. Older than 45 in this subject and you will be totally out of date. Why can't we advertise for what we need? Putting an age range isn't illegal is it?' He is right that it isn't illegal, but you know that age discrimination is inadvisable because it is unfair employment practice and you could lose a case if it came to tribunal. It would also restrict applicants and you want to attract as wide a field as possible.

For action:

What issues are raised by this case study and how would you go about dealing with this problem?
What arguments would you use to persuade the governors to change the wording of this advertisement?

Selection procedure

The criteria for selection

Establishing clear and agreed criteria will enable you to demonstrate why unsuccessful candidates were not shortlisted/selected if the appointment should be challenged. These should include, in addition to what is in your person specification, additional relevant training, outside interests relevant to the job and interpersonal skills.

Prepare the information the candidates will need

Sending the appropriate information to the candidates will help you attract suitable applicants. You want to encourage a potential applicant to apply by making the information user friendly, but you also want to ensure that the right people apply, so you need to provide information about the type of environment in which s/he will work and how the workplace is organized so that the applicant has enough information to decide whether or not the job is suitable.

The pack you send out should include a copy of the job description and details about the school. (It is sensible to develop a description of the school to use for all appointments.) Including an organizational chart is also helpful for candidates because it gives a clear picture of where the applicant will fit in. Finally, get the department concerned to provide information about the department or section of the school in which the applicant will work.

Other information should be available on request, but as it is expensive to send out a lot of paper you should send out sufficient information initially to attract the applicants that you want. Additional information can be provided for shortlisted candidates. Some candidates are addicted to phoning up and asking for copies of anything and everything ever produced by the school – resist this kind of unnecessary demand and think about what it tells you about the candidate! You may want to use some documents as tasks in the selection procedure, so think carefully about what you send to candidates in the initial stage.

Advertise the post

The costs of advertising are substantial, which makes it important to target your advertisement carefully. Remember that this is how possible candidates get their initial knowledge and understanding of the post on offer, so while stinting on the wording may save you money now if it is not clear to potential applicants what the job is and what kind of person is required, you are likely to attract a very small field and may have to readvertise, which is not cost effective.

The advertisement should concentrate on job title, salary, brief description of work/duties, indication of the kind of person who would best fill the post, location, benefits package and assistance given to successful candidate, how to obtain an application form and details, and the closing date.

No advertisement should be worded in such a way as to give the impression that applicants of one particular race, age or sex are preferred. Beware of gender specific job titles, eg headmistress. It is always wise to include a statement which makes it clear that the school has a fair recruitment policy and that applications are invited from all sections of society.

CASE STUDY 6.2. FOR ACTION

Bestwick Park High School – Head of Science – CPS plus 4
Following the retirement of Mr B Proudlove after 25 distinguished years of service, the governors wish to appoint a well qualified and experienced scientist to lead the faculty. A preparedness to lead from the front by example and an understanding of the likely needs of students of this successful and oversubscribed suburban school is essential. The ideal candidate is likely to be in the 30–40 age range and a graduate of a British university.

For action:

What are the main mistakes in this advertisement?
What advice would you give the headteacher and the personnel subcommittee?

What you put in your advertisement is not your only problem. You also need to think very carefully about where and when to advertise. If you advertise at the wrong time or not widely enough you could waste a lot of money.

You will have to decide whether to advertise nationally, locally or a combination of the two. The vacancy for a head or deputy headteacher must be advertised nationally throughout England and Wales. The main method is to use the specialist education press. Make sure that any local advertising does not exclude local church or ethnic papers. If the post is suitable for a first time applicant you may want to do a trawl of the colleges. This could increase the number of good applicants and you may find it useful to develop links with particular colleges who get to know your needs. This method should supplement the main methods of advertising and not substitute for them.

Ensure that your advertisement is non-discriminatory. Failure to do so could lead to a complaint which could be upheld by industrial tribunal. 'Word of mouth' is one example of recruitment which might save you money on advertising and bring you a candidate whose virtues and attributes are known, but could also result in you and your governors being taken to tribunal by someone claiming that the appointment was unfair because it was not advertised properly. In these circumstances it could be very difficult to justify your actions, so beware!

CASE STUDY 6.3. FOR ACTION

The librarian had announced her resignation. It was only a part time post, and the secretary suggested to you that one of her clerical assistants, who was also a parent, could easily take over the job, combining it with her existing post. Mrs Chattin is a lively person with a lot to offer. Her children are nearly grown up, so she could now take on a full time post. You think this is a good idea, as does the chairman of governors when you mention it to him, so you go ahead and offer her the job. Then you begin to receive letters of complaint – one from a furious parent who, as a trained librarian, claims that had the post been advertised properly she would have jumped at the opportunity of working for the school, and another threatening to take the governors to tribunal because the job wasn't advertised and she hadn't known it was available.

For action/discussion:

What mistakes were made in managing this appointment?
What advice would you give the head and governors?

There are specific circumstances, however, when internal only advertising is justified. This is when the school is involved in reorganisation or merger with another school. The governors could justify not advertising posts in order to protect the employment of existing members of staff.

Make sure that all posts are also advertised internally, even if you are unlikely to appoint an internal candidate. This is another safeguard.

Attracting candidates

The LEA package of benefits and assistance was designed to help attract candidates, but nowadays few governing bodies have the resources at their command to maintain this kind of incentive, so the post itself or the reputation of the school has to be the attraction. Setting the salary or grading the post at the right level to draw candidates is vital.

CASE STUDY 6.4. FOR ACTION

The school was expanding and I thought it only fair to create a second in the English department because it is compulsory to 16 and attracts large groups at A level. We reached this decision at the autumn meeting of the personnel committee and decided to go ahead with the appointment during this academic year rather than to wait for next September as it could be tied into a vacancy arising in the department for the Spring term. In the meantime I mentioned to the main scale teacher whom we appointed last year that we would be creating this post, and asked him if he would be a candidate. He's quite good and I wouldn't object to his appointment, although obviously I wanted to advertise properly. I was taken aback however when he said, 'No, for an A allowance, it's not worth my while.' When we did advertise the field was very weak and in the end we didn't appoint.

For action:

What mistakes were made in handling this post?
What advice would you give to this headteacher and the personnel subcommittee?

The point on a scale that you are prepared to appoint a suitable candidate can make a considerable difference to the field. Nowadays you have much more flexibility than in the past and this might incline you towards 'golden haloes', particularly in shortage subjects. Do look at the long term implications of the package, however, because in a climate of rising costs and inadequate funding, when schools are having to make staff redundant, the very idea of 'golden haloes' could raise a wry smile. A very real management issue for heads and governors is how to balance the need to attract quality staff in essential and shortage areas while shedding surplus staff elsewhere.

CASE STUDY 6.5. FOR ACTION

Your school is well down all the league tables, even in its own area it is hardly a market leader. It has its full complement of social and other problems and is seriously undersubscribed. Write an advertisement for the post of head of English for which a good field is essential to your plans for revitalising the school.

Timing

The closing date for applications is fixed before any advertisement appears, usually it is worked back from the date of the interview so that the necessary personnel can attend. Normally you will want a maximum of 14 days between the closing date and the interview, otherwise you may lose your best candidate to another post. Provide the candidates invited to interview with a programme of the day's activities and a list of names and functions of the selection panel. The letter of invitation should also set out what will be expected of the candidate.

Shortlisting

The selection panel will need a basic core of information – the job description, the person specification, the procedures being applied and anything else required to enable fair selection. Each member of the panel should have received a list of the applicants and copies of their application forms before the shortlisting session.

Don't forget that the chief education officer (CEO) (or his/her representative) has a right to attend meetings of the selection panel for teaching staff. The panel is required to consider any advice given by the attending officer. This is an advantage for you as the LEA officer is usually experienced in selection procedures, could warn you of possible pitfalls and help you gently nudge governors who stray from the agreed criteria. It is sensible to record who is present and what advice is offered, and, if it is not taken, why you have set it aside. If the panel decides to ignore the advice and the case comes to tribunal you must be able to justify the decision.

The way a candidate has filled in the application form could make an initial good or bad impression on the panel members. They will need to balance this initial impression by using the selection criteria to help them analyse the data in the application forms. Indeed your most difficult task could be to persuade the panel to apply the criteria rather than rely on gut reactions, both at the shortlisting and the interview stages. For this reason it is a good idea to use an evaluation grid which helps keep the process methodical and objective.

CASE STUDY 6.6. FOR ACTION

The selection panel at Bestwick Park High School is considering the applications for the post of second deputy head. The job description (see case study 6.9, p.118) makes it clear that it is a pastoral post. Both the existing senior teachers have applied. Neither are considered suitable, one because he has done little work in the pastoral side of the school and is generally regarded as having little to offer, the other because she has a tendency to be both aggressive and rather rigid. The head wants to restructure the pastoral system and improve the contact with parents.

For action:

Should either or both of the senior teachers be interviewed on tactical grounds? If the panel decide that it is more honest to remove them at this stage if they have no hope of being appointed and it prevents better candidates from being interviewed, how should they go about it?

Take up references

References are a problem area. When you should take up references and how far they should influence the selection of a candidate are issues that you will have to resolve quite early on. References have been discredited for a number of reasons:

■ often they tell you as much about the writer as about the candidate!
■ they can create an impression of the candidate which could influence the shortlisting or the selection

- ethnic minority groups have felt disadvantaged by the reference process
- a small number of LEAs will not use references at all because they do not consider them sufficiently objective.

Some heads/selection panels take up references on all or the most promising candidates as soon as the application forms are received, which can speed up the process. Most LEAs, however, recommend that references are taken up after shortlisting, and that they should act as confirmation at interview stage rather than forming a part of the selection procedure. This makes it difficult for a disappointed candidate to claim that an adverse reference prejudiced his/her chances. For the same reason LEAs discourage telephone references, although this is sometimes the only way to obtain a reference in time. Occasionally a post is offered 'subject to satisfactory references' if there has not been time for references to arrive before interviews.

Interpreting the reference should be approached with caution. References normally only contain positive statements, but can nevertheless damn with faint praise or somehow manage to create a negative impression, so treat them with extreme care. They can sometimes sound a warning bell that things are not quite right and this can be extremely useful. For example if they fail to match the candidate's application form in some important areas, say by not mentioning activities or qualities that the candidate has highlighted, you might begin to wonder what the candidate has actually achieved. Similarly, the choice of referee indicates something about the candidate, either because of the quality of referee that the candidate has to offer or because the applicant has omitted to give his or her present head-teacher as one of the referees. Inevitably you will wonder 'Why not?' You will want at least two references so you can check that they convey the same impression of the candidate. The reference is useful in enabling you to tick off the good points against the criteria that you have established.

Should you visit the candidates?
Visiting candidates in their own schools to help you gain an impression of them is nowadays discouraged for several reasons:

- you are unlikely to be able to visit all the candidates – visiting some, but not all, is unfair
- not all schools will want you to come – this may not be the candidate's fault

- watching the candidate teach in one school will not tell you how s/he will fit into a different institution
- if one person's impression and feedback influenced the decision it could be questioned later on
- the candidates may not have told their current schools about their application?

Candidates' visits to the school

You will have to decide your policy about allowing candidates to visit the school before the formal interviews. At one time this was very popular but, unless all candidates have the same opportunity and can all take advantage of it, it discriminates against those who live a long way away. It is probably wiser to send shortlisted candidates some additional information and take a full day for the interviews.

On the day

A well organized day is a priority. It is nerve racking enough for candidates to spend a day in an unfamiliar school and have to go through a formal interview. You do not want to make the experience either painful or unpleasant, nor do you want them to dine out on horror tales about your school. You will want to give any visitors, whether you appoint them to your staff or not, the best possible impression of the school. Making a group of candidates feel that this is a school they would like to join is an important public relations exercise. The day's programme should include an opportunity for the candidates to tour the school and meet appropriate people for long enough to gain an impression of the ethos of the school and the department. A good lunch in pleasant conditions is always appreciated. It needs to made clear whether this is part of the interviewing process or not, as sometimes it is used for staff to get a feel of the candidates and for senior posts the candidates are made to play musical chairs, changing places for different courses. If it is not part of the selection process it is only fair to tell candidates that over lunch they do not need to 'perform'. Serving alcohol can also be an unfair test, particularly if only some candidates have already had their formal interview.

Most schools appoint staff using a formal interview as the main selection test, but often there are additional tests. A linguist for example will be expected to demonstrate his/her competence in the language/s. Quite frequently nowadays for senior posts there will be a task such as working out a curriculum notation or suggesting strategies to deal with a current problem. The usefulness of such can depend on how well the task is set and whether the selection panel have given enough thought to what they want to get out of it. Sometimes candidates are asked to take part in a group discussion, to see how they interact or what ideas they have to offer. This can be so artificial that it fails to do justice to some good candidates. A recent trend has been to use psychometric tests, administered by outside agencies as a part of the process of shortlisting. As long as these tests are not the only method of selection they can be useful, but be wary of governors who place total faith in them. You should also perhaps bear in mind that some candidates may already have done these tests, which will affect both their speed and the general tenor of their answers.

At the interview

The areas that you want to explore at interview, the interview questions and how they are to be asked should all be worked out well before the interview and the panel clearly briefed about the procedure. The questions should be structured so that each candidate is treated fairly and given the opportunity to do him/herself justice. This does not mean that they must all be asked the same questions Although a few LEAs still insist on this it could actually penalise some candidates and could be challenged at tribunal as unfair practice. It is more important that each interview should have the same shape and that candidates face questions of the same level of difficulty. A solution to what remains a thorny issue, could be to have mainly the same questions with a few specific questions slotted in for each individual. Candidates are usually interviewed in alphabetical order, and if some other procedure is adopted the candidates should be told what it is and why it is being used. The length of the interview varies with the seniority of the post, but is likely to be a minimum of 20–30 minutes.

How to structure an interview

At the start of the interview the chairperson should introduce the panel members and attempt to put the candidate at ease. 'Icebreakers' or warm up questions should be used early on. These require the candidates to talk about themselves in a descriptive way, and you could ask them to explain their current job title or talk about the stages in their career. This question is an opportunity to see how well they can categorise.

The interview is the candidates' opportunity to talk, so make sure that they are given sufficient time to answer and that there is enough variety in the questions so that you get a rounded view of the candidates. Although most of the time you will use open questions in order to get the candidates to express their opinions, sometimes you will want to focus on a specific point and so use funnel questions. You may also use funnel questions to push a candidate into a more precise answer. Avoid 'Do you agree?' because it pre-empts a real choice – the candidate will think that s/he has to agree. At a senior level it may be a test of whether the candidates are too ready to agree with what they think your view is, but beware how you use it.

Some questions should test what the candidate thinks is important (eg attitude to a current initiative or what his/her priorities would be over the next three years if s/he is appointed head of department), while others should test what they know (eg about recent developments in their subject or about current educational issues).

You will wish to know how they would tackle a problem, and you could approach this by asking them how they would deal with a particular situation or by asking them how they would introduce a specific initiative. You may want to know how they view themselves – approach this through questions such as what they see as their strengths or weaknesses or how they see their career developing. In some interviews it is important for candidates to demonstrate a positive attitude to a particular issue (eg multicultural education or equal opportunities), and you will test this through such questions as, 'How do you ensure equal opportunities in your department?'

It is your responsibility to see that the panel get a full picture of the candidate. If an answer isn't clear to them, try to help the candidate clarify what s/he means, either through a supplementary question or by explaining a technical answer to the panel.

The answers to questions like these will give the panel an indication of the candidates' knowledge, what vision they have, how practical they seem to be and whether they can make points cogently and concisely.

After the interview

Making the appointment

Some candidates are good at interviews, others may perform in the job better than they interview. This is why you should work from an interview summary for each candidate, which should be set alongside the person specification at the end of all the interviews. The interview summary is also an insurance against trouble if for some reason the appointment is questioned. When all the interviews have taken place the adviser, or in the case of grant maintained schools the consultant, sums up the interviews, indicating the strengths and weaknesses of each candidate in order to focus the discussion and help the panel reach its decision. The officer or consultant does not have a vote, but can offer advice to the panel. Normally the weakest candidates are quickly eliminated and then the evidence about the remaining candidates is reviewed. This usually settles the matter, but sometimes there is a lot of discussion at this stage and the panel begin to argue about the merits of the candidates. The consultant or the head will have to make sure that this discussion does not reflect personal prejudices, but keeps to the criteria. Eventually a decision is reached and the candidate who has been chosen is made a verbal offer of the post. The unsuccessful candidates are usually offered a debriefing by the adviser, who bases his comments on the interview summary.

If the interview is for a headteacher or deputy headteacher post the decision will have to be referred to the whole governing body for ratification. A mechanism has then to be set up to call the governing body together as quickly as possible, usually on the same day, so that a substantive offer can be made. It is possible for them to reject the choice, although this does not often happen.

Accepting the post

A candidate's acceptance of the post constitutes a contract, although as yet there is nothing in writing. Successful candidates often worry about the lack of proof that they have the post, and you should try to reassure them by explaining the procedure. Normally the head writes to the successful candidate within a few days, as it can be some weeks before the legal documentation arrives from the education office.

Candidates may ask for time to consider your offer because of other interviews. It has not been the practice in education to allow this, but if it has been difficult to recruit for a particular post, you have to wait for the person to make his/her mind up.

Another problem is the candidate who verbally accepts the post, and then accepts another job with better incentives. This is illegal, as a verbal contract had been made. In this situation, if you are an LEA school, the LEA is your best source of advice, but it still leaves you with the problem of being short one member of staff and having to start proceedings all over again.

Not appointing

Sometimes there is no agreement or all the candidates are felt to lack the necessary qualities, in which case no appointment is made and the post is readvertised. If this occurs, the panel should be clearly advised whether this is such a shortage subject that it may not bring a better field, but it is now that the adviser or consultant's knowledge of the marketplace should carry weight. Readvertising is expensive and may not be productive. On the other hand, no appointment is better than the wrong appointment.

Advice for officers/advisers

Written record should be sent immediately to the governors in the event of disagreement. This may be needed if subsequently the head/deputy appointed proves to be incompetent and the governors decide to sack him/her. The LEA will then need to prove that their advice was not heeded, and therefore the school must bear the cost of any redundancy and/or tribunal.

This form should be used alongside that already devised by the advisory staff, which records comments made on the people interviewed for further reference for shortlisting purposes. It should include notes on the debriefing.

Associate staff

Appointing associate staff differs from appointing teachers in some important respects. The CEO must be consulted before you advertise a post which is for more than 16 hours a week and the LEA can veto the appointment on the same grounds as for other staff in the school. There are however no attendance or advice rights. The Education Act of 1988 is not specific about the precise method to be adopted, so you could in theory proceed on your own. It is advisable to bring in representatives from the department concerned and some representation from the governors, though with associate staff appointments it can be difficult to get governors to give their time. The recommendation for the appointment must include details of the hours to be worked, the grade (one of the existing LEA grades) and, if any discretion exists, the recommended salary.

Exemplar material

The case study material below follows through the appointment of a deputy head at Bestwick Park High School and provides exemplars of the kind of documents you would need to write. They are for reflection.

CASE STUDY 6.7.

The advertisement
Besthampton LEA
Bestwick Park High School, Bestwick Park Avenue, Besthampton PJ1 L34
Tel. Besthampton 2468. Roll 911, Group 5, Sixth Form 150
Headteacher Mrs B. Gatlin MA

Required from September . . .
A suitably experienced and committed teacher to join the senior management team of this popular and well resourced suburban comprehensive school as the second deputy head. Initially principal responsibilities will include co-ordination of pastoral care and some general administration, but there will be scope at a later date for the successful candidate to negotiate changes in role and task.

Application forms and further details of the post may be obtained from the headteacher at the school and should be returned there within a fortnight of the appearance of this advertisement.
Besthampton is an equal opportunities employer.

For reflection:

What would a prospective applicant learn from this advertisement? Is it likely to attract candidates?

What do you think should feature in an advertisement for a deputy head post?

CASE STUDY 6.8.

General information about the school

Bestwick Park High School
Bestwick Park High School was formed by the amalgamation of Besthampton Grammar School with the nearby secondary modern school, Park High School. It is an all ability 11–18 mixed school, which takes a five form entry of 150 pupils. The school is popular and oversubscribed. It attracts pupils from the neighbouring villages as well as from Besthampton itself.

There are 911 pupils in the school with 47.6 full time equivalent teaching staff. The clerical and technical assistance from 14 associate staff is very good indeed. Visiting Music teachers set high standards in a wide range of instruments and contribute to the two school orchestras and to senior and junior choirs. 'Foodfair' provides refreshments for sale at break and a comprehensive lunch menu, including a health food bar. Vegetarian food is always available and every effort is made to cater for special diets. Our excellent facilities are also a catering centre for the local meals on wheels service.

Our well maintained buildings are set within 14 acres of pleasant grounds. These include eight laboratories, three Art/Pottery rooms, a well equipped Technology suite, two gymnasia, a lecture theatre, a dark room with excellent facilities, a recording studio, drama studios, and a very well stocked library. As well as two modern computer rooms, a network of computers is available throughout the school. The latest commercial and educational software is used and IT is widely employed across the curriculum. There are online facilities and electronic mail links the school with schools abroad, including one in Moscow. There is a lively and active Music department, with its own suite and practice rooms, which provides opportunities for specialist tuition in piano, guitar, all orchestral instruments and solo singing.

The five forms in each year are of mixed ability. In Year 7 the work is differentiated according to need to ensure continued progression. Groups for Mathematics are set by ability during the first term. The National Curriculum is integrated into the programme for Years 7–9 and the school places an emphasis on active learning. Special provision is made for individual learning needs; enrichment and extension is provided for those who are very able, and specific support as appropriate for others, both in and out of lessons; Besthampton Achievement Project courses are offered in most subjects.

A common course continues for all students in Years 8 and 9, and a second Modern Language is introduced for most students. Students are taught in sets in some subjects eg Mathematics, Modern Languages, Science and PE) which means that they are taught with others at the level which is suited to their ability and most likely to bring out the best in them.

Year 10 students study a common core of subjects in addition to some guided choices. The aim is to give a balanced programme over the two years leading to Key Stage 4. As well as departmental assessments, profiling is used throughout the school leading to a Record of Achievement.

There is a large, popular and well established sixth form. We are able to offer a very wide range of subjects at this level. Following detailed consultation the school aims to provide the most appropriate course for each student. Twenty-two Advanced level courses are offered as well as GNVQs in Business and Finance and Health and Social Care, together with a range of complementary courses. Sixth formers also have the opportunity to participate in a range of extra curricular activities such as Young Enterprise and community service. Additionally a work shadowing programme for all Year 12 students is followed in all Besthampton schools during the last two weeks of the summer term.

There are numerous after school or lunchtime clubs and societies. At present some 90 pupils participate in the Duke of Edinburgh Award Scheme at all levels. Outside speakers and visits play a vital role in the life of the school and our pupils attend lectures, exhibitions, discussions etc outside school.

Pastoral care is co-ordinated by one of the deputy headteachers. Each year is managed by a year head. The role of form tutor is regarded as crucial in pastoral care.

The Parent Teacher Association is very supportive and active, arranging many fundraising and social events. They also take an active interest in the educational life of the school.

Inservice training is considered to be very important and we encourage all members of staff to become involved through both school focused initiatives and through attendance at county or other external courses. Staff development is managed by a staff development committee and co-ordinated by one of the deputy heads.

The headteacher is assisted by two deputy heads and three senior teachers, who work closely together as a management team and collaborate with staff through whole staff consultative meetings, heads of faculty, heads of department, departmental, heads of year and tutor meetings. Recently the school has been reorganised into six faculties: Mathematics, English, Science and Technology, Modern Languages, Humanities, and Expressive Arts. The 18 governors meet termly. They take an active interest in the school, attending working parties and social functions, and there are five governors' subcommittees: curriculum, finance, personnel, buildings and marketing. We believe in consultative management and are working towards collective management. Bestwick Park High School is proud to be an Investors in People organisation.

CASE STUDY 6.9.

Job description

Post: *Second Deputy Head.* **Salary Scale**: Group 5 **Spinal point**.

Organisational relationship
The postholder will be directly responsible to the headteacher

Service relationship
The postholder will be a member of the senior management team

Purpose
In the capacity as a member of the senior management team the postholder will contribute to:

- the formulation of the school's overall aims and objectives
- determining and maintaining norms of behaviour and discipline for the pupils
- the motivation of pupils and staff by personal influence and concern for human needs.

Duties

- to develop and implement a pastoral system which meets the needs of the school
- the oversight and co-ordination of the work of the year heads and their teams
- overall responsibility for the Personal, Social and Health Education (PSHE) programme
- overall responsibility for community links
- responsibility for leading the development of a school Record of Achievement
- liaison with external agencies such as Education Welfare Officers (EWOs), Social Services etc
- deputizing for the headteacher as required
- to undertake such duties as may be assigned to the postholder by the head from time to time.

CASE STUDY 6.10.

Person specification

Job title: *Deputy Headteacher Secondary Comprehensive School*

Category	**Essential**	**Desirable**
Qualification		
Academic	Good degree	Further relevant qualifications and/or Inservice training
Professional	Qualified teacher status	
Experience		
Teaching	Secondary school teaching across the age and ability range	Experience in more than one school/LEA
Curriculum	Familiarity and involvement with new curriculum initiatives. Experience of leading curriculum development	

Management	Successful experience as a middle manager	Variety of middle management experience
Community	Evidence of commitment to community and parental involvement	
Extra curricular		Evidence of involvement in/ leadership of extra curricular activities throughout career

Skills and abilities

To provide effective leadership

Ability to communicate with different audiences (parents, staff etc)

Ability to formulate, implement and evaluate short- and long-term objectives for school development

Ability to set and manage a budget

A thorough grasp of current educational issues

Chapter 7
Managing Performance

Your role in managing performance

One of your principal responsibilities is to ensure quality teaching, and to achieve this the staff have to perform well. This chapter looks at how you carry out this important aspect of your role and concentrates on the difficult task of dealing with the problem of poor performance.

The obvious first port of call in considering staff performance is appraisal (now in place throughout the British system of education), which looks at the objectives and performance of individual members of staff. Where it is working effectively in schools it makes an important contribution to assessing performance, but there are problems connected with centring quality assurance on appraisal alone.

First, the existing system provides appraisal for teaching staff every second year (only associate staff receive an annual appraisal), and this makes it insufficient on its own for monitoring performance. Second, it is largely seen as a developmental tool, rather than one targeting assessment, and as a management tool it is still in its infancy. Moreover there is still a problem in finding the right balance between the individuals' needs and those of the institution. Third, even if you can wait two years to assess how a teacher performs, appraisal does not always lead to an accurate diagnosis of problems because it is all too easy to buck the system. This is discussed more fully later in the chapter, but many problems combine to make appraisal a less than ideal mechanism for monitoring performance.

Managing staff who are not performing well takes considerable time and effort. The process can also be stressful for headteachers, who have to ensure that the problems are handled in a manner that both complies with employment law and is seen to be fair. So how do you go about managing performance? Obviously you need to get an indication of how the staff actually teach, and this is likely to involve you in a programme of lesson observation.

CASE STUDY 7.1. FOR ACTION

In my previous school I visited at least one classroom every day. I intend to maintain that habit as headteacher here. (Recently promoted headteacher addressing his first staff meeting.)

For action:

How realistic is this new headteacher?
What impact do you think his statement is likely to have on his staff? (The previous head kept well away from their classrooms.)
What are the management issues implicit in this case study?
Where do you as headteacher fit into a programme of lesson observation?
What should you expect to know about how the staff are performing?

Monitoring performance is a management function, of which appraisal (if it is working well) and visiting lessons are tools. You cannot, however, manage it all yourself. Your heads of department or faculty are key personnel here and it is they who must keep you informed about how things are going. The appraisal observation or a letter from a parent should not be the first indication you receive if things are not going well. This means that you have to train your managers in some of the necessary skills, so that, should you receive a letter from a parent about a particular teacher, the head of department has sufficient knowledge of his/her department to reassure you. It is also part of the middle manager's responsibility to keep the senior management team (SMT) informed if s/he has concerns about the performance of a member of staff in his/her section.

Sampling is obviously more realistic than trying to see everybody on a regular basis, and allows you to keep your finger on things without overcommitting you. It will also give you and your middle managers opportunities to observe good practice, and in weak areas or where new techniques need to be strengthened appraisal will help provide targets. The vast majority of teaching in schools would be adjudged satisfactory, but what happens if it is not?

What is meant by poor performance

In any organisation you will meet with a range of expertise and some of the staff will emerge as poor performers. But how do you recognise and deal with poor quality performance? Indeed, what precisely is meant by poor performance? There is no simple definition, but it may help to clarify things if you ask yourself, 'Is this member of staff performing the important areas of his/her job to a generally acceptable standard?' This will apply to any member of the organisation, but as Chapter 11 is specifically devoted to managing the associate staff this chapter will concentrate on poor performance in the classroom. When we begin to look at what constitutes effective teaching and conversely, what is poor practice, an obvious starting point is Ofsted guidelines.

CASE STUDY 7.2. FOR REFLECTION

Ofsted Framework for Inspection 6.1 Quality of Teaching

Where teaching is good pupils acquire knowledge, skills and understanding progressively and at a good pace. The lessons have clear aims and purposes. They cater appropriately for the learning of pupils of different abilities and interests and ensure the participation of all. The teaching methods suit the topic or subject as well as the pupils; the conduct of the lesson signals high expectations of all pupils and sets high but attainable challenges. There is regular feedback which helps pupils make progress, both through thoughtful marking and discussion of work with pupils. Relationships are positive and promote pupils' motivation. National Curriculum Attainment Targets and Programmes of Study are fully taken into account. Homework that extends or complements the work done in the lessons is set where appropriate.

Teaching is unsatisfactory where pupils fail to achieve standards commensurate with their potential. The teaching is ill prepared or unclear. Pupils are unable to see the point of what they are asked to do. They are not appropriately challenged, nor are they helped to form a useful assessment of their level of attainment and of what needs to be improved. Specific learning needs of individuals in the class are not recognised sufficiently. Relationships are insecure and inhibit learning.

As you become familiar with it, you will begin to appreciate that most of the attributes of good and bad teaching have been set out in the two paragraphs above. But Ofsted language is not user friendly and the following should further clarify poor quality teaching:

- failure to maintain discipline – the most common individual cause of unsatisfactory performance
- failure to demonstrate mastery of subject matter
- failure to impart subject matter effectively
- failure to form a working relationship with pupils
- failure to accept teaching advice from superiors or colleagues
- failure to produce desired results.

Research suggests that poor performance normally manifests itself as a series of recurring incidents rather than a one off crisis, and that the crisis, when it comes, is the result of mounting tension and escalating problems. Usually the poor performer will exhibit more than one of the above weaknesses and they will be or will become interrelated. Let us illustrate this with a case study.

CASE STUDY 7.3. FOR ACTION

Mrs A

Mrs A left the staffroom slightly after the bell, as she usually did these days, so the majority of the class was already in the room when she arrived. Most of the remainder trickled in over the next few minutes and Mrs A waited for them before commencing any activities. She had long since given up any attempt to make them stand up to greet her, and she had some difficulty in getting silence so that she could start the lesson. Eventually the class came more or less to order, but when she stood up to begin the lesson someone said, 'We can't start yet, Tim isn't here.' And she asked involuntarily, 'Why not?' This question produced the one completely silent moment of the lesson. The class's attitude made it quite clear that they might know or suspect where Tim was but no way were they going to tell the teacher. Mrs A urgently needed to teach a new topic before the examinations, otherwise the class would not be able to do the paper, so she gave up on Tim's whereabouts and started the lesson. The information was contained in a video, which she proceeded to play. Neither Mrs A nor the video succeeded in capturing the class's attention. There was a lot of talking (which she did not try to stop), pupils rustled papers, many were chewing steadily, one boy was even listening to his personal stereo; several quietly got on with work for other lessons. A few pupils did try to watch the video, but found difficulty in taking notes and the programme was punctuated with their questions about what they were seeing. Mrs A sat at her desk at the front of the class finishing off some marking while the video ran for 20 minutes. She did once attempt to reprimand a pupil who talked too loudly to her neighbour, but the pupil answered back and Mrs A backed off. Another pupil however turned to Jane and said, 'Shut up Jane, we're trying to listen!' and Jane nodded and ceased her conversation. At the end one pupil tried to ask a question about something that she had not understood in the video, but Mrs A said that it was her own fault for not watching properly and went on to the next stage of the lesson, which was to dictate notes about what they had watched. It was difficult for her to get silence and eventually she gave up and simply started the dictation. Her voice was monotonous, but quite audible if the pupils listened, but this part of the lesson was punctuated by comments such as, 'What did she say?' or 'What's she on about now?' and pupils loudly rephrased the notes to each other. This created more confusion and held up proceedings, so Mrs A had not finished when the bell went for the end of the lesson. She tried to set some homework, but no one was listening to her and, not waiting to be dismissed, the pupils left. Mrs A gathered up her things and headed back to the staffroom for lunch – another lesson was over.

This case study, which is further developed later in this chapter, describes poor practice rather than complete incompetence, but the scenario includes a lot of the classic features of teacher failure:

- Weak discipline – not complete breakdown because both sides backed off from confrontation, but silence and a good working atmosphere were never established.
- A lot of time was wasted, particularly at the beginning of the lesson. The teacher was late and so were the pupils.
- The class didn't really understand what they were doing or why and they certainly could not guess what the learning outcome of this lesson was meant to be.
- There were few attempts to interact with the class. The only direct question was administrative and provoked a hostile reaction.

- Bright pupils were not challenged, and there was no differentiation – the lesson was targeted to the whole class.
- Weaker pupils received no support. An attempt by a pupil to clarify a point was put down. Pupils resorted to explaining the topic to each other which added to the indiscipline and general confusion.
- The teacher did not scan the class or patrol it, so pupils used the opportunity to do other work.
- At no time was a pupil addressed by name – did she actually know their names?
- Timing was poor – she was having difficulty completing the syllabus.
- She was unlikely to receive any homework – no one wrote the instructions down.
- There was a basic lack of respect – no working relationship had been established with the teaching group.

For action:

You are the new headteacher of Bestwick Park High School. You are very aware of the Ofsted guidelines on satisfactory and unsatisfactory lessons. As part of your preparations for a forthcoming inspection you visit the lessons of the faculty in which Mrs A teaches and observe a lesson much like the one described above.

1. In what respects do Mrs A's lessons fall short of the guidelines?
2. It is clear that chaotic lessons are a regular occurrence for this teacher. What should you do about Mrs A?

Patchy performance can also constitute a problem, either through uneven overall performance or because one aspect of the teacher's performance is less good than others, as the following case study illustrates.

CASE STUDY 7.4. FOR ACTION

Kevin was a very unassuming young man, and when he was appointed to the Modern Languages department at Bestwick Park High School he failed to establish his authority with his classes, particularly some of the junior groups. Very quickly discipline problems began to emerge, and Kevin developed a reputation as a poor teacher with control problems, whom junior classes 'played up' relentlessly. As a result of colleagues' remonstrances and some parental complaints a support teacher was put in to help Kevin, but this didn't seem to make any difference. Indeed the support teacher went to see the head because she felt things were actually getting worse, so the headteacher sent the deputy in charge of staff development to observe a couple of lessons and report back. The deputy (Mike Wade) found, to his surprise, that Kevin's reputation as a poor teacher was undeserved. 'He has a specific problem,' said Mike:

> 'His poor class control prevents him from getting started. When I went to the year 8 lesson the pupils behaved themselves. They were quiet and Kevin was able to teach them. He actually teaches rather well. He explains clearly, questions sensitively and makes ideas clear to the pupils. He also listens attentively to their ideas and suggestions. I feel that he has a lot to offer pupils. The support teacher isn't needed to back up Kevin's teaching, but can't enforce the discipline. Obviously I can't go to every lesson. What can be done about this situation?'

For action:

You are the headteacher – how as a manager can you salvage Kevin?

Causes of poor performance

In order to tackle the problem of how to manage staff who are not performing well, we need to understand the causes – ie what lies at the root of poor performance. Obviously we have to be careful about stereotyping and need to appreciate that poor performance is rarely the result of one factor alone. When a teacher is experiencing difficulties, the unsatisfactory performance may arise for a number of reasons:

- the employee – the most common cause
- organizational factors connected with the job
- the way in which the employee has been managed
- external factors
- a combination of factors.

In the majority of cases the problem arises from the employee's lack of skill as a teacher. This could mean, crucially, that the teacher lacks the intellectual ability needed to establish subject credibility. The most damning statement about a teacher we have heard recently is: 'What this teacher knows about his subject could be put on the back of a postage stamp . . . and would not fill it.' Not surprisingly this teacher had difficulty in maintaining authority. He was all too obviously barely one step ahead of the pupils, could not answer any of their questions and very quickly lost their respect.

Another manifestation of lack of skill is when the teacher lacks the ability to impart information effectively ('Mr X's explanations are very confusing. They make matters worse rather than better, so everyone just talks and no one listens.') or where the teacher uses methods which fail to engage the interest of the group ('Mr Y's lessons are so dull. All we ever do is to write notes from his dictation.')

Sometimes however the poor performance arises from the teacher's lack of motivation. It is important to distinguish 'can't' from 'won't' when evaluating and dealing with unsatisfactory performance. Case study 7.5 however, suggests why the performance of the teacher concerned deteriorated over a period of time.

CASE STUDY 7.5. FOR ACTION

James – An example of poor management accentuating poor performance

James had been teaching for 15 years, most of the time at his present school. His performance never had been world shattering – his subject knowledge was good, though recently he had made less effort to keep up to date. But he lacks charisma, pupils find his lessons dull and almost from the beginning the head of department had to be careful what groups she gave him as his discipline was weak and confrontations could occur. She worked round James and he seemed unaware that he had a protected timetable. His four children are now reaching adolescence and financial pressure has made James ambitious for promotion. He went on a couple of counselling and pastoral courses and applied for year head posts, but his poor personal discipline and general lack of organisation meant that his applications were never seriously considered. Debriefing was always kind, but the rejections mounted up, and when James applied for a head of department post in another school in the borough he did not even get an interview. On the surface nothing has changed. He is still the life and soul of the staff social committee and his lessons are much as before, but his time keeping is deteriorating, he does as little marking as possible and he dodges duties if he thinks he can get away with it. At his last appraisal interview however he said that although he was reasonably satisfied with things as they were he sometimes felt very depressed that he was always passed over for promotion.

For action:

What are the causes of James' increasingly poor performance and how should the headteacher respond?

No effort has ever been made to improve James' performance, and now it is deteriorating noticeably. It is the almost classic scenario of poor management of an employee. James' head of department could be classified as an 'Avoider'. She worked round the problem rather than confronting it. We do not know whether this was from misplaced kindness or from a reluctance to tackle a difficult situation, but it has had an effect on James. External factors also played their part – the cost of raising his family motivated James to seek promotion. Once again poor management strategies shielded James from any realistic appraisal of his performance or hopes, but as rejection followed rejection James became more depressed and demotivated. Once again his managers, either at department or SMT level, did nothing to help and now, if remedial action isn't taken quickly, he could easily become a failing teacher.

How an employee is managed can have a considerable effect on motivation and effort. Case study 8.2 (p. 162) describes Fred – a very difficult head of faculty. The abrasive management style used by Fred, especially combined with his effective blocking tactics, would have deterred all but the most determined innovators. Similarly lack of resources or attention over a long period can affect performance and attitude, as can failure to provide support or praise good practice. This is explored much more fully in Chapter 5. Here a cameo indicates how a teacher can feel.

CASE STUDY 7.6. FOR REFLECTION

It didn't seem worth making the effort as you would only rubbish anything that I did. Even when I was second class, you made me feel fourth class. (Snippet from a teacher's appraisal interview.) She is responding to the head of department's criticism that she no longer volunteered for her share of the department's responsibilities and that she grumbled when asked to contribute to curriculum development. False praise for mediocre or weak performances such as James', however, is as bad as failing to give praise for good practice.

External factors can also affect a teacher's performance in the classroom or how s/he carries out his/her responsibilities. These can include problems with health, finances or family and may even encompass the journey to work.

CASE STUDY 7.7. FOR ACTION

Alex

The deputy head in charge of staffing matters has come to you. He went into the staffroom early this morning and for the second time this week he found the head of Spanish sitting with his head in his hands. He looked totally exhausted and admitted that he had not been sleeping well. He is in his early 30s, married, with a young family and a heavy mortgage. When the deputy probed a bit further he discovered that Alex was teaching Spanish at the local college three evenings a week and carrying out a whole range of paid building and repair work locally whenever he could get a commission. It was no wonder, said the deputy, that he looked tired out at 8.00 in the morning. You are particularly concerned because there are a couple of letters in your file about Spanish homework not being set or marked, and about the quality of the teaching. You are also aware that Alex has almost stopped mixing with the rest of the staff and seems irritable when approached.

For action:

What should you do about Alex?

Compare case study 7.7 with this comment made recently by a headteacher: 'My staff are busy finding ways to meet their families' needs by increasing their earnings from non-school sources with the result that they perform the basic jobs and then firmly turn their attention to an impressive array of part time jobs.'

Identifying poor performance

Initially you may think that poor performance will be revealed in teacher appraisal, but this is rarely the first indicator, although poor practice in the class room may reinforce what is already known. This is partly because teacher appraisal only arises every second year and the teacher gets some choice in what is observed, so it is easy to hide problems (especially as the teacher is likely to prepare better than usual and the pupils may well behave better than usual). Feedback about a teacher's performance should actually reach you regularly from a variety of sources. Feedback will come from lesson observation, complaints, and results. Dealing with complaints (from other teachers, pupils or parents) can take up a lot of your time.

It is unlikely that the lesson observation used in case study 7.3 was the first indication to the headteacher of Mrs A's difficulties. Teachers will quickly pick up vibes about other teachers, but tend to keep quiet about a colleague's problems. They are most likely to want action taken about Mrs A if her indiscipline has an effect on their own classes – either because they are nearby and the noise from Mrs A's class makes it difficult for theirs to work, or because the pupils arrive from Mrs A's lessons so high that it is difficult to teach them. It is much more likely that sooner or later a deputation of pupils will arrive to complain about Mrs A and express fears that they cannot achieve good results in this subject because of what they consider to be her poor teaching.

The most common source of information, however, is parental complaint. It has been suggested that the frequency of complaints about teachers is linked to the social class of the clientele, but most schools all too frequently receive phone calls, letters and visits about the performance of a member of staff or about how a pupil has been treated.

Telephone complaints are seen as less effective than writing or coming in person, although sometimes they are used if the matter is urgent. Most letters of complaint are addressed to the headteacher, as aiming at the top is seen as more likely to get action than writing to the teacher concerned (who may simply suppress the letter) or to a middle manager with limited powers. A typical letter of complaint is shown in case study 7.8; it expresses dissatisfaction, offers a reason and requests immediate or future relief.

CASE STUDY 7.8. FOR ACTION

Letter of complaint about Mrs A

Dear Mrs Gatlin,

I feel impelled to write to you because Andrea is making so little progress this term in Mrs A's group. I have talked to her and to her friends in the same group about this and they all say that the lessons are confusing, both because other pupils are not attending and are talking and because Mrs A's explanations are so difficult to follow. To make matters worse, when Andrea asked Mrs A to explain some things more clearly, Mrs A told her not to be rude and that she should have listened in the first place. Andrea says that she has given up trying to ask questions and cannot make sense of the lessons. Homework does not appear to be set regularly. When it is, Andrea finds it difficult because she does not understand the concepts on which it is based. My sister who teaches this subject in another borough tried to give Andrea some help during the last half term and commented that the group appears to be considerably behind the group she teaches. Andrea is doing very well indeed in her other academic subjects, but her lack of success in this subject in her GCSE year is influencing her choice of A levels and we are particularly disappointed about this. Some of Andrea's friends are in Miss X's group, where they are making very satisfactory progress, and trying to explain the work to Andrea. We should therefore be grateful if you would arrange to have Andrea transferred to Miss X's group forthwith.

Looking forward to hearing from you in the very near future,

Yours sincerely,

Mary Blane

For action:

You are the headteacher, how should you respond to this letter, and what action should you take about Mrs A?

N.B. If you transfer Andrea you will be deluged with similar requests. The option blocks don't fit – you can't transfer Andrea!

A regular surgery for parents will certainly produce parents who are dissatisfied with the performance of a particular teacher because this is an easy form of direct access to the headteacher. Otherwise parents will ring or write for an appointment. Sometimes they go straight to a parent governor, in order to ensure that the complaint is heard or because you have not acted fast enough or reacted in the way that they want.

CASE STUDY 7.9. FOR ACTION

Under the old head we stopped complaining because she just denied that there was a problem and suppressed the complaints.

She was a very authoritative person and you didn't dare challenge her judgement, but the problem didn't go away. It was suppressed and if anything, as time passed, we felt that it got worse. Then she retired and you were appointed. With a new headteacher we thought it was worth trying again as our younger daughter has now reached year 10 and is suffering from Mrs A's teaching, so we came to your surgery. It is more than six months now, and you haven't sorted it out either. Mrs A's still there teaching appallingly, yet you are trying to tell us that everything is OK because the volume of letters is dying down. Of course it is, because the parents can see that you haven't done anything. They have stopped writing because it is a waste of time as we are not getting any results. Mrs A's teaching hasn't improved, but the parents have given up! (An angry parent at the headteacher's surgery. It is clearly not her first visit about this problem.)

For action:

You are the headteacher – how should you respond to the parent? What should you do about Mrs A?

Parental complaints are the most powerful pressure on you to do something about a weak member of staff. Obviously a chronic complainer carries less weight than the parent who usually supports the school but comes in desperation about a particular issue. The volume of complaints about a particular teacher will also affect your attitude and your reaction, as will persistence on the part of the parents.

Dealing with poor performance

There are three main types of response to poor performance:

- tolerance/avoiding the issue
- salvage attempts
- induced exits.

Tolerance/avoiding the issue

This is an all too frequent response. Managers are often reluctant to confront incompetent performance or hope that over time a teacher's difficulties will go away, or perhaps that the teacher will go away. Case study 7.5 about James is a classic example of misplaced tolerance. The problem of his poor class control is not confronted early on and he is allowed to think that his performance is no worse than anyone else's and that he is giving satisfaction. Often the problem is compounded, because appraisal and other forms of evaluation put a good face on what is happening and either focus on soft targets or fudge the issue altogether. In James' case lack of motivation and effort led to depression as he was met with rejection when seeking promotion, and his managers continued to avoid tackling the problem of his unrealistic aspirations.

CASE STUDY 7.10. FOR ACTION

Exemplar of an evaluation report

Mrs A is to be commended for volunteering to be part of the team for this new initiative. She has worked hard to prepare the syllabus and although there have been some teething troubles, mainly concerned with interpreting the instructions from the board, I am sure that these will soon be ironed out and the course will prove successful.

This report could be interpreted in many ways, from 'Mrs A is teaching a course for which she is not trained' to 'Let us hope for a miracle . . . maybe she will leave.'

For action:

What advice should you as the headteacher give to this head of department?

Poor performance is tolerated for a variety of reasons:

- misplaced kindness (to whom?)
- reluctance to face possible conflict
- lack of relevant management skills
- possible cost in time and effort
- knowledge of how difficult it is to get someone out
- problems of competency procedures
- fear of lack of support.

Reluctance to confront the problem usually means that nothing is done and over time the situation gets worse.

Avoiding the problem takes other forms besides pretending it isn't there. It often includes damage limitation. Mrs A can't be allowed to teach A level classes because the volume of dissatisfaction will be too great to suppress, so what shall we do with her? The head of department identifies the classes where it is considered she will do the least damage and she is allocated to teach them. In America teachers can be transferred within a region, from school to school or to non-teaching duties. We do not have escape routes of this sort and it is largely untrue that the incompetent are promoted out of teaching.

Salvage attempts

CASE STUDY 7.11. FOR ACTION

Mrs A
There was yet another letter about Mrs A in the day's postbag, very much along the lines of Mrs Blane's letter in case study 7.8. This one, however, accused Mrs A of incompetence in the classroom and, among other things claimed that the teacher was destroying the pupil's enthusiasm for the subject which last year, when she had been taught by Miss X, had been her favourite subject. The letter requested a change of group for the child or a change of teacher for the group. It ended by saying that in the interests of the pupils it was high time the school 'did something' about this teacher.

You take this letter to the deputy in charge of staff development, with the comment that this is the third of its kind this term and that 'we really must do something', but you know that he will have tried already everything that you can think of to help this member of staff. This includes checking the subject content, and the head of department has assured him that it is no different from what is being taught to the other classes and that he monitors it regularly.

You have checked Mrs A's results against those achieved by other teachers in the department, and her results stand up. What is more, the take up rate for A level of her group is no lower than the other groups and this does not change from year to year. When you say this to any of the parents who complain, you are told that the pupils only pass because everyone in Mrs A's group goes for private tuition and you cannot disprove this.

He has worked closely with the subject head of department to try to develop Mrs A. You have both observed lessons on several occasions and feel that although this teacher may be pedantic and uninspiring, she is actually sound. Although her control is weak, she is delivering the required content. She finds it difficult to cover the syllabus to time because of her control problems and has difficulty in enforcing homework, but technically she is accurate and she has thought about what she has to teach. She is terribly dull and you can understand why the pupils tend to turn off, but she was prepared to listen when the head of department tackled her about the problem and they have worked together to try and increase the variety in her lessons. The trouble is that if anything this made matters worse because the change in style did not come naturally to her and tended to make her nervous so that she sounded tense and snappy. The deputy's observations indicate that she does not refuse to answer questions but that she lacks flexibility and is put off by questions. This makes her seem aggressive or negative when a pupil interrupts her exposition to backtrack on something and you feel that worrying about this and the other associated problems has made her even more uptight about her teaching than she was originally.

You are sorry for Mrs A, and consider that the real problem lies in her inability to establish a good working relationship with her classes. They don't like her, and this leads them to question her subject credibility. She has developed a not totally deserved reputation as a poor teacher, pupils try to avoid being placed in her group and complain if they are. This has been going on ever since she was appointed.

For action:

What are your strategies (a) in the short term and (b) in the long term?
What can you do about this kind of ongoing problem?
What should the school do?
To what extent does your role as the headteacher mean that you will consider this problem differently from the deputy in charge of staff development?

The legacy of avoidance and tolerance of poor performance makes it very hard not only to confront the problem when it will no longer remain buried, but to remedy it. The head of department and the deputy in charge of staff development have tried a number of strategies. These include:

- pep talks about the need to improve her image as a teacher
- getting the poor performer to watch a good performer, with advice on 'how to do it better'
- spending more time planning lesson activities
- frequent observations to see if progress has been made
- checking pupils' exercise books and homework
- sending Mrs A on courses to update her knowledge or practice
- holding department Inset sessions
- monitoring results across the sets.

These strategies do not seem to have brought about either an immediate or a wholesale improvement. From the sound of things Mrs A is marginally worse than before the salvage operation started. Why is this? First, it has been established in American studies of teacher incompetence that remedial action is more likely to succeed with *beginner* teachers, and even then the success rate is low. Mrs A, for example, is set in her ways, and changing her approach will be difficult for her. This explains why her performance is worse using methods in which she isn't secure – they are eroding her confidence. Second, the change from avoidance to confrontation brings its own attendant problems. It may seem abrupt, and is very hard on a teacher who has believed him/herself satisfactory (or at least no worse than others) suddenly to be labelled as the weak link in the department chain.

In the past praise was given easily, now the manager is wary of praising anything lest it impede competency proceedings. Yet praise and encouragement are very important to motivating someone to try to perform well, especially in the current climate of documentation.

Sometimes the problem is incorrectly assessed and the wrong kind of support is given. In case study 7.4 about Kevin the problem is class control, yet the remedy is to provide a support teacher to help Kevin with teaching techniques and methods. This doesn't help because it is unnecessary, and Kevin struggles on with no support for class control until the problem is reassessed by the deputy head. Improvement, when it occurs at all, is likely to be in small rather than large steps – parental expectations will be very high that you can 'do something about Mrs A's teaching'. They will not be easily satisfied and this will put even more pressure on the teacher.

Failing teachers are rarely if ever changed from ugly ducklings into swans, but more could perhaps be achieved. The sections which follow make some suggestions as to how you could improve your management of teachers who experience difficulties.

Diagnosis

Apart from catching the problem early, correctly diagnosing it could help you find appropriate solutions. You must be rigorous about collecting evidence, because to address the problem you need hard data, ie precise information about how the lesson was conducted, rather than soft data, such as intuitions or opinions. Case study 7.4, Kevin, showed us how easy it can be to misinterpret a situation, because no one had really investigated it properly. You must review the file on the failing teacher very carefully and focus your observations or other evidence collection precisely. You will need to give instances of the specific difficulty, when you became aware of it, and what action was taken.

You also need to be precise about the nature of the difficulty. Is it lateness, absenteeism, discipline, lack of content, appropriateness of content or what? It is important to try to work out how far the causes lie within the individual, how far they arise from the job or its context and to what extent they are external in origin. The ongoing case study about Mrs A's problems in the classroom indicates how difficult it can be to sort out which is actually the *key* difficulty. Some problems are temporary and, once they are over, performance should revert to normal. Many of the external factors could be eased through stress management or appropriate counselling. This is another reason why correct identification of where the difficulty lies is so important. Three kinds of information help in diagnosing whether the origins of the trouble are internal, ie within the teacher, or external. They are all concerned with observation.

- *Distinctiveness*: how does this teacher's performance in this topic compare to how s/he teaches other topics or year groups? If other tasks are done better then either performance is patchy or the cause is external.
- *Consistency*: how does the performance change with time? If the pattern repeats itself over and over again the problem is likely to be internal.

- *Consensus*: how does this teacher compare to others teaching the same topic? If his/her performance is similar to others carrying out the same task, then an external attribution is likely.

Appraisal has helped some middle managers develop their observation skills, but this is still an area where schools would benefit enormously from training their managers as lesson observation is usually far too general. An example of focusing observation in order to set targets against which you can monitor improvement is given below as case study 7.12.

CASE STUDY 7.12. FOR REFLECTION

From a discussion between the HOD and Mrs A:
As how much work is actually done in your lessons featured in several of the letters we have received, it might be a good idea if my lesson observation focused on how much material is covered in the time.

After the observation:

I noticed for example that a lot of pupils sat for several minutes at the beginning of the lesson while you waited for other pupils to arrive. During that time no one started work. You would gain at least five minutes per lesson if you set an activity during that time. You could set a short revision exercise to test whether the last lesson was fully understood. This would help the pupils with revision. Sometimes you could set a short activity as a lead into the lesson. It is important that you make it clear that the exercise or activity counts as part of the lesson's work and that those who arrive late make up this task, otherwise pupils will see this part of the lesson as a punishment rather than as a learning opportunity.

The observation focused on one aspect of a lesson – how much content there was/material covered within a 40-minute session. Gaps were observed and suggestions made as to how to get more work done.

Confronting the problem
Where poor performance has been diagnosed it is essential to involve the teacher concerned. How you go about this is as crucial to whether you can help the teacher improve as whether you provide the right support structures. Dealing with a complaint about a teacher by

making an appointment, confronting him/her with the letter and making the teacher defend him/herself point by point is almost as bad as raising it at a departmental meeting. A strong daily relationship within the department, in which openness and a willingness to give and receive feedback about performance is well established, makes it much easier to tackle difficulties when they occur. Nevertheless holding a disciplinary/investigative interview with a colleague is never easy and likely to be extremely stressful for both of you. Almost certainly you will meet with a defensive reaction, first because the teacher has probably tried to hide the difficulties for as long as possible. This may be followed by cover stories, the attempt to blame someone else (usually naughty pupils) and finally an attempt to allocate the problem to external causes (no one can teach under these conditions).

Stewart and Stewart (1983) suggest an agenda for this kind of session, which you may find useful as a basic framework around which to structure the meeting. You must first agree standards, and that there is perceived to be a gap. You need then to agree the size of the gap, who takes responsibility for it, what actions need to be taken to reduce it, and the timeframe. Finish the discussion by setting a date for a follow up meeting.

Stewart and Stewart also make some useful suggestions about possible approaches to this interview:

- make it as easy as possible for the person to do what you want – do not let the meeting degenerate into a battle
- handle the problem, not the person. This is a classic counselling technique which enables you to adopt a problem solving approach and takes some of the heat out of the debate. It also makes it easier to suggest changes to behaviour. If the session is perceived as a personal attack you are unlikely to get a positive outcome and the teacher will become more defensive/aggressive or depressed
- find the knot that is easiest to undo and begin there. Time management or lesson organization for example are easier to tackle and improve than is the failure to establish a good working relationship. Real lack of the talent to teach children is virtually insoluble, however hard you try, and it may be better to face this
- try to give the teacher some hope. Encouragement will help a teacher try to persevere even if things are very difficult. Yet you must not lie to the teacher – false hope is not doing him/her a service, and you have the problem that any praise you give the

teacher could be used in evidence against you later on if the teacher's competency reaches tribunal.

Induced exits

> We don't dismiss a teacher. We never have and we never will. We try to encourage teachers to leave, we don't kill them. (Quoted in Bridges, 1992)

Dismissal is the harshest solution to teacher incompetence and the most infrequently used, but sometimes as a manager you have to face the fact that whatever you do, the teacher experiencing difficulty is never going to improve – so what do you do?

Basically there are two routes to follow: competency procedures or induced exits. To prove a teacher incompetent can be very difficult, especially if the issue was dodged initially, criticisms were not documented early enough, and the teacher can produce positive appraisal statements.

From the evidence provided on Mrs A, for example, it would be difficult to *prove* that she is an incompetent teacher. Indeed, your own inadequate monitoring of the situation would support Mrs A's case if she appealed against dismissal on competency grounds:

- she is teaching the National Curriculum and other required content
- she attempts to set homework
- she does prepare and has made an effort
- she listened to the advice and tried to follow it
- she started as part time and the school asked her to increase her commitment to full time teaching
- the school drafted her on to teams running difficult new curriculum initiatives in the course of which the team experienced teething troubles delivering the project.

Difficulties here would count as external factors connected with the job. Her pupils' results are as good as other members of the department, and although Andrea, the pupil mentioned in case study 7.8, was deterred from doing the subject at A Level, other pupils taught by Mrs A were not, and the take-up rate at A Level from her classes were as good as from the other sets.

Although it could be shown that she is not regarded as a good teacher, with weaknesses in class control, this is not enough. If a competency issue goes to tribunal with insufficient evidence it could easily fail. Tribunals are expensive and win or lose, generate bad publicity for the school. Competancy therefore is used infrequently in dismissing a teacher. As one headteacher said, 'I will not carry a case to this stage unless I am sure that I can win'. Headteachers should look for other ways to edge out a failing teacher. In Mrs A's case the most likely route would be to see whether she can be persuaded to take early retirement.

CASE STUDY 7.13. FOR ACTION

I've got to tell her to go

I know that I have to talk to her about considering early retirement, because that is a much better option for her than being forced out and having to go through capability proceedings, but I just don't know how to handle it. How should I broach the subject? Just how do you go about telling a failing member of staff that it is better that she should go before she is pushed? (From a conversation between Mrs A's head of department and the deputy head responsible for staff development.)

For action:

What are the issues raised in this case study?
What advice should the deputy head give the head of department and why?
What support should be provided for (a) Mrs A and (b) the head of department?
How do you as headteacher prepare your deputy and the middle managers concerned so that they can manage difficult issues of this kind?
What is your role as headteacher in dealing with this situation?

Having to face the fact that a member of staff experiencing difficulties has come to the end of the road, will not improve and 'should go before she is pushed' is difficult enough. Usually all your instincts are to go on trying to work towards improvement well past the time when you really believe matters will improve. Having to confront the member of staff with the unpleasant fact that s/he is regarded as a failing teacher and that capability proceedings are being contemplated is even harder and managing someone through an induced exit can be an emotional ordeal fraught with difficulties.

In America some principals have been trained to use prospective counselling to help them deal with staff in difficulties. It has been appropriated from medical counselling, where it is used to help patients who have decided to undergo major surgery. The training involves the manager in experiencing the unpleasant consequences in advance, usually via role play, and helps him/her to make plans for dealing more effectively with the situation when it actually occurs. Although this does not seem to be available here at present, it is worth your while giving a lot of time and thought to how the employee is likely to react and what strategies you could adopt given different possible reactions.

To manage the situation effectively you will need not only all your counselling and assertiveness skills but also determination and perseverance should things get nasty. Success or failure in this area can also depend on your ability to be an effective negotiator.

> You need a strong ego and the conviction that the knot should be cut and that what you are doing is in everyone's best interests. I have been called inhuman, a Hitler, and have got used to staff claiming that I am the problem, not the teacher whose retirement I am negotiating. (From a discussion at a headteacher conference about managing induced exits.)

CASE STUDY 7.14. FOR ACTION

I don't see why we are having this discussion. I don't believe I can be all that bad. Early retirement doesn't make sense for me at the moment. What would I do at home? Besides I can't afford it without substantial enhancement and I am advised that this is unlikely. (Mrs A)

For action:

Exploratory conversations with Mrs A do not seem to be going according to plan. What strategy should the headteacher adopt now? What advice would you give this headteacher and why?

Very often a combination of strategies is employed to 'persuade' a teacher to resign or to take early retirement. Of these strategies pressure – direct or indirect – is the one most regularly used. It provides managers with a weapon to make a failing teacher think very seriously about whether s/he wants to continue.

Using *direct* pressure means that you confront the teacher directly with his/her inadequacies; this will be extremely hurtful for the teacher concerned. Applying *indirect* pressure involves changing the teacher's working conditions and your approach in such a way that s/he becomes reluctant to continue under the new circumstances. You need to always walk warily enough to avoid any suggestion of harassment.

Another strategy is negotiation, either directly with the teacher or through the union representative. A request for early retirement can sometimes be negotiated in this way. Early retirement schemes offer a way out for hardpressed headteachers with too many undevelopable ageing teachers, particularly if they are linked to inducements. LEAs however are no longer providing generous funding for such schemes and it can be difficult for an individual school to fund a package that might persuade a teacher to go early.

Induced exits through resignation or early retirement with enhancement provide a teacher experiencing difficulty with an opportunity to go gracefully. Beware however that it is not seen by others as the rewarding of failure, because this could demotivate your best teachers. You will also need to take into account the appropriateness of the request/s being made, fair treatment of the person making the exit, the state of your finances and any criteria the governors have developed for this contingency.

Capability procedures

To satisfy an industrial tribunal following dismissal the employer must prove that:

- dismissal was based on a fair and thorough investigation;
- correct procedures were observed and proceedings were conducted in accordance with natural justice:
  1. the employee knows the full case against him/her
  2. the employee or his/her representative is given an opportunity to explain or defend him/herself
  3. those conducting the hearing must be impartial.
- the decision was a reasonable one given all the circumstances.

Dismissal for poor performance may be because either the employee is incapable of performing his/her duties, or although the employee possess the necessary skills and abilities, he/she fails to exercise them. (Drummond, 1990)

Incapability means that training, exhortation or encouragement would not enable the employee to do the job, either because of incompetence or ill health. The teacher experiencing difficulties would have to be given at least one written warning by the manager which clearly defined the deficiencies, provided with training and given prolonged support before incapability proceedings could be put in process. The procedure is summarised in the following checklist.

A checklist for handling incapability

Formal procedures – who does what?

- first written warning – headteacher
- second/final written warning – headteacher
- dismissal by a disciplinary panel of governors
- appeal to governors' appeals committee – comprised of different governors from disciplinary panel.

What should be included in the written warning?

- Performance standards and the gaps between performance and standard explained
- period of assessment appropriate to circumstances and details of how this has been/will be carried out
- what support is/has been given
- next stage of procedure explained.

Employee's rights – ignore these at your peril

- to prior acknowledgement of complaint
- to state case at hearing
- to question witnesses
- to be represented by someone of the employee's choice
- to be treated reasonably.

If incapability is due to ill health the position is different from that of incompetence. Here dismissal is acceptable if there is no possibility of a teacher's health improving sufficiently for him/her to continue in the post. It is not regarded as a disciplinary matter and is usually approached sympathetically in consultation with the teacher.

CASE STUDY 7.15. FOR ACTION

In the end Mrs A could not afford to seek early retirement and the school decided not to risk capability proceedings. As headteacher how do you manage the ongoing problem of Mrs A? Her presence is like a red rag to a bull for a minority of vociferous parents, who argue that you should remove her from teaching their offspring. The department finds having to provide ongoing support a strain, and the whole affair is demoralising for all concerned. How do you manage this extremely difficult problem?

For action:

What advice can you give this headteacher and where can s/he get support?

CASE STUDY 7.16. FOR ACTION

Gordon

Gordon was scanning the *TES* when you passed through the staffroom. You heartily wish he could get promoted, but you know how unlikely this is. He has been applying for posts unsuccessfully for years now, and his hopes remain undiminished in spite of numerous rejections. He also applies for every opening within the school, regardless of whether he has the relevant abilities or experience and this has now gone beyond a joke. Gordon does not seem to mind these disappointments. He works exceedingly hard and is on a lot of working groups, especially the ones that you can volunteer for, but Gordon is a man of minutiae, not a fount of ideas, and he can bog down any meeting he attends in a morass of detail. He is a year head, but his punitive attitude to the pastoral system is such that a pupil will do anything rather than seek his support and staff avoid involving him if at all possible. You would dearly like him out of the pastoral system as he provokes a constant stream of letters from angry or irritated parents and he has no place in your long-term plans for the school. Gordon already applies for every possible Inservice course and his training record fills pages of Inset file, but training seems to make little difference to his performance and you feel that sending him on yet more courses will not substantially improve his prospects.

For action:

You are the new headteacher of Bestwick Park High School, what should you do about Gordon?

Chapter 8
Managing Conflict

Every so often you will find that you have to resolve conflict between individuals or groups of staff. The case study below explores a dispute that sometimes arises in a school when one of the parties is a member of the senior management team.

A conflict situation

CASE STUDY 8.1. FOR ACTION/REFLECTION

Chloe, an excitable, but much respected member of staff, has arrived in your office. It is the day before the end of term, and she is in floods of tears. She declares:

> I can't stand any more of it! She's always shouting at me. She's done nothing but shout at me for the last three days, and now she's made me look foolish in front of the pupils. I know it's almost the end of term and we're all tired, but I can't take any more. If she shouts at me again, I am going to resign!

The member of staff who has reduced Chloe to this tearful state turns out to be your new deputy head, Sonia. She was internally promoted to the post only six months ago, but has had a great deal to contend with, because your other deputy, George, has been absent for much of the time having a serious operation, from which he is still convalescing. Sonia is an extremely conscientious deputy, who works all hours and finds it difficult to delegate. She likes things to be done her way, and is suspicious of Chloe's more intuitive approach and flow of helpful suggestions, which somehow always lead to major upheavals.

Although she accepts that the more volatile Chloe is also a hard worker she deplores the outbursts that seem to be a component part of all Chloe's activities. Chloe, in turn, never makes allowances for the difficulties of Sonia's position, or appreciates that her own interventions do not always seem to others as altruistic as they seem to her. Relations between the two women have never been good, and seem to have deteriorated with Sonia's promotion. Recently there have been a number of clashes between the two, mainly connected with cover and communications, and now, just before the end of term, matters have come to a head.

For action:

How should Erica, the headteacher, deal with this sensitive problem in which her deputy is one of the parties to the dispute?

For reflection:

The case study is an extreme example of the kinds of personality clash which can occur in any organisation: conflict has built up between two members of staff until, just as term is ending, it has emerged as a public clash and now one of the combatants has asked the headteacher to intervene. Obviously so violent a breakdown in the relationship between two members of staff cannot be allowed to continue and it is important to minimize the effects of the confrontation as quickly as possible.

Erica needs to start by breaking the problem down into short- and long-term issues. In the short term she needs to resolve the public row between two members of staff, where one has complained about how she is treated by the deputy and threatened to resign.

What should Erica do about Chloe's threat to resign? She should be aware if Chloe has threatened resignation before (and if so how regularly). This is quite likely because Chloe is clearly well known for her outbursts. The incident is certainly unfortunate, but may be less significant than if it had occurred with a normally calm member of staff. This prior knowledge should influence how Erica deals with the situation. Chloe has appealed for help and clearly needs to vent her feelings somewhere, and Erica's full attention and sympathetic ear will probably relieve the immediate tension.

She certainly needs to see Sonia, because she has not heard Sonia's side of the story. It is important to get the two members of staff to make things up, at least on the surface, as soon as possible. As the senior manager Sonia will lose most face, which is another argument for a speedy resolution of the problem. It would also help to retrieve the situation if Sonia took the initiative and made some gesture of reconciliation to Chloe.

On the other hand, Erica could play it down and see what effect a cooling off period has. It is not impossible that, with time to reflect, Chloe might regret having involved the headteacher, or she may wish to withdraw the complaint – after all it has been heard. Certainly it would be better if they were able to sort it out for themselves than for the head to act as arbitrator. If Erica chooses to take this path, however, she must ensure that Chloe, and possibly other staff, do not perceive her as doing nothing, or interpret it as 'the management always sticking together'.

Once Erica has dealt with the short-term issues, there remains a much more complex problem for her to resolve. A personality conflict between two forceful members of staff is potentially very damaging for a school – factions could form from the supporters of each side (arguments were already occurring in front of pupils and could involve pupils), and if the conflict were allowed to continue the quality of education provided for the pupils could be adversely affected. It is an essential function of management to create a harmonious working atmosphere in which the talents of a diverse group of people, each with different skills, abilities and personalities, can complement each other and contribute to the effective running of a school. But in this school harmony was breaking down.

To deal with this situation in the long term Erica must first analyse the underlying issues inherent in the problem. This will involve diagnosing the problem, categorising the symptoms, considering the viewpoints of the people concerned, suggesting possible causes and breaking the problem down into its component parts. The exercise is worth doing because it will indicate what the management issues are and so help to generate solutions.

Analysing the issues

Issues connected with Sonia

Although we only know about the problem that Sonia is experiencing with one member of staff, there are indications that she seems to be preoccupied with her role as deputy to the detriment of her effectiveness in managing staff. She seems to be low on the interpersonal skills needed for the job. Sonia's use of her power as a deputy head in charge of the daily running of the school affects the way that she relates to staff. She seems to be using an authoritarian style, which has provoked Chloe's resentment.

The case study suggests that Sonia is having to work very hard and is under some stress. There are two reasons given for this: the long-term absence of the other deputy (was she doing both jobs?) and her own attitude to her role (unable to delegate and rigid in her approach). There was probably also a confidence issue. Sonia was recently promoted and the description of her behaviour suggests that she is anxious to prove herself 'up to the job'. The promotion is likely to have additional effects – to make her reluctant to admit to even minor errors and to see Chloe's advice or interventions as unnecessary interference.

Issues connected with Chloe

The issues connected with Chloe are much more personal, although only suggested by the case study they emerge from speculating about Chloe's motives. The dispute is clearly very important to Chloe and seems bound up with her own personality, self image and how she thinks she is viewed by the establishment.

Chloe visibly dislikes Sonia's management style and is dissatisfied with how she is being treated by the deputy. The present quarrel could easily have its origins in Chloe's attitude to Sonia's recent promotion. Sonia's skills and abilities are very different from Chloe's, and the head clearly valued Sonia's in making the appointment. Whether or not Chloe was actually passed over for promotion, the institution appointed someone for whom Chloe has neither liking nor sympathy, and she may have had difficulty in understanding and adjusting to the appointment. Chloe did not support Sonia for the post, but now has to live with her appointment. It is possible that Chloe sees Sonia as blocking her access to the head, ie if she has an idea, she now has to go to an unsympathetic deputy.

Chloe's visit to Erica indicates that she is very anxious to put her version of events, perhaps before anyone tells the head that there has been another outburst. This could be as much a call for attention as a genuine complaint – Chloe wants to be noticed and valued for her good work. Whereas it is important to Sonia to prove that she can manage, Chloe is clearly admitting that she cannot cope with the situation that has arisen. It is also likely that, whether she realises it or not, Chloe is taking the opportunity to draw the head's attention to what she sees as Sonia's deficiencies, implicitly criticising her appointment as deputy head.

Issues connected with Erica

How did Erica manage the induction of her new deputy and what training or support was provided? The first year in a new post is usually hard, but internal promotion is particularly difficult to manage and can lead to all kinds of jealousies amongst the staff if not handled sensitively. There are always plenty of people waiting for mistakes to be made and the opportunity to say, 'We always knew she wasn't up to the job.' The incident involving Sonia and Chloe thus raises the question of whether enough support was provided for Sonia as a new senior manager.

Chloe's reaction to Sonia's appointment also raises issues about how Erica manages and motivates her staff.

Possible management approaches

Erica clearly needs to monitor her deputy more closely, so that situations such as the row with Chloe aren't allowed to develop, but she must not do this in a way that seems to undermine Sonia.

She has to make Sonia more aware of the other dimensions to her role as a manager, perhaps particularly her role as a manager and developer of personnel. She has to look for ways to provide Sonia with the support and encouragement to develop the confidence to manage more flexibly. Later (so that it is not linked in the staff's minds with this incident) she should provide Sonia with management training to develop her interpersonal skills, especially perhaps in dealing with difficult or intransigent staff.

She really ought to lighten Sonia's workload, but she must approach this sensitively or Sonia will interpret it as a judgement on how she has coped so far. If George is going to be absent for the following term then Erica should make arrangements for his responsibilities so that they are shared amongst the management team or someone is given an acting responsibility. It would be wise to ask Sonia which tasks she would like to keep. Sonia will probably argue that she can manage, but she shouldn't be allowed to prevail as lightening her task and cutting down the number of hours she has to work should eliminate a lot of errors and generally help her relationships with staff.

Chloe's need to be noticed could be met by a job appraisal interview delivered by Erica in person. This would give the attention and encouragement that she needs and the reassurance that she is a valued member of the community; it would also give Erica the opportunity to address the issue of the effect on the school of Chloe's all too frequent outbursts. Erica may have to approach this issue through Chloe's own promotion hopes – Chloe can hardly expect promotion if she is likely to have violent altercations with the staff she has to manage.

The cycle of conflict

If conflicts are not resolved they are likely to escalate, moving from a minor disagreement to a major battle. Such conflicts often start with a disagreement over some substantive issue – perhaps each party wants more of a limited resource, or has a different and incompatible view of how to deal with a particular problem. Whatever the issue, the parties differ and take a position of 'either/or', which means 'Either we do it the right (my) way or the wrong (your) way' and 'The more I get my way, the less you get your way'. Such an interaction is fairly unpleasant for both parties and even more so for the rest of the staff, who get drawn into the conflict as each side seeks supporters.

As the conflict escalates, the parties develop negative feelings towards each other. This mutual dislike may eventually turn to loathing, especially when the conflict is compounded as a second argument develops over another issue – the parties are likely instinctively to disagree with anything that the other supports. At the same time they are likely to avoid each other. They may have to attend the same meetings, but they will not voluntarily seek situations in which they have to work in association. This serves to minimise the immediate feelings of frustration and impotence of one to the other, and helps create a stereotype of their opponent, either as someone generally undesirable who will take advantage of others, or as someone totally unreasonable. It does not matter who lost or won the first round, the so-called 'winner' is just as likely to dislike, avoid and expect a fight as is the 'loser'. This tendency repeats itself in an ever increasing cycle of animosity and fear until finally it comes to a head, possibly over a less important conflict than the original disagreement. This is why, as headteacher, you will from time to time find yourself dealing with violent disagreements between staff over what seem to you to be trivial issues.

Case study 8.1 had many of the features described in the classic cycle of conflict, but unusually one of the combatants was a member of the SMT. This needs particularly sensitive handling, but all conflicts will make considerable demands on your ability to manage people. If

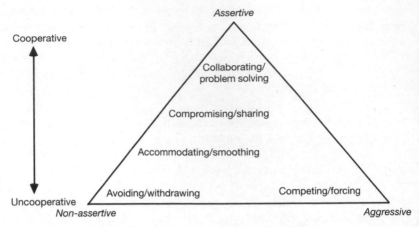

Figure 8.1   Styles of conflict management

disagreements between members of staff such as those described above are not to affect the well being of your school, you need to become the kind of headteacher who is able to resolve conflict and reconcile the warring parties. Although it may not come naturally to you, you can learn to manage conflict constructively.

Styles of conflict managment

Different people use different strategies in managing conflict. These methods are usually learned in childhood and become habits. We use them automatically, without thinking. We are often not aware of how we act in quarrels, we just do what comes naturally. But we do have a *pattern* of how we deal with conflicts with other people and, because it was learned, we can always change and improve it by learning new and more useful strategies. The first direct steps to managing conflict successfully should be a review of one's own typical style. There are five main styles or possible approaches:

Competing/forcing
Competing is aggressive and uncooperative. If you use this approach you try to overpower those involved by forcing them to accept your solution to the conflict. Your goals will be more important to you than personal relationships or the needs of others, and you tend to assume

that conflicts are settled by one person winning and the other losing. You want to be the winner because it will give you a feeling of pride and achievement; losing would give you a sense of weakness and failure. Your methods will include attack, use of power or position and intimidating the opposition. It is useful:

- when quick, decisive action is needed, eg in emergencies
- where important but unpopular courses of action need implementing
- on issues vital to institutional welfare, when you know that you are right
- to protect yourself from people who will take advantage of soft/ non-competitive behaviour.

This approach is typified by such statements as:

I'm not prepared to change my position.
I want to make my position quite clear.
My view is the most logical.
If you don't agree to do this, I'll. . . .
I know best, you had better. . . .
Do as you are told.

Accommodating/smoothing

Accommodating behaviour is unassertive and cooperative. It involves making concessions to avoid conflict. You might adopt this approach when it is important that nothing rocks the boat – ie a period of stability is essential. A subset of this approach is smoothing – 'Let's put this aside and agree to disagree for now.' A smoothed over conflict has a disturbing habit of resurging, but it can be useful if it allows you to deal with other more urgent issues. It is also useful:

- when you realise that you are wrong
- when the issue is more important to the other person than to you
- to build up credit for later use
- when you are outmatched or losing
- to allow people to make mistakes.

This approach is typified by such statements as:

I concede that point.
I agree with you there.
I will do as you think best.

What is your preferred outcome?
You have convinced me.
I'm glad we agree on that.

Avoiding/withdrawing

Avoiding behaviour is unassertive and uncooperative. You tend to feel helpless, that you can't resolve the issue and you shy away from dealing with it. Sometimes this is because you know that you will not be supported by the staff/governors/LEA, eg if you have had trouble in the past and not succeeded or you adopt this approach because relationships are so important to you that you are not prepared to endanger them and you do not think that any conflict or clash of interests is worth the uproar. Sometimes this strategy will include passing the buck, eg to governors, so that someone else has to deal with the problem. Deputy heads avoid by referring the matter to the headteacher. It is useful:

- when an issue is trivial, of only passing importance or when more important issues are pressing
- when you see little chance of satisfying your concerns
- when you need time – to think, to let people cool down, to gather information, to discuss the issue with others
- when the issue seems symptomatic of another, more basic issue.

This approach is typified by such statements as:

I can't take the responsibility for this decision.
I'd prefer not to discuss it now.
That's outside my brief.
I won't be drawn on that.
Let's talk about that later.

Compromising/sharing

Compromising behaviour is assertive and cooperative and falls in the middle ground between competing and accommodating. If you adopt this approach you are seeking a workable solution and are prepared to give up part of your goals in order to persuade the others involved in the conflict to give up part of their goals. Compromising involves bargaining: you offer some concessions provided that they offer some, and you will sometimes see this approach to handling conflict described as bargaining. You are seeking a solution in which all parties can be seen to have achieved some points and no one loses too much face. It is useful:

- to provide the parties to a conflict partial satisfaction or achieve temporary settlements to complex issues
- when goals are moderately important, but not worth the effort of more assertive modes
- when two opponents with equal power are committed to mutually exclusive goals
- to arrive at expedient solutions under time pressure
- as a backup mode when collaboration or competition fail.

This approach is typified by such statements as:

I'll give you . . . if you'll give me. . . .
Let's find a quick solution.
I suggest that we meet half way.
Let's split the difference.
I'm prepared to . . . if you . . . .

Collaborating/problem solving

Collaborating behaviour is assertive and cooperative – the opposite of avoiding. You tend to view conflict as a problem to be solved, as in case study 8.1, and you want to achieve a solution that will resolve the conflict both in the short and the long term. You are not frightened of conflict, but regard it as a challenge. You want to confront the problem in order to clear the air and begin to work towards a solution which can be mutually acceptable. You value both relationships and goals and are prepared to work with both parties, perhaps initially individually and then together in order to clarify the issues and to work out how to rebuild the relationships. It is useful:

- to find a solution when both sets of concerns are too important to be compromised
- when the objective is to test your own assumptions, understand the views of others and to learn
- to gain commitment by incorporating others' concerns into a decision
- to merge insights into a problem from different perspectives.

This approach is typified by such statements as:

How can we solve this?
Let's work together on this.

Where do we differ?
What is mutually acceptable?
Let's investigate the problem.

How do you find out what your dominant style is?

You may have recognised yourself instantly in one of the above descriptions, but if not there are tests available commercially to help you work out your natural or dominant style of conflict management. They normally involve answering questions designed to see whether you are relationships or goal centred (people or task) and to which of the five categories you are most inclined. You may score quite highly in more than one category as you often have to adopt the most effective approach to deal with a particular situation. In that case look for which column is the longest. If you are feeling brave, ask some of your staff to assess you and compare the results with your own score. They may perceive you very differently – you may think you are a collaborator, but they may think of you as an avoider!

Not surprisingly the most common styles involve fighting and avoiding, as these represent the reflexive, built in fight or flight response to a threat. Bargaining is the next most frequently used approach, with smoothing and problem solving by far the least used of the five. The most effective approach to managing conflict is usually collaborative or problem solving. Success, however, depends largely on your ability to handle the situation and on your interpersonal skills.

Key interpersonal skills for managing conflict

Active and attentive listening are key techniques when the combatants are telling their stories. You need both to get the story straight and demonstrate that you are prepared to give your full attention to those involved. Attending behaviour gives important clues to the individual who has sought your help: an open posture indicates that you are willing to hear what s/he has to say, regular eye contact that you are paying attention and verbal signs that you are following the story and willing to hear more. Similarly, nodding from time to time encourages the speaker to continue. Active listening ie repeating what the speaker has said, and restating it in your own words, is also important because it helps to clarify what is meant and eliminates misunderstandings.

Sensitive use of questioning also plays a major part in handling conflict. You need to get the balance of open to closed questions right in order to elicit the most information. Whereas open questions can appear to be counter-argument denying the validity of the other person's viewpoint and closed questions will simply elicit 'yes' or 'no', sometimes an appropriately focused 'in-between' question can move forward sharing information which may generate ideas for problem solving. An example of this kind of question could be, 'What common interests do we share in solving this problem? Often you will want to probe into a situation. You can do this verbally with a follow up question such as 'Then what happened?' or non-verbally eg by raising your eyebrows. A very good probe is an expectant pause (but you have to resist the impulse to jump in and fill the silence) because it can often extract more information than a direct question.

Developing your conflict management skills

It has been repeatedly observed that using interpersonal skills effectively seems hardest just when they are needed most and indeed, when involved in conflict some people abandon them altogether. For example, instead of active and attentive behaviour they use the opposite behaviours: closed posture, lack of eye contact or dead silence. This seems to occur because the body's response to a conflict situation is to manufacture large quantities of adrenalin which raise blood sugar levels in preparation for fight or flight. Restating another person's feelings is also difficult in a conflict situation because conflict seems to cause people to focus on their *own* emotions and to ignore or deny someone else's. The problem is connected to the fact that conflict makes people behave aggressively and, whether you are personally involved or attempting to mediate, the aggression makes you feel threatened. It is thus physiologically difficult to confront conflict in ways that are productive. So what can you do either to improve your skills in handling conflict or to ensure that you do not lose them at a crucial moment? One way is to learn the interpersonal conflict management skills so well that they become almost reflexive, 'conditioned responses' to conflict situations. The most useful strategy, however, is to use a structured step by step framework for dealing with the conflict.

A structured approach
This approach assumes that the situation is a problem to be solved rather than a battle to be won or a danger zone to be avoided. If you

get used to using the format and practise frequently it becomes second nature. Automatically you will begin to think 'Where have I reached in the cycle?' and be able to stay on track when things seem to be getting difficult. You will begin to recognise the tactics the various parties are using as tactics rather than being drawn into the contentious areas of the dispute. Remember that when we reviewed the various styles of managing conflict we commented that the problem solving approach is the least used, yet it is the most effective. It will take you a while to master the technique. It will not come overnight, nor by magic, but like most other management skills it can be learnt and improved.

Using a structured approach enables you to present the issue far less emotionally than might otherwise be the case. You turn it into a problem on which you collaborate in attempting to solve it. It contains an appeal for assistance to both parties: 'Can we agree to work together to try to sort this situation out?' rather than the accusations or threats with which the incident will have started. Case study 8.1 showed how the approach brought together the interpersonal skills, the attention and listening the parties required, and the detachment necessary to make the problem more manageable.

What are the steps that you have to take in order to use this approach?

Provide an opportunity for the combatants to talk to you individually
This is when you have to demonstrate your listening skills. You have to draw the parties out, get them to tell you what the problem is and how they feel about it. However busy you are, you must never hurry this stage.

Clarify and define the issue
This is when you have to get each person to make a clear statement about what they see as the cause of the conflict and precisely what they are arguing about. If it is difficult for you to understand what it is all about, or if it takes a while to work through the emotions and accusations and arrive at the underlying issues, go on probing. You do this either by restating what you think is the problem and asking if you have interpreted it correctly or by asking for further explanation or more detail until you have got it perfectly clear. Some conflicts are caused by differences in perception rather than any real difference of interest or opinion, and you may be able to sort them out simply by clarifying things.

Explore possible solutions
This could mean brainstorming ideas or bargaining for concessions. You will have to establish under what conditions both parties will be satisfied. It is their problem, and only indirectly yours in that it affects the smooth running of the school, so beware of *providing* the solutions, otherwise they will be regarded as imposed and not owned by the parties involved and the conflict could re-emerge. If this happens there is likely to be the added complication that they will blame you. So you have to work slowly and carefully towards an acceptable solution by getting them to generate the ideas and discuss them. In case study 8.1 the issues were separated into short and long term – taking this approach will also affect the solutions suggested.

Decide which is the preferred solution
Each person will have to decide which of the possible options is their best alternative. If you haven't handled the early stages too well this could provoke some selfish responses, but collaboration should have set in and if the preferred solution is itself open to modification at any stage you are well on your way to reaching agreement. Sometimes you will have to do some persuading – if this occurs try to avoid things becoming personal again. Discuss the implications of the preferred solution so that everybody knows what it entails.

Create an action plan
It is important to clarify what has been agreed and what is to happen next. The best way to do this is by creating an action plan and setting a review date, because this helps the parties to be clear about what they are going to do, how they are going to do it and by when.

For action:

Case study 8.1 described a conflict between the school's deputy head and one of the teachers. The problem solving approach was adopted, but the problem was not completely resolved. You are Erica, the headteacher, draft an action plan for resolving this conflict.

Managing difficult people

In addition to managing conflict you may also have to manage difficult staff. Case study 8.2 which follows provides an almost classic example of a difficult member of staff, whose own performance made it difficult for others to give of their best.

CASE STUDY 8.2. FOR ACTION

Fred had been head of faculty for as long as anyone could remember. He had a reputation as a survivor of the vagaries of the educational system and very clear views about current developments – he didn't like them. No initiative was worth bothering about; he had seen it all before and it wouldn't last. Fred knew to an inch what was essential in order to get by, and he did the absolute minimum. He arrived each morning at the exact time stated in the staff handbook, and left dead on 3.30 unless there was a scheduled meeting. If the meeting over-ran, Fred would get up and leave. He had no ambition, no desire for early retirement, and no notion whatsoever of his role as a developer. Fred had very little interest in any of the projects initiated by members of his faculty, and even less in helping or supporting his team when problems occurred. Indeed, he tended to be very unsympathetic and sarcastic in his dealings with other members of staff. He could be very difficult and aggressive, and, on a bad day, his bad language could empty the staffroom. Anyone allocated to Fred for appraisal had subsequently requested a change of appraiser and students could not be allocated to this faculty. His attitude engendered considerable frustration within the faculty where many of the staff would have liked to have seen the faculty play a more active role in school affairs. Anyone of ability tended to seek promotion elsewhere and, of course, Fred's longevity blocked promotion opportunities for others.

You have been putting off dealing with the problem of Fred, who you consider doggedly undevelopable. But now there has been a deputation from the faculty and the deputy head in charge of staff matters insists some action be taken. What do you do about Fred, whose poor performance is affecting how people do their jobs and whose aggressive behaviour is affecting the whole staff?

Bramson (1981) has identified seven stereotypes of difficult people. They are:

Hostile aggressives
They are the bullies, often very aggressive and confrontational. Fred

fits into this category absolutely. They can be very destructive of people and ideas. Their sarcasm and cutting remarks can also adversely affect the morale and performance of other staff.

Complainers

Nothing is ever right for these members of staff and they never do anything to help solve a problem. Their constant whingeing is wearing for everybody, and some of it can rub off, affecting the attitude of other staff. The problem for you as a manager is that complainers have an unerring talent for putting their finger on real difficulties. You ignore these at your peril, even though you can't always see when they have identified a major flaw in a scheme. Whether they feel powerless or simply don't like taking responsibility themselves is difficult to tell, but they can be extremely irritating.

Silent unresponsives

Putting over a scheme to a group of silent, unresponsive staff is every headteacher's nightmare and can be very depressing. They are clearly not enthused by your scheme, but won't tell you why and won't enter into any kind of dialogue, indeed they won't communicate at all beyond the occasional monosyllable. What is really infuriating for you as a manager is that you don't know precisely what it is that they don't like, but their non-cooperation speaks volumes. You will never make these staff even part owners of any initiative or their own development.

Super agreeables

These members of staff are OK to be with at the time, when to all intents and purposes everything is fine, and they seem to be totally in support of anything and everything you want to do. Then you wait for them to carry out the things they have agreed so readily to do. You can wait a very long time, because these members of staff fail to deliver. Avoidance of conflict is more important to them than doing the job, and getting these horses to water can cause you a lot of hassle.

Negatives

These members of staff will happily rubbish any and every scheme you put up. Basically they are anti the organisation, the rest of the staff, you, the education system and anything else you care to name. Opposition is their blanket reaction to any change or new idea, especially anything that could mean more work for them. It usually takes the form of: 'I can't see why we should want to do that', or 'It can't possibly work!', 'The pupils won't do that', 'We'll only get a lot of letters of complaint from parents', or 'We've done it before and it didn't work then!' What makes it worse is that negatives can't resist the opportunity to say, 'I told you so!' if things do go wrong. Their negative reaction is a classic blocking manoeuvre, not reasoned but intuitive. Sometimes negativism is the result of burn out; more often, for whatever reason, the negative feels defeated and doesn't want to be involved in further change. The reason can be more personal: s/he has been passed over for promotion and is resentful of you, the school or both, and will determinedly make life difficult for the management.

Know-it-alls

We have all suffered from people who are absolutely sure that they are right and insist on doing everything their way. Some know-it-alls have genuine expertise, which if used well can benefit the organisation, so you can't simply turn down their offers of assistance – however infuriating you find their attitude. In their arrogance and self confidence however they erode and pre-empt others and you have to watch teams being taken over because they threaten other staff and can make them feel inadequate. As a senior manager you will have to monitor this very carefully as it could damage an important initiative. Other know-it-alls are in a different category altogether. They are the phoneys, who claim to know everything but everything they touch is a disaster. They can be relied upon to make a difficult situation worse. You have to learn which know-it-all is which and work out appropriate strategies for each.

Indecisives

These staff 'witter on' for ever but never make any progress because they hate making decisions. Getting these horses to water can be very difficult indeed. They seem to think that if they put off the decision for long enough the whole thing will go way. You have to watch them very carefully or, despite hours spent talking about a project nothing will ever get done. Sometimes indecisiveness is linked to a desire to please everyone, but it can be infuriating for colleagues. Another facet of indecisiveness is avoiding taking responsibility, and you will find that problems are either constantly referred back to you or a policy produced by a group led by an indecisive makes you responsible for everything. This kind of buck passing can leave you with an impossible workload and a staff who are unable and unwilling to think for themselves.

To this list we can add minimalists. They exist in all organisations and have got doing as little as possible down to a fine art. They can seem to be very busy, but their output is low. They go on about how hard they are working, and may even believe it, but they are making work expand to fit the time allowed rather than seeking new projects. It is difficult to get much work out of minimalists, who usually protest that they are fully committed already and can't undertake any more.

Some people have more than one of these characteristics at the same time and this makes them even more difficult to deal with. Fred in case study 8.2 is an example: he is a hostile aggressive, a negativist and a minimalist. His rudeness and bad language are bullying tactics designed to ensure that he gets his own way. He rubbishes every new initiative, both to avoid work and to make things difficult for others. He knows absolutely how little work he can get away with and operates within this framework.

How then do you deal with difficult people?

Listening and counselling
Some people have become difficult because things have gone wrong in the past, but the situation may be retrievable. Chloe, described in case study 8.1 must have been difficult to deal with both because she all too frequently had emotional outbursts and because she felt threatened and ignored. Such people respond to genuine attention and to deal with them you will need your listening and counselling skills. Using the problem solving approach described earlier (pp 159–61) allows you to detach problems from personalities and this can enable you to move forward.

Deflecting aggression
With others such as the hostile aggressives who are using bullying tactics, you cannot be seen to allow them to win as they are testing out your authority, – very like when pupils misbehave to see what their teacher will do. Fred for example cannot be allowed to go on insulting and swearing at his colleagues. The interview in which you insist that he controls his language could become very unpleasant so it must not

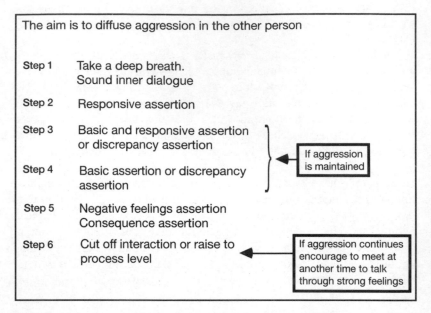

Figure 8.2   Guidelines for handling aggression

Key: *Basic*: a straightforward statement that stands up for your rights by making clear your feelings/opinions. *Responsive*: you try to find out where the other person stands. *Discrepancy*: you point out the difference between what has previously been agreed and what is actually happening. *Negative feelings*: you draw attention to the undesirable effect the aggressive behaviour is having on you. *Consequence*: you inform the other person of the consequences of continued aggression. You also provide a let out so he or she can change the behaviour. (Back and Back with Bates, 1982)

be allowed to get personal and you will need all your skill in handling aggression. I am grateful to Rod Young of SIMS Management Services for providing the guidelines for handling aggression which follow.

Demonstrating assertiveness
You will also need to show assertiveness because you must not allow the aggressive teacher to see that s/he has got to you, and your ability to take charge of the situation is central to your success in dealing with difficult people. What exactly is assertiveness and how can you be assertive when dealing with someone like Fred, whose rudeness gives him the initiative?

Assertive behaviour is interpersonal behaviour based on honesty. It is demonstrated by clear statements of needs, opinions and feelings, directly stated, without apology. This is balanced by sensitivity to and respect for the rights of others. It involves demonstrating that you understand the other person's position, stating your own views and feelings on the matter calmly and clearly and making it quite clear what you want the outcome of the situation to be. Don't sound apologetic, because this allows the aggressive person to take the initiative.

In dealing with Fred you have to show that you are not intimidated by his bullying or his bad language, which are not going to deter you from your purpose. You need also to show Fred that you are in control, eg by turning his time tactics on him: 'I need to be away by five o'clock, so there is no point wasting time abusing the system. If you have serious criticisms of the new scheme, I am prepared to hear them.'

Combining empathy with firmness is another useful assertiveness technique, eg 'I appreciate that you don't like the new procedure, Fred, but it has been agreed by the staff and now that it is in place I'd like you to see that your department follows the new practice.' This kind of statement contains an element of empathy but goes on firmly to insist that he conforms to current organisational practice. Sometimes you have to repeat the statement or put emphasis on what you want in order to get an aggressive person to listen.

Sometimes it is helpful to offer an alternative to the unacceptable behaviour: 'Fred, I was unhappy about how you expressed yourself. Abuse is never productive. I understand you don't like what is happening, but it would be much more helpful if you tell me why you feel as you do. Making personal comments helps neither of us sort the problem out.'

Drawing attention to how *you* feel, rather than concentrating on how someone else feels is an assertiveness technique which you might find helpful with a difficult member of staff. For example, 'Fred it is unpleasant and unfair to go on at me like this' or 'I really don't enjoy having to talk to you like this, but when a senior member of staff behaves in this way, it has an adverse effect on the rest of the organization and it makes things much more difficult for me.' This technique is also useful with those staff who don't deliver the goods, such as the super agreeables:

Because you haven't completed the task, it means that I shall have to do the job myself and will now have to do the work over the weekend to get it done on time. I feel annoyed about this as I had planned to do several other jobs this weekend and now they will have to be postponed. Next time I should be grateful if you only promise what you are sure that you can deliver. I am very disappointed about what has happened.

This makes it very clear what the effect of the super agreeable's inactivity has been. Peer pressure could also be employed. For example if a staff committee exists it could censure or put pressure on Fred whose use of the staffroom could be made conditional upon 'good behaviour'.

It can be helpful to make clear to the person the consequences of non-co-operation. It also gives him/her a letout, ie the opportunity to change his/her behaviour. Say for example that one of the technicians persistently took home equipment but never bothered with the proper procedure to check it out. He took no notice of the head of department's remonstrance and was rude to her. She has come to you. The technician maintains that it is all very stupid, he doesn't see why he should bother with all this red tape and is generally difficult. In the end you have to spell out the consequences of defiance: 'If it occurs again I shall be left with no alternative but to proceed to the formal disciplinary procedure. I'd prefer not to.' Disciplinary procedure (dealt with in Chapter 7) should only be used as a last resort.

Chapter 9

Managing the Partnership with Governors – 1

'Governors govern, heads manage'

As a result of the Education Reform Act of 1988 governors are much more important to the running of a school. Their vastly enhanced responsibilities include deciding budget priorities, determining staffing complements and gradings, selecting staff at all levels and making decisions about staff discipline and dismissal.

The powers of the governing body have also expanded. LMS, open enrolment, the National Curriculum etc have placed emphasis on the role of the governors in determining the future direction of the school. It has become fashionable to use business terms to describe the working relationship between governors and the headteacher. Indeed one CEO wrote to governors recently saying 'It may be helpful if you see your role as that of a non-executive director, who sets the direction that a school should take' and this kind of terminology has generally been adopted. The word direct however is the key to the governors' new role – the governors' concern should be with policy and determining priorities, not intervention in the daily management of the school. This kind of comparison fails to take into account your role as chief professional and educator and case study 9.1 perhaps puts this in perspective.

CASE STUDY 9.1. FOR REFLECTION

Main roles of the governing body – DFEE advice

To provide a strategic view

- The governing body should focus on where it can add most value – that is in helping to decide the school's strategy for improvement.

- It should help to set and keep under review the broad framework within which the headteacher and the staff should run the school.
- The governing body should focus on the key issues of raising standards of achievement, establishing high expectations and promoting effective teaching and learning.

To act as a critical friend

- Its role is to provide the headteacher and staff with support, advice and information, drawing on its members' knowledge and experience.
- It is responsible for monitoring and evaluating the school's effectiveness, asking challenging questions and pressing for improvement.
- It is a critical friend because it exists to promote the interests of the school and its pupils.

To ensure accountability

- It is responsible for ensuring good quality education in the school.
- The headteacher and staff report to the governing body on the school's performance.
- It should not rubber stamp every decision of the headteacher – it has a right to discuss, question and refine proposals.
- It should however always respect the professional roles of the headteacher and the staff and their responsibility for the management of the school.
- It is answerable for its actions and for the school's performance to the parents and the wider local community.

The changes in education have affected the traditional pattern of powers and responsibilities and have altered the whole relationship between the headteacher and the governors. The days when governors nodded when the headteacher spoke are long gone. As the head you have lost some powers, including much of your power to determine the school curriculum. This is not because curricular responsibility now resides with governors (which technically it did in the past) but because central government, through its directives, has taken control of much of the curriculum and left you with only the fine tuning. Where governors have gained additional powers and responsibilities is in the areas of finance and personnel, although even here (for maintained schools), the LEA retains last resort responsibilities, a factor which has led to some tensions between governing bodies and LEAs.

If it so chooses to exercise its powers the governing body can become the magnet, but most governing bodies remain content to take the advice of professionals in the field. The fact that the CEO quoted above felt he need to put out advice in the vein he did indicates that some governing bodies must, however, have flexed their muscles. There have been clashes between headteachers and either a group of governors or the whole governing body, which have received considerable attention from the media and led to demands (including some from influential bodies such as the National Association of Headteachers (NAHT)) that the powers of governors be more clearly defined or severely restricted.

The change in power and responsibilities has led to a growing awareness that a new relationship is needed between governors on the one hand and headteachers and the SMT on the other. The relationship is intended to be a working partnership. It usually takes time in any organization for new partners to learn to work with each other and in some schools there has been a steep learning curve. It has not proved easy for a working partnership to develop and there have been some hiccups.

CASE STUDY 9.2. FOR ACTION

Compare the two quotations which follow and comment on what they tell you about the nature of the relationship established between governors and headteachers.

1. 'The art of working together may be delicate but it can also be fruitful.'
2. 'The governors are happy to exercise power, but far less happy to take responsibility when things go wrong.'

Your predecessor may have been resistant to change, clinging to his/ her residual powers and reluctant to implement the new arrangements fully. If this was the case the governors may see the change of personnel as an opportunity to alter the balance of power. At other times a basic lack of respect or trust on one side or the other has made an effective working partnership difficult to establish. One of the main reasons for this is uncertainty about the nature of the partnership and the precise role each partner should play. Indeed, a question frequently asked by new governors is: 'Who does what?' It is not only new governors, however, who have difficulties with role definition and establishing where the boundaries should lie, and although the legislation has been in place for several years there are still issues about 'who does what'.

As a new head teacher, it is very important for you to be able to form a good working relationship with the governors. Each side should understand its own role and responsibilities and those of its partner, and be prepared to undertake both its own responsibilities and stay within the boundaries of its authority. The next section suggests how the division of responsibilities might work in a number of the key areas connected with running a school. Bear in mind, however, that even a definitive list of who does what will not do more than paper over the cracks in a poor relationship. Mutual respect for each other's role must be established.

Roles and responsibilities – who does what?

In broad terms, *the headteacher has responsibility for day to day decisions* about the management and curriculum of the school and *the governors have a strategic overview*. To make this work in practice, however, the full governing body should agree the general framework of activities:

Planning and policy making
The governing body has the responsibility for planning and policy making and for producing the school's management/development plan, which is officially the governing body's development plan. The governors determine the aims, ethos and priorities of the school, but much of the nitty gritty work of formulating the development plan is likely to be done in practice by you and your SMT.

Curriculum
The governors determine curricular policy in consultation with the headteacher. In practice this is restricted by central government directives (such as the National Curriculum) and by the LEA's curriculum statements. The latter may be modified with the LEA's approval. The governors are also required to have policies on specific

areas of the curriculum or aspects of education such as religion, health or drugs, and the governors are held responsible for the delivery of the curriculum. The head or SMT will probably supply the information, advice or indeed the first draft of the school curriculum plan for discussion and subsequent approved by the governing body. As head-teacher however you are responsible for the detailed *implementation* of the curriculum.

Staffing establishment

The advent of LMS means that governors, not LEAs, determine school staffing levels.

As headteacher you will draw up the initial staffing plan based on the school's needs and the overall development plan. The governors, however, either as the full governing body or as a staffing subcommittee, are responsible for the major decisions about staffing, for example what the staffing complement should be, what proportion of the overall budget should be devoted to staffing, whether to use any surplus for staffing or spend it on other areas. Their decisions must be informed and largely based on the information you supply through the staffing analysis and proposed plan, and this illustrates the nature of the partnership and just how closely you have to work together.

Appointments

The governors now have the responsibility for managing appointments, although in maintained schools the LEA remains the ultimate employer. Drawing up advertisements, drafting job descriptions and person specifications and criteria for shortlisting are the governors' tasks. Ensuring that the governors work within the rules is your responsibility, and this means in practice that you do much of the initial drafting, offer professional advice and guide the governors through the procedures, avoiding possible pitfalls. A full discussion of how to manage staff selection can be found in Chapter 6.

Salary issues

The governors' personnel responsibilities include determining salary levels for all members of staff, which can be a minefield. The governors must master the terms of the current pay award and work out how to apply it – often the head has to act as interpreter for a new scheme whose implications s/he has barely had time to analyze him/herself. The governors will have had to develop a pay policy, but you will have to assess how adequate it is and advise them of any necessary changes. Getting the pay policy right is one of your most important tasks as the criteria provide the governors with their best defence against criticisms of their individual decisions. Drafting a pay policy is described in Chapter 10, where an exemplar is provided.

Personnel issues

The governors' deal with personnel issues, but the day to day management of staff is very much your responsibility as headteacher, and it is only the complex problems which you need to refer to them. The governing body could be described as the adjudicator between the headteacher and the staff on personnel issues. This enhanced responsibility for personnel requires considerable expertise and has involved the governors in much new learning, making courses on personnel issues the most oversubscribed area of governor training. The position of staff governors on committees dealing with personnel matters is sensitive, but essentially they are expected to attend, and withdraw only if their own or relatives' employment is to be discussed, or where they have a greater interest in the matter under discussion than other teachers at the school. Personnel issues are discussed in detail in Chapters 7, and 10.

Finance

The governors are responsible for approving and monitoring the budget. Your role is to draft the budget as part of the school development plan through the school's finance sub-committee. Once the budget is approved the daily management of the money must be your responsibility.

Charging/premises

The governors determine the policies for charging for school activities and the use of the premises outside school hours. The headteacher implements the policies, oversees site inspections and reports to the governors.

Marketing

The marketing plan is usually drawn up by a governors' subcommittee or staff working party for the governors' approval. It is rarely the work of the headteacher. Implementing the plan is your responsibility, though you may choose to delegate many of the proposals to individuals or groups.

Resources

Here you would expect to act as adviser to the governors on policy because they are dependent on your professional expertise. But you also need their advice about how to get some of the resources that you need. Usually the governors work through a resources subgroup, whose task will be to assess what the needs are over a period of time, but it is for the governing body to decide the priorities and allocations and for you to apply them.

Discipline

The 1988 Education Act makes the governors responsible for producing a written statement of general principle for pupil discipline, of which you as headteacher must take account. You are responsible for the maintenance of order and good behaviour on a day to day basis – making the school rules, deciding how they should be enforced and dealing with individual cases.

When serious indiscipline occurs it is the head who excludes a pupil, but s/he must inform the governors and, if it is a maintained school, the LEA must be informed – there are clear procedures which must be followed. The parents have the right to make representations to the LEA or to the governors and need to know what their rights are. (The prospectus informs parents how to go about this. They can apply either to the school or for a maintained school they can go directly to the LEA.) The headteacher is not usually a member of a governors' subcommittee formed to hear representations or appeals.

Responsibilities in respect of information

Schedule 3 of the Education Reform Act 1988 established the flow of necessary information from the governing body on the exercise of its responsibilities. The governors have to supply the LEA, the Secretary of State DFEE, parents and teachers with any information requested of them.

These are some of the main areas about which the governors must provide information and for which they are accountable:

- an annual return to the LEA about the curriculum in the current year
- an annual return to the LEA about pupils for whom the National Curriculum has been disapplied or modified
- an annual report for parents

- an annual general meeting to which all parents are invited.
- they are responsible for ensuring that all policies and procedures relating to employment have been fully communicated to staff.

Although they have the responsibility to provide the information, the governors are dependent on you and the SMT for analysing or supplying their data.

The above listing of governors' responsibilities indicates the magnitude of their task. They decide direction, determine priorities and allocate resources. In reality the governors have been empowered with responsibility for all the really important decisions (except those reserved by the DFEE) and, in spite of LMS, your power as headteacher has been reduced.

Although it is rarer now for governing bodies to rubber stamp a head's proposals, they would be foolish to disregard them altogether. As neither professionals, nor full timers, they are dependent on you and your SMT to interpret legislation and guide them through complex or detailed information and, most of the time, this will make them anxious to listen to your advice and be guided by you. They will be keen to do whatever is felt to be in the best interests of the school. Individual prejudices can cause hiccups, but governors have power as a group, not as individuals, and the common sense of the group usually prevails and improves the quality of decisions. As headteacher, you may exercise your option to become a governor, which most heads do. Even of you do not become a member of the governing body you can still exert influence through drafts and briefings, so most of the time you can still expect to get what you want.

Where the adjustment has come is in the *relationship* – there needs to be give and take, trust and common sense if the partnership is to work.

There is evidence that many headteachers are struggling with the new relationship. Many only seek approval when the decision is irrevocable. Some wonder how the motley crew, who sit round the table once a term or more, can ever be shaped into a decision making team and hope that if they keep calm, the politicians too will eventually see that it is impossible. Most, if they are honest, yearn for the days when the governors came to the school's big events, made encouraging but futile noises about the school's achievements and occasionally stood by them when a difficult decision had to be defended.

This extract, from a contribution by Joan Sallis at a governors' training session, indicates that not all headteachers have really come to terms with the changed relationship. Neither, of course, have all the governors. The extract below is from the Governors' Training project, 'Working Partners' and sums up the current position rather well. You may find it useful if there comes a time when the governors need reminding of what their role should be.

The role of a school governor is to:
- support the school, but not uncritically
- explain its policies to parents and the community, but not blindly
- watch its standards, but with care, humility and with an open mind
- oversee its policies and its use of resources, but not in tiresome detail.

These responsibilities should be carried out as a governing body and they should be carried out with the knowledge and understanding of the school.

Making a success of the partnership is yet another test of your management skills, and a crucial one. If you try to pretend that the legislation of the 1980s hasn't happened and that the governors' power has not increased, sooner or later you will find yourself on the road to confrontation.

Making the partnership work – some guidelines

- make the framework of responsibilities clear to each side – try to avoid boundary disputes
- think positively and constructively about the relationship and work at developing it
- utilise the strengths that governors can bring to the school – they should complement your professional skills
- provide full information – don't hide things, share disasters as well as triumphs.

■ involve the governors in the life of the school – the more they are involved the more they will understand.

Case studies – the partnership in practice

Your governing body should be an asset and an important source of support for you. The case studies which follow explore the kinds of situation which might arise and suggest ways to make the partnership between the governors and the SMT more effective.

CASE STUDY 9.3. FOR ACTION

I am aware that there isn't time for us all to become experts in every aspect of school life and that some areas are so hedged about with legislation that it is genuinely difficult for governors to have more than a very general overview, but I am beginning to feel strongly that we should be more involved and be given more information. We just seem to be there to rubber stamp things. At the last governors' meeting we were given the health and safety policy to approve. It was actually drawn up by a senior teacher who is in charge of health and safety in the school. When I got home I read the policy and realised that there were a lot of references to LEA memoranda about reporting of accidents, letting of kitchens and such like. I'm a fairly new governor, but I've been on the governing body long enough to know that I've never seen any of these documents. It seems to me that the school is operating a policy of 'Keep your fingers crossed and leave it to the headteacher'. How are we meant to take responsibility for what we haven't seen? (From part of a conversation at a governors' conference.)

For action:

What does this extract tell you about the relationship between the governors and the headteacher in this school?
What role are the governors taking?
What advice would you give this headteacher and why?

CASE STUDY 9.4. FOR ACTION

The induction of new governors should include the following.

■ Briefing material
  – about the functions and responsibilities of the governor
  – about the school.
■ The opportunity to spend time in the school.
■ Time to talk to the headteacher – before and after the first meeting.
■ Information about the area Governor Training programme.
■ Opportunity to observe some subcommittees at work.
■ Linking the new governor with a mentor on the governing body.

For action:

Plan the induction programme for a governor who is elected during the 4-year cycle. Are there important differences in managing the induction of a group of new governors from that of an individual?

CASE STUDY 9.5. FOR ACTION

Observing lessons
The head's aim in inviting Gerald Duncan to spend a day in the school observing lessons was to help him learn about the school by seeing it at work, to give him the chance to talk to the staff and to the pupils and help him appreciate what studying Science and Technology in the National Curriculum actually meant. Bestwick Park High School was justifiably proud of its Science and Technology; not only had a lot of money been invested in equipment and facilities, but the school had been involved in a number of exciting curriculum projects, some of which had been published. Brenda Gatlin hoped that Gerald would enjoy seeing this work and report back positively to the governors and perhaps inspire other members of the governing body to spend time in the school observing lessons.

The visit duly took place, but the immediate feedback from both the teachers and the pupils was extremely negative. Gerald had been highly critical of what he had seen, had made his opinions quite clear to staff and pupils alike and intimated that he would raise the whole issue of unsuitable teaching methods and the poor standard of classroom discipline at the next governors' meeting. Brenda was appalled. It had taken time and considerable effort to persuade the staff, who were unused to governors visiting lessons, to accept the idea that this could become a regular feature, so it was a major setback for the policy. On enquiry she discovered that Gerald seemed to regret the passing of the GCE examination, had no faith in current qualifications and no experience of active child-centred flexible learning. Although he had been given some information about what to expect this clearly hadn't been assimilated, and he had expected to see didactic teaching with pupils sitting neatly in rows. What he actually saw was group work, assignment based teaching and a lot of movement around the school. He interpreted what he saw as progressive methods, leading to chaos and the complete breakdown of discipline, and he viewed it as his responsibility as a governor to get something done about this dreadful situation.

For action:

What are the lessons of this case study? For this headteacher the disastrous visit raised a number of issues.

- It highlighted the need for governors to heighten their awareness of current teaching methods.
- It created the problem that a negative visit will make it more difficult in future to persuade teaching staff to welcome the governors into their classrooms.
- Active child-centred learning was a feature of the school's curriculum policy – this could only be changed by agreement of the governors' curriculum subcommittee. As an individual governor, Gerald Duncan could not reverse this policy, but the governing body could decide to review the situation in the light of his criticisms. This could lead to conflict with the staff, who believed in the present policy, and cause problems for the school because it was receiving special funding for the technology project.
- It highlighted the need for established procedures for classroom visiting – governors' criticisms or concerns should be voiced in private to the head.

For the partnership to work, the governors needed the opportunity to see the school at work. The door should be open to them, but equally, they should come with an open mind or their visits will be seen as interference.

CASE STUDY 9.6. FOR REFLECTION

Dealing with a complaint

Yvonne Perkins, the deputy head at Bestwick Park High School, was working in her office when the secretary rang to say that as the head was out at a meeting she was putting through a call from one of the parent governors. Mrs Cunningham sounded perturbed. 'I've had a phone call from the parent of one of the year 7 pupils,' she said. 'It's about a music exam tomorrow. Sara Phillips has apparently been told that she has to go to the Music Centre at Besthampton Heights for the exam, and that a sixth former will drive her there in her car. Mrs Phillips is most unhappy about this.

The deputy head wondered why, if Mrs Phillips was so worried, she hadn't rung the school instead of complaining to a governor? Yvonne asked Mrs Cunningham for the background to the case. The examination was grade 4 piano, for which Sara was being tutored by one of the visiting music teachers. 'Are you sure that Sara didn't receive a letter explaining the arrangements?' she queried. 'We have a standard procedure for these things, and the letter should have been signed by Mr Wrench, our head of music.' 'No,' replied Mrs Cunningham. 'And I did ask her that, because my own daughter, Gwenneth, has taken some music exams and I always get a letter from the school. So I asked Sara if she had lost it, but she said that Mrs Martin had simply sorted it out during the lesson.' Mrs Martin, the new visiting music teacher, had clearly got the procedure wrong, and Yvonne would need to see both her and the head of music. More urgently she had to sort out the actual arrangements, as not surprisingly Mrs Phillips was not happy about a sixth former driving her daughter to an exam. Yvonne laughed: 'We have enough problems with staff and insurance for driving pupils, without adding sixth formers to the list. I don't suppose Mrs Martin realises all this as she is new to the area. We'll make other arrangements when I've found out how many pupils are involved.'

She suggested that Mrs Cunningham tell Mrs Phillips that the school would sort it out, and asked the governor to ring back after lunch. She needed some time to locate Mrs Martin, who only came in once a week and was probably teaching at another school. She would also need to talk to Mr Wrench, as she needed to find out whether the head of music was aware of the arrangements and what, if any, part he had played. She had a shrewd suspicion, though she did not intend to share it with the governor, that the cause of the problem was Mr Wrench, who was artistic rather than practical and had probably forgotten to tell his new part timer what procedure to follow. She in turn had probably not informed him about the exams. Yvonne was cross about this – the standard procedure had been introduced precisely because some departments (including music) tended to be stronger on performance than procedure.

A busy hour or so followed. Yvonne's suspicions turned out to be correct and she spelt out to Mr Wrench that the head had a right to know if a pupil had to go out of school for an examination and that parental permission was also needed. Yvonne, continuing to use the parent governor as an intermediary, apologised to Mrs Phillips for what had happened and explained the school's normal procedures for music exams when they occurred during school time, and she negotiated more suitable arrangements. In the end Mrs Phillips, much mollified by Yvonne's prompt action, offered to drive her daughter to the exam. The other pupils, accompanied by the teacher, travelled on the local bus. The parents of each pupil were contacted to appraise them of the arrangements, as they hadn't had the annual letter about travelling to music exams on the bus. The sixth former was allowed to drive herself to the exam as the car was her normal form of transport to and from school.

This incident, minor but irritating for all concerned, illustrates the role that governors are often asked to take and how a school should react. Parents often use a parent governor as an intermediary when they want to make a complaint because the parents expect him/her to understand the problem and to be sympathetic. This strategy reinforces the complaint and indicates their lack of confidence in the school's ability to solve it without some outside pressure.

This case study sought to illustrate how each partner understood the other's terms of reference and worked together to solve a problem. This was a relatively straightforward case, so it was easy for the deputy to resolve it and for the two sides to cooperate, but they succeeded because of the goodwill that already existed on both sides. All too frequently a complaint escalates because one party has an axe to grind or it becomes personal. Where a really sensitive issue arises, there is an even greater need to operate as partners, and to respect each other's role, otherwise the school could find itself defending itself from the governors as well as from angry parents.

CASE STUDY 9.7. FOR ACTION

The gap between policy and practice

At the annual governors' meeting for parents the governors found themselves facing criticisms from a small but vociferous group of Asian parents, who asked what the governors were doing about the racism that was occurring in the school. The chairman of governors was nonplussed, as no racist incidents had been reported to him. He asked the speaker to elaborate and the parents described name calling and harassment of the girls (who wore Muslim dress to school) by a group of year 10 boys. 'How,' asked the parents, 'does this fit in with the equal opportunities policy statement recently distributed by the governors?' The governors found it difficult to answer the questions, but pledged themselves to look into the problem and to take appropriate action. The following morning an irate chairman of governors sought an appointment with the headteacher to discuss the problem.

For action:

What are the issues raised by this case study?

What should the respective roles of the headteacher and the chairman of governors be in dealing with this matter?

What advice would you give this headteacher and why?

The chairman of governors, having pledged himself to look into the matter, had to find out whether the criticism of racism in the school was justified and, if it proved true, how serious it was. He would have to report his findings to the governing body, and they would then have to meet to consider the problem and decide what strategies to adopt.

Where does the headteacher fit into all this? The complaint had not been made to the head, but to the governors, so the headteacher cannot act without reference to the governors and must take direction from them. It is however the head, as the person on the job, who would have to undertake the initial investigation, with the governors, through the chair, monitoring the situation closely.

It is clearly not enough for the governors simply to have all the necessary policy statements, they have to see that they are implemented by the headteacher, who is directly responsible for implementing policy. It is his/her task to establish and maintain a multicultural ethos and equal opportunities for all members of the organisation. S/he is also responsible for the good order and discipline of the school. If the school's hidden curriculum and actual practice differ substantially from its published aims then the headteacher and the governors have to face the fact that a serious problem exists and that corrective action is needed. Both parties have a responsibility in the matter and if the situation is to be put right they must work together to find solutions.

If the accusations turned out to be true a number of issues needed to be addressed:

- what to do about the pupils responsible
- how to improve pupils' attitudes
- how to help pupils cope with harassment if it occurs
- how to make staff more aware of and more active in dealing with such incidents
- how to ensure that name calling and teasing were recognized as racist and not regarded as trivial.

In many ways the problem was one of awareness. Both the headteacher and the governors seem to have been unaware that a problem existed, and the staff seemed unaware of what constitutes racism. Awareness training that centred on recognition of different categories of racist behaviour and which suggested some partial responses would probably be beneficial for both staff and governors, and running the sessions as joint Inset open to both staff and governors would demonstrate that it was not only the staff who needed this training. A governors' working group, which included staff representation, could be given a brief which included organising the necessary training, exploring ways in which to support the victims and deal with the perpetrators and continuing to monitor the situation. Recording each incident that occurred and acting to check all cases of possible racism would deter some pupils from the more overt racist bullying. It would take longer to deal with latent racism. The curriculum and materials used in the school would also need to be checked for racism, as although most textbooks had changed with the times, some old books were still in use. Addressing the issue through the Personal, Social and Health Education (PSHE) curriculum was a more obvious, longer-term solution, but it would only become effective once the teachers' awareness and understanding of the issue improved, otherwise their teaching would lack credibility. The school's pupil council also needed to be involved. It would probably be a sensible move to make the governors' working group permanent, because of the need to monitor equal opportunities on a regular basis.

CASE STUDY 9.8. FOR ACTION

Making appointments

1. You are the headteacher of Bestwick Park High School. Your deputy is retiring this summer and you are hoping to appoint someone who enjoys managing change and development. You have drafted the job description and the person specification in consultation with the governors, and had thought that they understood what you wanted. In addition you have taken the CEO's advice about the procedure to follow, the criteria for selection and the wording of the advertisement. This duly appeared in the national press and because Bestwick Park is a popular school it attracted a good field. The time for shortlisting had arrived. Faced with the pile of application forms, the appointments panel (a governors' subcommittee) seem uninterested in the criteria that had been so carefully devised to provide a basis for the shortlisting. What really worries you is that they seem oblivious, or in some cases actively hostile, to equal opportunities considerations, and inclined to rely on 'gut reactions' to applicants' letters and forms.

For action:

What strategy should you adopt in this situation?

2. You are holding interviews for a head of department post. Three candidates had been shortlisted and all three arrived for interview, but Mr X, a candidate with very good references, withdrew because it became clear that his high pay demands would not be met. Your budget could not accommodate a C allowance for a department which usually merited a B, and you had had to inform candidates that the school could not afford to offer the successful candidate a relocation package.

The appointments panel, which consisted of two governors, one of whom is the chair of governors, an LEA representative, your deputy, Mrs Perkins and you, interviewed the remaining candidates, and then tried to reach a decision. Neither candidate precisely fitted the criteria, and the governors on the panel initially wanted to readvertise, but you have to advise them that these candidates are the best you are likely to attract and that readvertising is unlikely to attract a better response as it is a shortage subject. The LEA officer supports this view, so the panel review the two candidates.

At this stage the chair of governors becomes convinced that Mrs Y should be appointed, because she is the more accommodating of the two candidates. She has no shopping list of items for the department, and is likely to prove very easy to manage. He is worried lest Mrs Z, the younger and much livelier of the two candidates, but also the more ambitious for the department, would prove demanding and difficult to manage. You feel that, although not perfect, Mrs Z has the greater potential of the two candidates, and although there could well be problems you believe you could manage her successfully. On the other hand you fear that you could be saddled with Mrs Y for the rest of her teaching career. The criteria don't help you, as it is your years of experience in making appointments and managing staff that lead you to suspect that Mrs Y lacks any initiative and will prove personally unpopular with pupils. The department needs building up and modernizing, so there is a lot of development work for the new head of department to do and the appointment is a crucial one for the school. The chair of governors usually listens to you, but once he develops a view, he holds to it tenaciously.

For action:

What strategy do you adopt in this situation?

CASE STUDY 9.9. FOR ACTION

The role of the chair of governors

Mr Robbins, a parent who managed a large carpet firm, telephoned Brenda Gatlin in response to an item in the parents' newsletter to offer the school some carpeting. He said it would not only cover the library, but the reception area and her office as well, and he could sell it cheaply because of a cancelled order.

Brenda was eager to take advantage of this offer and went to inspect the carpet that afternoon, taking with her the chairman of governors, Miles Standish. Mr Robbins clearly understood the quality of carpet needed for a school. It was an attractive colour, and the price seemed to her very reasonable compared with quotations from other companies. Her instinct was to snap it up, and Mr Standish agreed with her, so they bought the carpet using moneys from the reserve accumulated in the previous year, and immediately put in hand arrangements to have it laid in the library and reception area.

A few weeks later there was a governors' meeting. All went smoothly until, in his closing remarks, Miles happened to mention the purchase of the carpet, congratulating the school on getting such a bargain. The governors' reaction wasn't quite what he had anticipated. There was uproar. It wasn't that the governors didn't think that the carpet was a bargain. Their complaint, expressed in no uncertain terms was that they had not been consulted. They were extremely angry at what they regarded as his usurpation of their decision making rights. 'What about the finance subcommittee?' asked one governor. 'It's their job to decide how the reserve is allocated. Why didn't you consult them?' 'Why on earth haven't you even bothered to tell any of us until now?' intervened Mrs Cunningham (who never had much liked Miles Standish), 'just who do you think you are?'

Miles was both injured and extremely aggrieved. They didn't seem to appreciate that he had taken time off from work to go and inspect the carpet on their behalf, nor to realise what a bargain they had got. Why did it matter so much that he hadn't consulted them? They had never got angry like this in the past when he acted in his capacity as chairman. Surely they understood that as chair of governors he had 'emergency powers' which gave him the right to take important decisions? 'If it were an emergency, maybe,' came the reply, 'but this wasn't an emergency. There was plenty of time to refer the matter to the finance subcommittee.' That led them on to discuss the role of the chair of governors in relation to that of the finance subcommittee, and to realise that the terms of reference for the group were rather vague and needed to be clarified (see Chapter 10).

The governors, several of whom thought Miles needed a lesson, were not prepared to approve the purchase and referred it back to the finance subcommittee. Mr Standish got angry at the thought of losing a bargain for the school simply because, as he put it, 'I had omitted some of the red tape.'

'Don't you shout at us!' retaliated, a normally very mild man. 'That's no way to go about things.' The governors were so infuriated with Mr Standish that they passed a motion of censure of the chairman's behaviour, at which the enraged Mr Standish stormed out of the meeting, and the vice chair, Mrs Cunningham had to take over.

In the end, as well as temporarily blocking the purchase, they severely restricted the headteacher's power to spend large amounts of money without reference to the finance subcommittee, whom they instructed to work out spending priorities for the reserve.

At the end of this turbulent meeting the headteacher was left with an embarrassing problem on her hands.

For action:

What had gone wrong?
What are the issues underlying this conflict?
What strategies should the headteacher adopt in order to retrieve the situation?
What advice would you give the headteacher and on what grounds?

CASE STUDY 9.10. FOR ACTION/DISCUSSION

Evaluating the governors

Some time before the annual governors, meeting for parents Brenda Gatlin reminded Miles Standish that some form of evaluation of the governors should take place. This entailed discussing the strengths and weaknesses of the governing body and whether it should make changes to the way it carried out its business. They decided that, since the rest of the organization had recently been asked about customer satisfaction, they should construct a questionnaire for use with governors and that the main item for the next full governors' meeting should be evaluation. They agreed that Brenda should draft a questionnaire, as it was better to start with something other than a *tabula rasa*, and that it should be issued to governors a week before the meeting to give them time to reflect on it. The meeting itself would be divided into two parts. In the first half the governors would form small groups and discuss the questionnaire, with the second half used as a plenary in which they would report back and discuss ways in which they could improve the system. A small working group would then be formed to write an evaluation report and to continue working on any recommendations which might need further refinement. This group could also be used to consider what form governor evaluation should take in future.

Bestwick Park High School – Governors' effectiveness questionnaire
Policies and priorities

1. Are the governors sufficiently involved in the school?
2. Do they help the school with daily tasks?
3. Do individual governors play an active part in specific areas of the school?

4. Are the governors sufficiently informed about the school?
5. How often do the governors visit?

Relationships inside and outside school

1. How often do the governors meet the staff or pupils formally or informally?
2. Do they know whom to approach at the LEA for help and advice?
3. Has a 'link governor' been appointed and how much use is made of him/her?
4. Do the governors know the community the school serves?

Roles and relationships within the governing body

1. Do all the governors know each other?
2. Are new governors made to feel welcome?
3. Are the governors encouraged to take on responsibilities within the group?
4. Does the governing body regularly share ideas, skills and knowledge?

Meetings

1. Are the meetings interesting and stimulating?
2. Does everybody have a reasonable opportunity to say what they want at meetings?
3. Are the meetings of reasonable length and frequent enough to cope with tasks effectively?
4. Do governors' meetings get things done?

For action/discussion:

What form of governor evaluation operates in your school? Who organises it? How is it reported?

The DFEE booklet *On Governing Bodies and Effective Schools* (1995) lists six features of effective governing bodies: working as a team, good relationship with the headteacher, effective time management, effective meetings, knowing the school, training and development. How far did the evaluation operated by Bestwick Park match the DFEE list? What other aspects of the governors' work would benefit from evaluation?

Chapter 10

Managing the Partnership with Governors – 2

The spate of government legislation of the late 1980s and early 1990s greatly enhanced the powers of individual schools at the expense of LEAs in respect of resource allocation, salary and employment. These powers have not been delegated to you as headteacher, but to the governing body of the school. Chapter 9 sought to demonstrate how essential it is that you make the partnership with governors work because of the closeness of your linked roles. This chapter continues to develop the theme of your relationship with the governing body, explores the structures and mechanisms you will need to establish the policies and offers guidelines for dealing with some of the problems involved in managing resources and personnel.

Creating structures – governors' committees

One of the problems that governors have had to address is how to divide up the work. It is simply unrealistic for the whole governing body to deal with every task. The growth of the volume of work has led to a mushrooming of committees, but the two structures most regularly used are: governors' working groups and subcommittees of the governing body.

A governors' working group/party is much less bureaucratic than a committee and does not need a formal agenda or minutes. Its advantage is in being a useful way of getting a group of governors and staff to work together. It lacks any real power because its recommendations have to be referred back to the whole governing body for discussion and ratification. This can be a major advantage for you because it prevents power being concentrated in a small group of governors. A subcommittee of the governing body is a formal organization which must have a chairperson and a vice chair, who must be governors (but not staff governors). Its membership and terms of reference are decided by the full governing body and it has the same procedural arrangements as the parent body, eg chairperson's casting vote and withdrawal criteria. These are designed to prevent ambiguity or overlap of functions between the various subcommittees. Subcommittees have much greater power than working groups because their decisions have the status of decisions of the full governing body, and are reported in the minutes of the governing body. They do, however, have to refer the pay and conditions policy, where the regulations make it clear that this must be formulated by the full governing body.

You may well have to advise the governors which structure they should adopt and, although they may have definite ideas, it makes sense to use a mixed system. Where there is a clear task, and it will hold things up to keep referring back to the whole governing body, then use a subcommittee. Where the issues are controversial, or there could be conflict between subcommittees, or where a clique could develop which may try to abrogate power properly belonging to the governors as a whole, then use a working group.

GM schools are bound by their instruments and articles of government which usually require them to have committees on admissions, (pupil) discipline and staffing (to deal with matters related to staff discipline). Appeals committees are also required to handle complaints from parents and staff.

Whether or not it is grant maintained each school makes its own decision about its preferred number of committees and their format. Each group has to have both governors and teachers (most frequently members of the SMT, so there should not be too many, as they will all have to have regular meetings. The most commonly used groups, whether working parties or committees, are:

- finance
- resources
- buildings
- curriculum
- personnel
- marketing
- community

There is obviously some overlap between these groups, which is another reason why it is important to establish clear terms of reference for each of them. Most schools find that they need five of six subcommittees to manage their affairs – creating more is usually counterproductive. An appeals/grievances subcommittee must be in place, however, and this must be formed from a distinctly different group of governors from those serving on the personnel subcommittee.

CASE STUDY 10.1. FOR ACTION

Terms of reference for Bestwick Park High School finance subcommittee

- to advise the governing body on financial strategy and policy within the resources available
- to receive, consider and present to the governing body annual estimates of the school's budget
- to keep under review the staffing establishment of the school and to recommend to the governing body and to the personnel subcommittee the financial limits for salaries and wages within the overall school budget
- to receive regular reports on the school's income and expenditure, to set these against the annual budget and to report to the governing body on their findings
- to provide the governing body with advice on resources and services to the school and in particular to undertake the setting up of contracts for services as required by the governing body
- to review from time to time and update the governing body on the financial memorandum, DFEE and LEA circulars and other documents pertinent to financial matters.

For action:

Compare this subcommittee's terms of reference with that of the finance subcommittee of your own school. Do the terms of reference cover everything necessary for the committee to function effectively?

Draft terms of reference for either the buildings group or the personnel subcommittee.

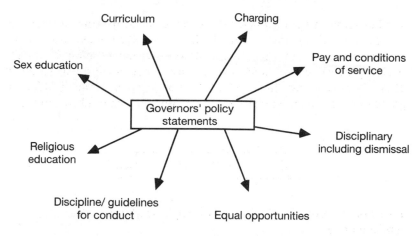

Figure 10.1   Governors' policy statements

Statutory policies

It has become essential for a governing body to have a clear set of policies on a range of educational issues. Many of these policies are now statutory, resulting from the Education Acts of 1986, 1988 and 1990. Others arise from issues confronting the school. How do you set about constructing the policy statements?

Guidelines for constructing policy statements

Given the need for a range of policy statements (and some schools now have so many that they are producing them in booklet form), it makes sense to adopt an inhouse approach towards them all. It also makes it easier for the governors to understand the methodology and what the person who has done the initial draft is trying to achieve.

1. Create a working group which includes both governors and pro-fessionals. Co-opt or seek advice from outside the school if you need particular expertise.
2. Define the terms of reference clearly so that the group understands the task, the deadlines etc.
3. Set the objectives – this can be done by the whole governing body, who will instruct the working group, or the working party will have to start by determining the guiding principles and the desired outcome.

4. Create a standard format or model for all your policy statements. This creates not only an inhouse style, but ensures that you cover all the areas which should be included in a policy statement.

Some of the exemplar policies available are virtually pamphlets in themselves and have perhaps lost their way. If you group your policies into one handbook there is no need to keep repeating the background of the school as a preamble to each policy. A page at the beginning can include the relevant information about the school.

A model policy statement

Aims
Keep the aims distinct from the objectives. Aims should be general, objectives are your achievable targets. Sometimes you will need to start the policy with a rationale section of what you believe, or eg in the case of a school's pay policy, with some general principles.

Content
The school's curriculum policy section will explain the main features of the school's curriculum. In a specific area of the curriculum, eg economic awareness or sex education, the policy statement will list the main curriculum areas through which the policy is delivered and describe what is covered. An exemplar is given below as case study 10.2.

Methodology
This section describes teaching methods or your general approach. It is most commonly used for policies dealing with aspects of the curriculum, but can also be used to spell out the steps you are going to take to enforce the policy. Sometimes it works better to combine content and methodology under the heading 'Delivery'.

Management
This describes who is responsible and for what. As well as describing how the policy will be managed, this is the section where you include 'liaison with' and list the 'other relevant policies'.

Evaluation
This section spells out how the policy will be reviewed, how regularly and by whom, ie the evaluation procedure. Many policy statements are

good on statements of intent, weaker on methods of delivery, and there is a tendency to skip evaluation altogether, so this last section is not only a test of whether you have grasped the general principles of writing a policy, but of where you intend to apply it. (See case study 9.7 in Chapter 9 which described a governing body being taken to task for its failure to implement its antiracist policy.)

The two case studies which follow provide exemplars of governors' policy statements which you can test against your own policies and the model.

CASE STUDY 10.2. EXEMPLAR

Bestwick Park High School – multicultural/equal opportunities policy

Rationale
This policy statement defines multicultural in its widest sense – ie not only referring to colour or ethnicity, but including all the factors *influencing* culture, including gender, class, religion, where individuals live etc. Therefore every classroom has a multicultural range of students, who bring to the school a selection of different cultural understandings, influencing how they learn and interpret the world.

Education for equality ensures that learners develop autonomy over their learning in a secure environment in which their understandings of the world are valued and used as a basis for learning.

Aim
Bestwick Park High School aims to provide for all pupils access to the full range of educational and personal development opportunities so that pupils reach their full potential physically, socially and academically. The school aims to provide for its pupils a curriculum and learning environment that values cultural diversity and builds on the experiences of all the members of the organisation.

Objectives

■ to develop a commitment to equality throughout the organisation
■ to develop a curriculum which delivers our aim

- to develop teaching methods and learning approaches which help us to create a learning environment, which will promote equal opportunities
- to provide the educational context which promotes awareness and positive attitudes.

Delivery
1. Curriculum

Both the content and the way it is presented can address issues of equality. All curriculum subjects can contribute, and the list which follows is intended merely to provide exemplars.

PSHE

PSHE has an obvious contribution to make through curriculum content (eg the syllabus contains a unit on stereotyping). In addition discussions on issues relating to equal opportunities and prejudice raise awareness and help promote positive attitudes. The rationale of the PSHE programme is to support personal development and to equip pupils with the means to challenge inequality, racism or prejudice wherever they find it.

History

The syllabus includes units of world history eg World War II, which encourage pupils to view events from a number of different perspectives. Through the study of the past pupils can begin to understand inequality in society. Contributing units include:

- the industrial revolution (KS3) – nineteenth century working and living conditions, working class movements – class, economic and political inequality
- revolutions which reordered society (KS3 and 4) eg France 1789 or Russia 1917 – the inequitable distribution of power and wealth and the move towards democracy
- suffragettes (KS3) and humanities GCSE – gender inequality
- black peoples of America – colour and inequality.

Evidence work helps our pupils recognize bias and appreciate the extent to which the cultural heritage or personal prejudice of a writer may influence his/her interpretation of events.

Science

The Science curriculum emphasises that it is not neutral or value free, but a cultural activity practised in a particular political/economic context. It endeavours to avoid tokenism and to give Science a wide context. The Science curriculum addresses racism through its discussion of pseudoscientific genetic theories, which divide humanity into distinct racial groups and justifies the doctrine of master and inferior races.

2. Teaching and learning

Pupils receive overt and covert messages from the way in which a classroom is organised and from their role in the classroom. A variety of teaching and learning strategies and differentiation are used to promote equal opportunities:

- to enable our pupils to interact in a variety of ways with the teacher and to reach their potential (see our special needs policy)
- the pupils' own experiences are valued and built on
- ideas and assumptions are challenged
- team work and collaborative strategies are regularly employed
- materials are regularly monitored and pupils made aware of their context
- displays represent social, linguistic and cultural diversity
- resources are relevant, open and accessible, enabling pupils to negotiate and develop their own ideas and take some responsibility for their own learning
- regular audits are carried out to check where we stand.

3. School policies and practice

A number of school policies contribute to equal opportunities, eg behaviour policy and code of conduct, anti-bullying policy, special needs and pastoral policy.

These policies should ensure that the organisation and its members will react to any incidents which occur and lead by example.

Some of our current initiatives will also contribute to equal opportunities, eg our monitoring programme will help us record what pupils achieve in terms of value added and will influence future planning, and the Investors in People initiative will contribute to the promotion of the school as one community.

We shall continue to take advantage of training opportunities which raise awareness or inculcate good practice. Appointments should follow good practice and equal opportunities procedures.

Management

The named person in respect of equal opportunities is Mr S. Tucker, head of Science. Heads of department are responsible for subject delivery. Year heads are responsible for pastoral aspects and for the PSHE programme. Staff development is coordinated by the deputy head. The ultimate responsibility for the school's policy rests with the governors.

Evaluation

Sampling and monitoring will be used to check the tone and language of our documents, how regularly incidents occur and how we react to them. Curriculim audits will be used to check where we stand in respect to content and methodology. Feedback will help us monitor awareness and perceptions.

Drafting a pay policy

CASE STUDY 10.3. FOR ACTION

Schools now have much greater discretion in determining the pay of the staff they employ. They have had to draft a pay policy and to do this they have had to work out the criteria on which to base it. This case study follows through what happened at Bestwick Park High School. Although it centres on pay policy, it can be used to compare how to approach any new structure which the governors may need to put in place.

As details of the recent pay awards and new structures were circulated the chairman of governors, Miles Standish, put down an agenda item for the governors' meeting. He had been briefed by Brenda Gatlin, the headteacher, and gave a summary of the main changes saying that the school would have to change its procedures to bring it in line with the new awards. There was concern as the meeting failed to grasp the implications of this, 'What exactly does it mean we have to do?' asked a parent governor. 'There seems to be so many potential pitfalls.' 'How do we make sure that we treat everyone fairly and consistently?'

Brenda Gatlin intervened. 'You're quite right,' she said. 'We could face a lot of trouble in the future unless we draw up a pay policy which will provide us with clear principles by which we can operate.' There was general agreement with this view. The governors were quite experienced in drawing up policy statements and were happy to do this for pay, but some could see that the complexity of the new regulations and the sensitivity of this particular issue made drafting the policy and getting it accepted by the staff a difficult undertaking.

'It's clearly going to take a lot of time and hard work,' said Peter Leigh. 'The obvious thing is to set up a working party. It doesn't make sense to devote full governors' meetings to drafting a pay policy.' 'You also need to be sensitive to how the staff feel about this,' interjected one of the staff governors. 'If the teachers have some imput, the policy will be much more acceptable than if it is imposed on them.' The meeting agreed to get the staff views at informal lunchtime sessions. These would be given to a working party of governors and staff, who would be entrusted with the task of producing the first draft of the new pay policy.

The governors set the group clear objectives. The policy should:

- help the school achieve its aims and objectives as set out in the school development plan
- apply to all staff, not just teachers
- reward staff fairly and equitably
- help motivate staff
- enable staff to understand the basis of pay decisions
- ensure that all decisions were fair and consistent.

The terms of reference also spelt out a number of considerations which the working party had to take into account. The policy would have to:

- be in line with the school development plan and the LEA's pay policy
- take account of the school's budget proposals and pupil number forecasts
- take into account national or local factors which could affect decisions or implementation of the policy
- be consistent with the school's equal opportunities policy
- be brief but sufficiently precise to meet the needs of the school
- provide the opportunity to create a mix of annual and continuing payments, and keep a balance between allowances and discretionary scale points
- ensure that proper relativities existed, eg between the pay levels of the head, deputies and other staff.

It was also decided that, because a good working knowledge of the new pay regulations was essential, the first meeting should be a briefing/ training session for the working party. The Besthampton governor

training scheme provided someone who briefed them on the regulations and took them through the LEA's own policy statement. They
also looked at pay policies which the headteacher borrowed from
colleagues elsewhere.

Once the working party had grasped the implications of the new
regulations and received feedback from the staff sessions they moved
on to determining the general principles of the policy and deciding how
it should operate. The area which provoked the most difficulty was in
deciding what criteria to use, but finally they decided to stick to the
criteria listed in the pay and conditions document. Once general
agreement had been reached two members of the group volunteered to
do the drafting, and the working party amended and agreed the draft
before it went to the full governing body, where it was debated in detail
and amended. The governors had complied with the regulation that the
pay policy has to be the work of the whole governing body. The final
text of the Bestwick Park Pay Policy is given below as case study 10.5.

When the head reminded them of their duty to communicate the
policy to all staff the governors sought the advice of the teacher
governors. It was decided that copies of the draft document should be
displayed in the staffroom for ten days, with personal copies made
available on demand and that the next staff meeting should include
discussion of the draft as a major item. The members of the working
party (where possible) and the chair of governors were to attend. This
session led to some slight redrafting, after which the policy was finally
adopted by the governing body.

For action:

What are the issues which arise from this case study?
Why was the initial task given to a working party and not to a
subcommittee?
How do the procedures adopted at Bestwick Park compare with those
in your own school?
How could they be improved?

CASE STUDY 10.4. FOR ACTION

Key issues to be considered in drafting a pay policy

- Have all of the employees who work in the school community been
  considered?

- Does it deal effectively with the most relevant issues such as recruitment, retention and motivation?
- Will it promote the staff's professional development?
- Is it compatible with the school development plan?
- Is it compatible with the school's budget arrangements?
- Has it taken due regard of all relevant legislation?
- Does it consider all discretionary payments and any other pay related elements, which can give rise to costs within the school's budget?
- Does it ensure that appropriate differentials will be created and maintained between posts held within the school?
- Who is to manage and administer it?
- Does it determine the power of appointment for new and temporary staff to be delegated to the headteacher?
- What criteria does it establish for special payments such as relocation packages?
- Does it provide a practical appeals procedure?
- Is it clear how the policy will be disseminated both now and in the future?
- Will it be reviewed annually and by whom?

CASE STUDY 10.5. EXEMPLAR

Bestwick Park High School pay policy

General principles

The governing body of Bestwick Park High School seeks to ensure that all teaching and associate staff are valued and receive proper recognition for their work and contribution to school life and will endeavour, within its budget, to use the national pay scales and discretions available to it as the 'relevant body' to recruit, retain and motivate teachers of quality to ensure the best possible delivery of the curriculum.

Aims

1. To maintain and improve the quality of education provided for pupils in the school by having a pay policy which supports the school's mission statement and development plan.
2. To have a staffing structure related to the school's development plan.

3. To show all staff that the governing body is managing its pay policy in a fair and responsible way.

Management of the policy
The governing body has responsibility for establishing the school's pay policy and for seeing that it is followed. It considers and approves the overall pay structure for all staff. The governing body delegates authority to a personnel subcommittee to administer the pay policy on its behalf. The subcommittee will comprise the headteacher, vice chair of governors and four other governors. It requires its members to treat information about an individual's earnings as confidential. Its responsibilities are exercised within the constraints of the school's delegated budget and in accordance with the school's financial plan.

A second subcommittee, for appeals and grievances, will comprise the chair of governors and five other governors.

The two subcommittees will be appointed annually by the full governing body. No governor may be a member of both the personnel and the appeals subcommittees.

Consultation
A representative group from the governing body will consult fully with all staff when drawing up the pay policy and during each annual review of the policy in line with best practice. Each member of staff and each governor will be given a copy of the pay policy. The governing body will also consult with the LEA where appropriate.

Equal opportunities and employment legislation
The governing body seeks to provide equal opportunities for all staff, in accordance with the school's equal opportunities policy and equal pay legislation.

Vacant posts
Full information relating to vacant posts, including those carrying additional points, whether permanent, temporary or acting, will be made known to staff in time for them to apply for posts for which their training and relevant experience are appropriate.

Job descriptions
The headteacher, on behalf of the governing body, will provide these for all staff when s/he is first appointed and at an annual review in

consultation with staff in the summer term. Written statements of the terms and conditions of employment will be provided by the LEA.

Appraisal
The governing body acknowledges that appraisal is primarily to assist staff with their own development in the context of the school. There will be no link between appraisal and promotion or additions to salary except in the case of associate staff who are employed under Besthampton pay regulations. The only impact of appraisal for such members of staff is in relation to the annual increment, if they are not at the top of their pay scale.

Job relativity
The governing body will seek to ensure that there is proper relativity between jobs within the school.

Records
Records of salary will be confidential to the individual concerned and to the personnel subcommittee.

Grievance
If a member of staff has a grievance relating to his/her salary she should follow the grievance procedure.

Associate staff

Pay and conditions

1. The governing body will work within the national and local structures agreed with the unions in accordance with the employer's contractual conditions of service. These are Besthampton Pay, national conditions for APT&C staff (protected), national conditions for manual workers and local amendments. The governing body delegates decisions on salaries, job descriptions and gradings to the personnel subcommittee.
2. The personnel subcommittee will evaluate the range and grade of each post based on the requirements of the job description and personnel specification. These will be compiled from the LEA's model job descriptions, which have undergone job evaluation in accordance with the legal requirements.

3. The personnel subcommittee will grade all new appointments on either Besthampton Pay or the manual workers' pay scale. Employees who have not previously elected to transfer to Besthampton Pay will be protected on APT&C conditions until their post is evaluated and regraded or until they are contracted to a new post.

Manual workers
Once the personnel subcommittee has decided the grade of a manual post, the postholder is on a fixed wage, paid weekly, subject to a national pay award whenever it occurs.

The site manager and assistant site manager's pay will include 15 per cent performance related pay. The governing body will withhold this element if specified performance is not attained. Performance related pay is not paid during sickness absence.

Besthampton pay
The personnel subcommittee will determine the starting salary within the range and will base this decision on the following criteria:

- level of experience
- qualifications
- added value to the school
- level of training required to fulfil the needs of the post
- present salary
- protection in cases of redeployment
- next incremental due date (if appointed between October and March this will be 18 months).

The minimum starting salary at age 21 is ISN 5.

The governing body can award merit or accelerated increments within the range at any time during the financial year. Criteria for this decision will be:

- achievement exceeding normal job requirements but at an equivalent level of responsibility
- completion of key tasks to a degree which exceeds the line manager's recorded expectations
- undertaking a specialised project at an equivalent level of responsibility to the post holder's current job description.

Annual increments are payable on 1 April each year subject to satisfactory performance. They are managed through the appraisal process.

Honoraria

The governing body will award an honorarium to an employee temporarily carrying out work of a higher level. This will be calculated on the difference between the postholder's substantive salary and the bottom ISN of the appropriate range for the new tasks or a minimum of one increment, whichever is the greater, pro rata for the number of hours worked and the period of time involved.

The personal subcommittee will review job descriptions annually and will re-evaluate the grade if responsibility or accountability are increased, decreased or changed.

Teachers

1. The governing body will follow the requirements and guidelines of the current school teachers' pay and conditions document in exercising a pay policy for the teaching staff. The discretion allowed by this document and the accompanying circular will be used according to identified school needs and based on clearly laid down criteria subject to annual review and available funding.

2. The personnel subcommittee together with the headteacher will review on an annual basis all teaching staff salaries and will make an assessment of each teacher's salary. An individual assessment report will be given to each teacher for implementation the following September. Any teacher who wishes to query his/her salary should raise the matter in the first instance with the headteacher. If the matter is not resolved the grievance procedure should be invoked.

3. The headteacher may at any time during the year make recommendations to the governing body regarding changes to a teacher's pay and conditions in the light of unforeseen circumstances. The governing body delegates authority to the personnel subcommittee to give approval for changes required during the course of the school year.

Teachers on the common pay spine 0–17 points

1. Qualifications

   The governing body, in line with the current school teacher's pay and conditions document award two points for a good honours degree (first class, upper and lower second class) or equivalent, or for a higher qualification. In some cases a teacher in post without such a qualification may subsequently so qualify and therefore become entitled to two points, unless that teacher already has the maximum of nine points allowed for experience and qualifications. These points once awarded are a permanent entitlement in any post.

2. Experience

A. Mandatory. The governing body will award one point for each year of recognised teaching service up to a maximum of nine (seven for those with two qualification points). A year of recognised service is one in which the teacher has taught for part of at least 26 weeks in the school year.

B. Discretionary. The governing body has determined the following number of points for directly relevant experience outside teaching:

1–3 for maternity/paternity – up to a maximum of two points

1–2 for particularly relevant experience – up to a maximum of five points.

Mandatory and discretionary points once awarded remain a permanent entitlement in any post.

3. Responsibility

The governing body will need to determine the number of posts with additional responsibilities and the corresponding number of points each will carry. Such additional responsibilities will be clearly defined and linked to job descriptions. Such posts could carry up to a maximum of five points. They may be either fixed term or permanent as determined by the governing body, which will seek to ensure that similar responsibilities carry similar points.

4. Excellence

The governing body will annually determine whether to exercise its discretion to award up to three points for excellence. These points may only be awarded on an annual basis. If the governing body decides to award such points, it is essential to agree clear and objective criteria before any awards are made. Further advice on this will be issued.

5. Recruitment and retention

The governing body will need to determine whether of not it wishes to exercise discretion in awarding up to two points for recruitment and retention.

6. Special needs

A. Mandatory. The governing body will award a minimum of one point to teachers who wholly or mainly teach pupils with statements of special needs.

B. Discretionary. The governing body will use its discretion to award a second point to teachers who wholly or mainly teach pupils with statements of special educational needs.

7. Frozen payments

The governing body will exercise its discretion to preserve existing permanent discretionary scale points over and above the assimilated salary.

Heads and deputies

1. General

The governing body is aware that heads and deputies do not receive annual increments and they will therefore ensure that careful consideration is given to these salaries in the annual review. The following guidance from the school teachers pay and conditions document will be followed and used when and if it is appropriate: awards may be given on a temporary or permanent basis; it is in order to pay a higher salary than that falling within the normal range if that salary is considered inadequate.

2. Criteria

The criteria to be taken into account when reviewing the salaries of the head and deputies include the responsibility of the post, length of service, whether the post is difficult to fill, and the overall performance by the head or the deputy, assessed by a defined procedure taking into account overall management objectives.

3. Process

The process for considering an award for the head/deputy will be as follows:

a) The subcommittee appointed by the full governing body to make recommendations on the pay of the school's head and deputy will, when considering the salary to be paid on the first appointment to the school, need to have regard in particular, but not exclusively to the first three of the statutory criteria set out in the school teachers' pay and conditions document

b) Thereafter the subcommittee should establish an annual time-table for its work. This will be concerned particularly with the fourth of the statutory criteria to which the governing bodies are required to have regard. The timetable for reviewing this should include:

- At the onset of the school year, setting the basis on which performance will be reviewed, including the personal and school-based objectives and some indication of the exceptional standards, which need to be achieved to justify progression up the pay spine.

- During the school year, reviewing the progress towards meeting personal and school-based objectives, taking into account any new factors that may have arisen.
- At the end of the school year, considering the performance achieved over the year as a whole.

c) The subcommittee should consult the head and deputy/ies at each stage and report periodically to the full governing body. A brief written report should be submitted at the end of the year with recommendations as to whether any changes should be made.

d) In making its recommendations, the subcommittee should also give due regard to any other factors which might affect the pay of the individual/s concerned, including changes in responsibilities and evidence about the pay of heads and deputies in other schools in the area.

e) When the full governing body has come to a decision, which should be final, on the recommendations made by the standing committee, the outcome and its basis should be confirmed in a written statement from the Chair of Governors to the individual/s concerned.

This policy was agreed by the governing body on
It will be reviewed annually thereafter.

Signed: Miles Standish
Chair of Governors, Bestwick Park High School.

Personnel issues – managing staff cuts

The largest part of any school's budget is spent on staffing, and if the budget is tight invariably the money spent on staff comes under scrutiny. Although there is evidence to show that schools look at non-teaching posts first, because such a large part of the staffing budget is spent on teachers governing bodies may be forced to consider reducing the number of teachers they employ. The case study which follows explores this scenario.

CASE STUDY 10.6. FOR ACTION

Managing staff cuts

On receipt of the budget figures for the following year, Brenda Gatlin phoned her chair of governors to give him the bad news. Miles Standish was furious. 'What was the point of our ensuring our budget is properly managed if the LEA can't keep its own house in order? The head sympathised with his feelings, but their priority had to be solving the immediate problem. They agreed that the bursar should analyse what the cuts would mean in practice while the governors' finance sub-committee looked at areas in which cuts might be made.

Brenda Gatlin felt it only fair to warn Miles that trimming budget headings would not be enough, and that they might have to look at staff cuts: 'I don't see any alternative. And we must inform Mark Tulley, the LEA area manager, of the position we are likely to be in. Under the current Education Act the Chief Education Officer or his representative is entitled to attend proceedings of the governing body relating to the removal of a member of staff.'

Mr Standish was rapidly coming to the conclusion that the school should apply for grant maintained status as soon as possible. 'It would give us a great deal more money and solve most of our budget problems, as well as freeing us from an LEA which I am increasingly convinced is an albatross around our necks.' Mrs Gatlin pointed out that it took time and lengthy consultations to acquire grant maintained status, and although going GM could be a long-term solution to their problems, they needed something more immediate. It was essential to calm the chairman's anger and keep him to the point, so she drew on her experience of managing Mr Standish and added that, in the short term, it was essential to follow procedures precisely as redundancy was the one place where the LEA still picked up the tab and surely he wouldn't want to put that at risk? They would also need to act swiftly because there were only three dates in the financial year on which teachers could be dismissed on grounds of redundancy (31 August, 31 December or 30 April). Teachers have a statutory entitlement of one week's notice for each year of service up to a total of 12 years, so a teacher with 12 years' experience, who is to be dismissed, needs to be given notice by 30 September. If a school fails to complete all the necessary steps in time to give proper notice contractual and/or statutory, then it is liable for salary until 31 December.

The finance subcommittee meets
At the finance subcommittee's meeting it became clear that trimming was not going to solve the problem. There had been too many lean years for them to have accumulated savings substantial enough to help them now, so they were left with the problem of staff cuts. They would need to reduce the complement by at least one, possibly two. Mr Standish was still angry: 'The staff will blame us for this, not the LEA' he said. This outburst made the subcommittee realise that they had to decide both what staff cuts to make and how best to handle informing the staff. In view of the gravity of the situation and the need to ensure that procedures were followed absolutely, the matter was referred back to the governing body and a special budget meeting was called.

The governors' meeting
The governors were appalled at the situation and spent some time composing a less than polite letter to the LEA, suggesting that it improved its forward planning in future and deploring the cuts. In considering the staff cuts they quickly realised that they could not simply ask the head to nominate a suitable member of staff, although a few parent governors would clearly have liked to suggest some of the less popular and effective teachers. 'We have to be seen to be fair,' said Tessa Baines, one of the co-opted governors. 'Otherwise we shall simply compound our problems.' They decided to set up a governors' working party to create a possible formula for debate by the whole governing body. This would mean additional meetings which would eat into people's time. 'We have no choice,' said Trevor Davis, another of the co-opted governors. 'With such a sensitive issue we must share the responsibility, however much time it takes.' The head asked for advice about how and when to broach the matter with the staff:

It has always been my practice to be open with them. If we tell them nothing, in an affair that so intimately concerns them, we should forfeit all goodwill and put the staff governors in a very difficult position. There are bound to be rumours of what we are doing, and I have already heard that Besthampton School, Bestwick Park's nearest rival, is in an even worse position than we are. The contractual problems also make it essential that people are given notice within the time limit and may lead us to issue more notices than we eventually need. Yet if we say too much too soon, especially as we cannot even say which staff stand in danger, we shall worry people unduly and be accused of scaremongering.

It was decided that the head should use the next weekly staff meeting to give an update on the school's budget position. Staff would be made aware that a serious problem existed, that a governors' group had been asked to look at ways in which cuts could be made and that this could lead to the issuing of redundancy notices. A longer staff meeting would be held after school next month, when the position was clearer, and at that meeting the situation would be fully explained and discussed with staff. The governors asked Mrs Gatlin to produce a consultation paper for the staff meeting and one of the staff governors proposed that some governors should attend the staff meeting. The governors weren't used to attending staff meetings, and some thought that the staff would find their presence threatening. Most agreed, however, and Mr Standing and Nandish Samani, one of the parent governors, were nominated

Informing the trade unions
Mrs Gatlin proposed seeing the union representatives at the same time as the issue was raised with the staff.

The rules say clearly that the recognised trade unions must be consulted at the earliest opportunity and, even if the rules didn't insist, I should want to brief them and clarify the processes of consultation. We want to avoid any unnecessary problems and I have always considered it important to cooperate with them as far as possible.

The working party meets to determine the criteria
At the meeting it quickly became clear that they could not apply industrial techniques (first in, last out) for handling their redundancies. If different criteria are applied, however, the school may need to demonstrate that they are more important. Yvonne Perkins, the deputy head in charge of curriculum and timetabling was especially horrified by the suggestion. 'You can't possibly do that!' she exclaimed. 'It will wreck our whole development plan. We've recently made several appointments which will benefit the school in the long term and the last thing we want now is to lose these staff.' 'Can't we simply seek volunteers?' asked Nandish Samani. 'My firm always asks for volun-

teers first, and this quite often means that the management don't have to nominate people for redundancy. There must surely be staff who are near the end of their teaching careers or who want to leave teaching.' Mark Tulley, the area manager, agreed that this was an excellent suggestion. 'It would give you a starting point. But you still need to establish priorities, in case you attract more volunteers than you need.' 'But what happens if the volunteers are from the subject areas where we can't afford to lose staff?' asked Mrs Perkins, preoccupied by her vision of a timetable with all the wrong teachers. 'This is the drawback of a voluntary system,' replied the area officer. 'You could save money if you replace an experienced but expensive teacher with a younger teacher who is not at the top of his/her scale, or with a newly qualified teacher.'

He then went through the factors they would have to take into account. The criteria had to take account of the school's needs and priorities and the specific skills, experience and potential of staff in managing and developing the curriculum and managing the school as a whole as well as considering volunteers and those on fixed term and part time contracts. The area officer had to make clear that cutting down a part timer's hours could help, but ending a fixed term contract counted as dismissal, and if the reason for dismissal is really redundancy, then the governing body must follow proper procedures in accordance with employment legislation.

The discussion on the skills and expertise of the staff made the working party realise that staff had potential as well as current value, and that suggesting teachers with qualifications in shortage subjects or teachers who had been appointed specifically to play a major role in the school's future development for redundancy would be counter-productive. Qualifications and experience in National Curriculum core and foundation subjects, RE and special needs, or qualifications to teach a wide age range or to switch between subjects all had a quantitative value. They therefore tried to establish criteria using the school's development plan staffing and curriculum sections as a starting point. This was extremely complicated and time consuming, and the area officer suggested that the group draw up a matrix to display how individual members of staff met the criteria (see Figure 10.2).

Using the matrix made it much clearer which posts and therefore which members of staff could be considered surplus to requirements. The next step was to get the governing body to agree to the criteria matrix, and then to consult the unions and establish what their view is.

SPECIFIC SKILLS AND EXPERIENCE	STAFF INITIALS									
MANAGING THE SCHOOL	a	b	a	b	a	b	a	b	a	b	a
Team leader										
Special needs coordinator										
Staff development/INSET										
Probationary support										
Middle school liaison										
Early years										
Management of SATs										
MANAGING AND DEVELOPING THE CURRICULUM										
Mathematics										
English										
Science										
Technology										
Humanities										
Art and Display										
Music										
PE										
RE										
ESL										
Assessment										

a = current   b = potential because of skills and experience

Figure 10.2   Criteria matrix – reduction in staffing

The staff meeting
After talking to the union representatives, who were naturally unhappy at the prospect of any redundancies, but who could not improve on the criteria suggested by the governors, another staff meeting was held to put staff fully in the picture. The headteacher announced that she would see personally all members of staff who met the criteria in order to discuss the position and establish whether anyone wished to volunteer for redundancy. If there was more than one volunteer the governors would resolve the situation in the best interest of the school. 'The LEA selects the volunteer with the longest continuous service record,' intervened Mark Tulley.

Volunteers are interviewed
The staff to be interviewed were given the choice of having their union representative present. Where the teacher chose this option, Brenda

Gatlin asked Mark Tulley to be present too, so that both sides had an adviser. Most staff preferred a less formal session, and the chance to talk privately to the headteacher. Clive Draper, head of Geography, was first in the queue: 'If there's an opportunity for early retirement, preferably with a couple of years' enhancement, I'd like to take it. I'm really uncomfortable with the endless stream of innovations, I feel pressurized all the time and I don't approve of most of the changes.' This request created a problem for Brenda as Geography was a National Curriculum foundation subject, and as such had not been identified by the working group as surplus to requirements. Yet both the headteacher and the area officer could see advantages for the school in taking up his offer, particularly as within the Humanities faculty there was a very promising candidate for the head of Geography post and Clive could be replaced with a newly qualified teacher, which would save the school money. Brenda told the governors:

> I shall have to talk to the LEA, as the current package is not very good, but Mark has offered to negotiate on our behalf. We certainly don't want to reject Clive's offer out of hand, and it does give us some flexibility. It means however that we require more than one person to go. Let's hope that Miss Cline, the head of Classics, feels as Clive does. We really don't need a full time Classics teacher any more, let alone a head of department.

Ultimately three staff left as a result of the cuts. Clive Draper and Celia Cline were offered and took slightly enhanced early retirement, and Miss Rossiter, a part time teacher in Home Economics, accepted redundancy. This enabled the headteacher to make an internal promotion to the vacant head of Geography post, appoint a newly qualified teacher to the Geography department and a part timer to teach the Classics, which was all the school required in this subject area.

Counselling out
The area officer offered to make redundancy counselling available to Miss Rossiter. The staff exhibited a noticeable lack of confidence in the LEA's expertise in this sensitive area, and there were comparisons with what had been provided for appraisal training. The advice from her friends was to avoid it at all costs, but Miss Rossiter said that she was interested in retraining in Technology, requested details of available courses and went ahead with the interview.

Discussing the affair with Miles Standish before the final governors' meeting of the year, Brenda Gatlin thought that they had come out of it reasonably well. There had been remarkably little acrimony and, as a result of the cuts, the school's budget was in the black again. In the circumstances it was as much as could be hoped for, though they were all too aware that there was nothing left to trim next year. The chairman of governors agreed, but still thought the situation wouldn't have arisen if the LEA hadn't unloaded its financial problems on to the schools. He remained disenchanted with the maintained system. 'Now,' he said, 'we should take the initiative and opt out before there is another financial crisis.'

For action:

What are the main issues raised by this case study?
Compare what happened here to the flow chart (Fig. 10.3).
What strategies were adopted in dealing with the problem? How effective are they likely to be in practice?
How would you have dealt with the problem?
Write your own checklist for handling staff cuts.

What can you learn from this case study?
You manage a budget but do not, even if you are a GM school, determine how much you will receive. You plan your budget as best you can, but definite information about your budget share often arrives well after the planning has been done and sometimes cuts are made at a very late stage. This case study explored the kind of problems you might have to face as a manager when things go wrong and about how you react to a financial crisis. Can you keep calm and cope in a crisis, can you think on your feet, can you get the best out of your partners (the governors) in this situation and can you manage the stress of making a long serving colleague redundant?

Handling staff cuts is a delicate exercise. It encompasses the kinds of skills you need to manage today's schools – negotiation, communication and ability to manage public relations as well as the budgetary concerns around which the scenario revolves. It also involves managing decline. Unlike innovation, the most you can hope to achieve is the best of a bad job.

This kind of crisis puts the partnership with governors to a real test. This case study showed the partnership with governors operating

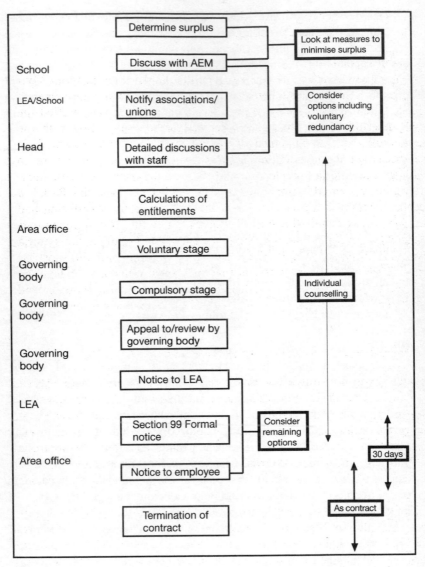

Figure 10.3 A flow chart for managing staff cuts

effectively. It is when things go wrong that the partnership falls apart and individuals act unilaterally, overstepping their boundaires and not showing respect for other members.

It also indicated how important it is to be aware of employment legislation, such as the Education Reform Act of 1988 and any subsequent modification, or the governors may find themselves at the losing end of an industrial tribunal in which a protective award gives the trade unions a 28 day delay. European legislation also affects you, and urges you to undertake consultations which should cover ways and means of avoiding collective redundancies or reducing the number of workers affected. Not only do you have to ensure that there is consultation, but you must make it meaningful. Remember however that consultation is not quite the same as negotiation.

Chapter 11
Managing the Associate Staff

Support staff and their position

It is easy to forget, when you refer to the staff of a school, that you are not only talking about the teaching staff but something like one third of the total staff who may not be teachers at all. They are the support or non-teaching staff. School secretaries, technicians and caretakers have served as members of the school staff for many years and have established roles and patterns of work. The creation of other posts has been much more recent. The expansion in the area of non-teaching staff seems to have been spurred by a number of different factors. Some of the new posts were specifically designed to service new needs, others have evolved or developed from existing posts, as a postholder had a good idea which led to the expansion of his/her role. The main catalyst for growth was perhaps the Education Reform Act of 1988 and the introduction of LMS because the legislation provided new needs and created the flexibility to meet them. Most of the resulting expansion has been within the well established boundaries determined by LEA rules and procedures, but the growth of the GMS sector has allowed considerable innovation in the kind of posts created.

The support staff in a large secondary school include site managers, caretakers, clerical and office staff, librarians and library assistants, financial officers, welfare assistants, technicians, classroom/curriculum support staff, dinner supervisors, cleaners and contract staff. Most schools also have a lot of volunteer helpers, who are not members of staff but who come in on a regular basis. All these people need managing and developing, and as the headteacher you are responsible for their performance and job satisfaction.

Case studies

This chapter explores, through a number of sequential case studies, the problems and issues which may arise in managing the non-teaching staff. If you want to use the case studies for group sessions on different aspects of managing the associate staff you may find it useful to have read them all first as some of the initial ones raise and discuss ideas or issues that are assumed in later problems. Nevertheless most of the scenarios can be used individually if required.

CASE STUDY 11.1. FOR ACTION/REFLECTION

'Why was Mrs Adams at the staff meeting again this week?' Ian Clarke asked a colleague at the end of the weekly staff meeting. 'I particularly noticed her last week and meant to ask "Why?" What is a member of the ancillary staff doing attending our meeting? I don't remember being consulted about whether she should be allowed to come, do you? What do you think the head is up to? Is she quietly infiltrating Mrs Adams, hoping we won't notice? Will this prove to be the thin end of the wedge? It's meant to be a staff meeting isn't it? Does she get to vote when we do? It worries me because confidential issues about pupils may arise and we won't be able to talk freely.'

The person whose presence at the weekly staff meeting this teacher so clearly resented is the school's bursar, Sarah Adams.

For action:

Why does this teacher resent the bursar's presence at the staff meeting?
What issues are raised by the case study?
How well has the headteacher handled/managed the situation?
What advice would you give the headteacher and why?

For reflection:

In this case study, Brenda Gatlin, the headteacher of Bestwick Park High School has asked the bursar, Sarah Adams, to attend the weekly staff meetings. This decision by the new head to include a member of the non-teaching staff in a meeting hitherto attended only by teachers raises a number of issues.

What was the motive?

The role of the bursar varies from school to school. He or she may be an administrator, carrying out clerical tasks with little or no power to influence decisions, or a highly paid and influential member of the senior management team (SMT), responsible for making the school's finances work, or may operate on a level somewhere between these two extremes. However much real power he or she has, the bursar has become a pivotal figure in the daily running of the school. Getting Sarah Adams to attend the weekly staff meeting could fulfil two purposes. First, Mrs Gatlin may see it as good for the bursar to learn more about what goes on in the staffroom, and consider the sessions to be developmental for Mrs Adams, whose knowledge of education is limited. It could help her to understand better what the school is about and how the staff feel about things, and could help to integrate her into the staff. Second, the presence of the bursar could lead to the teachers rethinking who attends staff meetings as a first step towards creating one staff rather than two separate entities – teaching and non-teaching staff.

How well was the situation managed?

Was it a good idea simply to introduce a member of the support staff, even if she is the most senior, into the teachers' meeting without prior consultation or informing the staff? Ian Clarke was clearly angry about the bursar's presence, but there is no indication that his reaction was typical of other staff, or whether his suspicions about the head are based on her previous track record or have arisen because he feels threatened by this change. There are signs however that the bursar's presence could easily develop into a confrontation between the head and some of the staff, in which case the head may have misjudged her tactics. It might have been wiser to have at least explained why she had asked the bursar to attend, even if she wasn't prepared to seek the staff's consent. The element of surprise contributed to the distrust that Ian Clarke felt.

Did the head adopt this approach because:

- she genuinely regarded the matter as uncontroversial
- she was totally insensitive to how the teachers might feel
- she feared resistance and wanted to pre-empt it?

The incident raises questions about her dominant management style and her relationship with the staff, and it may be useful to think about what approach you might take in these circumstances. If you want to make a change to the personnel included in the staff meeting, would you:

- act without giving the staff prior warning
- inform and then act
- consult, but use your own judgement
- consult and only act if the teachers agree?

Should support staff be present during confidential discussions of pupils?
This is the most problematic of the issues raised in this case study. Staff meetings are often used to bring to the attention of teachers issues involving individual pupils. Often there has been a deterioration in the pupil's work, perhaps because of family problems, and the teachers need to know that there is a problem, discuss how to monitor it and what approach they should take. Most teachers would not want support staff present during these discussions as they would regard it as important to share this kind of information only with those who needed to know. Yet some support staff should be included amongst those who need to know, because they interact with the pupils concerned and need advice about how to react or deal with potentially difficult pupils. Providing relevant information could prevent an unnecessary clash between a technician or a dinner supervisor and a pupil with problems. The teaching staff might argue however that sufficient information could be conveyed by the support staff's line managers without their having to be present at the meeting. Perhaps the solution to this is to classify the meetings (though this obviously reduces flexibility) with issues about pupils being raised at particular meetings or at the end of meetings. When confidential matters are being dealt with those for whom the information is not essential could leave.

Should the staff meeting be purely a teachers' meeting?
Bestwick Park High School needs to clarify whether or not the staff meeting is purely a teachers' meeting. If it is a teachers' meeting then support staff may not attend, but if the school wants to create one staff then all staff should attend the staff meeting, even though to make this possible some logistical issues might need to be resolved. It is a sensitive issue, and one which should be faced and discussed openly in order to reach a decision that reflects the views and culture of the

school. If the headteacher of Bestwick Park wants to change the prevailing culture in order to create a partnership between the two sets of staff, then she should reflect on how best to approach this. Judging from the case study above, staff might not be open to change without being made more aware of the issues involved and the benefits that might accrue.

One of the main problems in managing two sets of staff is the almost total lack of respect each group seems to have for the other's professional expertise. The case study which follows explores what can happen when a well qualified and efficient bursar's administration of financial matters brings her into regular contact with the teaching staff.

CASE STUDY 11.2. FOR ACTION

The bursar, Sarah Adams, and the teaching staff are grumbling in the staffroom over coffee:

1. I might have guessed that one of them would hand in photograph money today. I told them quite clearly I wanted it all in by the end of last week so that I could have everything clear for the end of term. I totalled up all the money that had been given in and the photographer came into school and collected it on Friday afternoon, but they didn't listen to me and now all this money comes in today. Where has he been keeping it all this time? It's a lot of money and it could easily have been stolen. Now I shall have to contact the photographer to come back and collect the additional money. It's duplicating work that I've already done and I don't know whether the photographer can come back before the end of term, and anyway he'll think we're utterly incompetent.

2. She simply didn't or wouldn't understand that the children only brought in the money this week, although I had been asking for it every day for ages. You know what my form is like, and anyway she said at the staff meeting that she wanted it all in together and not in dribs and drabs. But when I handed it in she shouted at me and virtually accused me of being late on purpose and storing away huge amounts of money in a cupboard or something! She was quite unnecessarily nasty about it. She gave me a lecture

about not keeping to the deadline, talking to me the whole time as if I were a particularly stupid child. Who does she think she is anyway?

3. I tried to get Mr Draper to understand that he couldn't place an order for that set of books because his department has already overspent its allocation. He seemed to think that the head could simply find him some more money. Where does he think she'll get it from? There's no pot of gold out there. Some of those teachers don't seem to live in the real world and have no understanding whatsoever of what it means to work within a budget. Absent-minded professors are all very well, but I have to balance the books.

Sarah Adams is an extremely efficient and conscientious member of staff. She is a methodical and well-organised person who enjoys her work and doesn't suffer fools gladly. With her in charge of the bursar's office you don't have to worry that orders will be placed incorrectly or that anyone will be allowed to spend over the limit. The reconciliation of the monthly statements is meticulous, goods are carefully checked in and reach the right department, bills and parcels really meant for the primary school across the road are noticed and dispatched to the correct address, staff are bullied into seeing that their account books are in order and petty cash is always in credit. You know that any task given to Sarah will be handled capably and completed well within the deadline. She relishes making sense out of a lot of detailed financial information, keeps up with the constant changes of codes uses by the LMS system and is quick to pick up on mistakes made by the teachers or by the LEA. Nothing escapes Sarah's eagle eye.

Unfortunately Sarah's relationship with the teaching staff is nothing like as good as her administration of finances. She expects the teachers to understand budgeting and why it is so important to get their orders right, and she sees their mistakes as inefficiency. Her experience so far has not led her to rate teachers very highly because many are much less efficient than she is (especially about money matters), they dislike deadlines and never read her memos. She often feels exasperated at their behaviour, which seems to her worse than the pupils' with less excuse, and she can be quite curt and aggressive when they get things wrong. She always sorts it out for them later, though, because she likes things to be straight, and she is upset when the teachers do not seem to appreciate her efforts after all the extra work they have caused her.

The teachers, who tend to think that administration is far less important than their classroom teaching, feel strongly that such tasks should be kept to a minimum (and preferably done by somebody else), find Sarah's behaviour equally exasperating. Many of them regard her as a petty tyrant who makes mountains out of molehills, but it is the way she talks down to them that really puts their backs up. 'We are the teachers, yet she talks to us as if we are idiots who can't get anything right!'

For action:

What are the issues raised by this case study?
What staff development should be provided for the bursar?
What strategies should the headteacher adopt in order to resolve this problem?

In dealing with financial matters Sarah is a gem; in dealing with staff Sarah is a disaster, and the headteacher must address this problem before it worsens.

Analysing the problem
Sarah's problem arises partly from her lack of knowledge and under-standing of the education system and partly from her own inflexible personality. She doesn't have the interpersonal skills needed to make the staff want to cooperate with her; she hectors them as if they were naughty children, which makes them feel both guilty and inefficient, and they respond by belittling her efforts. The problem is compounded by the fact that what is very important to Sarah is low priority for the teaching staff. For teachers, administration is something they have to do but largely would prefer not to. It's not surprising that they don't feel sorry that they cause her extra work or are not grateful for what she has done for them.

Confronting the problem
If the issue is not addressed it will become increasingly difficult for Sarah to do her job effectively, so Mrs Gatlin has to talk to Sarah about the problem – ideally at Sarah's annual appraisal. The feedback from staff could legitimately be sought, especially if communication was one of the areas being monitored. Mrs Gatlin would need to ensure that Sarah received plenty of praise for the parts of her job she did well, before she embarked on the more difficult stage of the appraisal, and then she must ensure that it is not too negative for Sarah to handle. The

headteacher will need to use all the sensitivity of which she is capable in order to get Sarah to accept how she is perceived by the staff. Sarah will be hurt and initially defensive, saying that it is all because of careless staff. She will have to be persuaded that this is not the whole truth, and if the headteacher fails at this stage no progress can be made. (The skills needed to handle conflict or difficult staff are discussed in Chapter 8.)

Suggested strategies
Mrs Gatlin will have to reassure Sarah by offering her some support in the ongoing battle with the teachers. She could reinforce the importance of administration at a staff meeting, have a chat to the heads of faculty to make it clear that she needs their co-operation in improving relations with the bursar's office. If the staff knew that the problem was being addressed they could be persuaded that it was in their interests to co-operate.

Mrs Gatlin had already decided that one way of helping Sarah appreciate what the teachers do was to have her attend the weekly staff meeting. We have seen the furore this caused with one teacher, and that the head might have consulted the staff meeting first.

It could be useful to arrange for Sarah to have some sessions with heads of faculty so that they could give her a clearer idea of their administrative needs. In turn this might help them to appreciate her problems and concerns. The teachers themselves could also usefully learn from the bursar about her role and perhaps receive more training about how the finances of the school are run. Establishing a dialogue of this kind could benefit both sides of the battle.

It could be very beneficial for Sarah to observe some lessons, because this would give her some idea of the craft of teaching. Sending Sarah on a course dealing with interpersonal skills for administrative staff could also help her overcome her difficulties – at the very least it would show whether she was developable.

The headteacher would need to monitor progress and, since ancillary staff appraisal is annual, she can set fairly short term targets.

Managing a two tier system
The case studies so far have been dealt with the question of the status of the non-teaching staff. It is not merely that you manage two sets of staff, but that you are managing a two tier system. Within the organisation the non-teaching staff are considered second-class citizens

and the names given to this section of the staff reinforce this impression: non-teaching staff, ancillary staff, support staff. The teachers have the status of starring roles, the non-teaching staff of supporting cast. Two research studies (Mortimore *et al*, 1994) highlighted this problem: 'To name such a group of people according to what they did *not* do, rather than what they *did* contribute to the school was not only demeaning but unjust' and in the second survey the non-teaching staff are retitled associate staff.

Pay reinforces the problem: it tends to be very low and, in stark contrast to teachers, support staff appraisal is directly linked to pay, so to earn a rise they have to give satisfaction, and this can lead to exploitation. All too frequently, for example, a good technician finds him/herself working over time to complete work requested by teachers, sometimes way beyond what s/he is paid for. They are doing more than the job, yet there is no scope for promotion and no extra money to pay them for all the work they do. The line between giving people their heads and exploiting them is very narrow, and an honest school should at least face the problem and discuss the issue with its technicians.

The academic qualifications of the non-teaching staff will vary. Women technicians for example are often graduates and considerably overqualified for the jobs they are doing This is for a number of reasons: sometimes they are using the post as a means of re-entry to the labour force, sometimes because of family commitments they have sought a less demanding position or they have opted for a part time job because it enables them to be home before their children. Where this is the case and the well qualified technician finds herself treated with little respect or consideration by some of the teachers there can problems.

CASE STUDY 11.3. FOR ACTION

'I'm going to resign,' Anne, the Physics technician, has arrived in the headteacher's office. Although she sounds belligerent, she has clearly been crying. The head knows from the comments made by the head of Science and from her own observations that Anne is a highly competent and responsible technician, and usually she is a very willing worker, capable of using her initiative in a crisis. As tactfully as possible she enquires what the problem is, and it's like opening the floodgates.

He treats me like dirt, ordering me about all the time as if I were a servant. 'Prepare this, clear that up, do the ordering.' It's non-stop. He never says thank you or seems to appreciate what is done for him and he complains at every opportunity. Each time something goes wrong he makes a point of mentioning that I am a graduate and so I should be able to cope better. He talks to me as if I can't even follow a simple instruction. I think he gets a kick out of making me seem a fool in front of the pupils. I like to plan things out well in advance, but he gives me so little notice, often simply telling me in the morning what is required for the afternoon, that I can't always manage to do it in time, and then he blames me and implies that I'm not working hard enough. Sometimes I'm in the middle of preparing something for Mrs Brown and he arrives, late as usual, and demands that I set up an experiment for him. But I can't just stop doing the other job, which was properly booked in. This makes him angry and he shouts at me. It upsets me each time it happens, but I've put up with it because I do like the school, and everyone else is very friendly, but now I really think it is impossible to go on. I had taken this job, rather than look for something in industry, because I only want a part time post until the children are a bit older. But now almost every day, just before it's time for me to go home, he comes to me with another big job to do, and if I suggest leaving it until the next morning, he's really sarcastic, and implies that I'm not pulling my weight. I have been late home every day for the last fortnight and Ruth cannot get in and has had to go to the neighbours. She's only six and yesterday, when I finally got home an hour late, she was quite weepy. I can't go on like this, so I shall have to resign.'

For action:

What are the issues involved in this case study?
Should the headteacher accept Anne's resignation?
What advice would you give this headteacher and why?

The head of Physics in this case study has been treating his technician with so little consideration that it almost amounts to harassment, and as a manager he seems to be singularly unsuccessful at creating a good working relationship with his technician. We do not know how regularly he loses technicians, nor how he treats his teaching colleagues, but his overall behaviour suggests that he is selfish, high-handed and inconsiderate. Nor does he seem to value any of Anne's work. If we take this scenario a little further, and picture what might happen if Anne resigns, this head of department could be left without a technician until a replacement is found. If his previous behaviour is anything to go by he is likely to grumble and be critical of how long it takes 'them' to find a replacement and the quality of what he gets. If this is a fair picture of what has happened, he cannot be allowed to continue in this way and the problem must be confronted.

If the headteacher wants to keep a trained and responsible technician Anne will have to be convinced that her work is valued and generally be treated better. Inviting Anne to attend Physics department meetings could make her feel more a member of the team, but her time constraint would make participation in after school sessions difficult. The headteacher should involve the head of Science, as the head of Physics' line manager, to resolve the immediate problem and to devise a longer term strategy to improve working relations. Management training for the head of Physics seems an obvious move but, for it to be successful, he has to understand why he needs it. (See also Chapter 8.)

Sometimes, however, the very experience and competence of a technician can create problems, as case study 11.4 indicates.

CASE STUDY 11.4. FOR ACTION

The head of Science has come to seek your advice. The problem centres on the Chemistry technician, Mrs Dodds. She is both knowledgeable and experienced, a graduate, who is working as a technician to keep her hand in while her family are still too young for her to seek a full time career. She has been with the department for a number of years. The head of Science regards Mrs Dodds as an asset to the department and values her judgement so highly that she frequently consults the technician about the best way to handle a topic. This year the department has taken on an NQT, a conscientious and hardworking teacher, whom she feels will eventually develop into a valuable member of the department, but who is currently experiencing some teething problems. She is rather shy and hesitant and Mrs Dodds' competence and confidence are making the NQT extremely nervous.

This is beginning to affect her relationship with the classes she teaches, and even more unfortunately it is inspiring Mrs Dodds' contempt and she is now treating the NQT in a rather high-handed way: 'There is almost role reversal, Mrs Dodds is giving Jane orders, not vice versa, and I think that she is becoming too dependent on her. What should I do?'

For action:

What are the issues raised in this case study?
You are the headteacher, what is your role in the situation?
What advice would you give the head of Science and why?

CASE STUDY 11.5. FOR ACTION

A deputation of angry technicians has arrived in your office clutching this week's edition of the local paper. They point to an advertisement which the school has placed for an assistant systems manager for Information Technology. 'What is wrong with the term technician?' they demand. 'We know that you are advertising for an IT technician. Why is he to be a systems manager, while we are called technicians? Are we being downgraded?' The biology technician is particularly incensed:

If I had realised that more hours were available, I would have offered to work them. Now that the kids are older I would have been pleased to have extended my time. Now there won't be any opportunity for me to do more. Why weren't we offered it first? Aren't we worth talking to? Why should we have to find out what is going on in this school by reading about it in the newspaper?

For action:

What are the management issues raised in this case study?
You are the headteacher – how should you respond to this deputation?
What advice would you give this headteacher and why?

Whereas some of the problems that concern technicians have arisen because they are overqualified for their jobs, the problems connected with the school office tend to be different in nature. The following case studies illustrate the kind of problems that may occur.

CASE STUDY 11.6. FOR ACTION/DISCUSSION

They think they know best!
Mike Wade, the deputy head in charge of staff development, is grumbling to his colleague, Yvonne Perkins:

> I put some forms into the office to be duplicated as part of our Investors in People initiative. I wanted a form to go to every department or section of the staff. I estimated this required about 40 forms and told the secretary so quite clearly. When I returned to collect the forms the pile was much smaller than I expected and so I counted it. There were only 19 forms, so I queried it with the secretary, only to be told self righteously that they had counted up, and as there were only 19 subject departments they had done the right number. I was horrified, as the whole point was to target every section, not just the subject departments. I was so angry that I made an issue of it. 'Is the office on the list of subject departments?' I demanded. 'No,' they said. 'Well, then you have not done a copy for your own department. Now please duplicate the additional 21 forms and next time check with me before you change my instructions!' The problem is that, because they process a lot of information, they get a superficial overview of things and then pass judgement on what the teaching staff do, when a lot of the time they have very limited understanding of what is really going on.

For action/discussion:

What issues are raised by this case study?
The deputy has raised the matter with the headteacher, what action should she take and why?

In case study 11.6 the deputy head has identified one of the problems which may arise if the office is not well managed. The previous head had not concerned himself with the activities of the school office and as a result it had developed bad habits. Case study 11.7 explores this situation.

CASE STUDY 11.7. FOR ACTION

The office at Bestwick Park High School was a very friendly place. Visitors who came into the school were made welcome, teachers would stop for a chat when passing through the office and the pupils queued at the office window for attention. It seemed a hub of activity. What Brenda Gatlin found, however, after she had been in the school for long enough to see things for what they really were, was that productivity in the office was very low. This was due partly because the telephone never stopped ringing, and the secretary seemed to do little but answer the telephone, making her output in terms of secretarial work extremely low. The office was actually very disorganised. Brenda would go through the week's priorities with her secretary on Monday morning, but unless she chivvied constantly no progress seemed to be made and the priorities did not get through to the other office staff. Important letters were neglected or mislaid and deadlines seemed to be an unknown concept, yet the secretary and two part time assistants always seemed to be working. Their work appeared well presented, but you had to check it carefully because the incidence of errors was high and you could not be sure that letters had been sent to their intended destination, or indeed that they had been sent at all. On a number of occasions Brenda had found herself faced with a different set of parents from those she had been told to expect, presented with the wrong set of pupil notes or, even more embarrassingly, double booked. 'Sorry, we forgot' or 'Whoops, we've got it wrong again!' became an increasingly irritating feature of life with the office. Indeed her deputy, who was thoroughly fed up with this state of affairs, claimed that if you weren't told it was the office, you'd think it was the school social club.

For action:

What were the main problems and why were they occurring so regularly?
What strategies would you suggest for improving the performance of the office staff?
What advice would you give this headteacher and why?

The school office holds a central position in ensuring the efficient running of the school, but the office at Bestwick Park had become a liability instead of an asset. The new headteacher must confront the problem because the office clearly could not continue to perform so ineffectively. She would have to raise the matter either through a meeting with her secretary or with the whole office staff. She should record the meeting and subsequent actions in case the matter should become contentious. One way of approaching such a sensitive issue is to explain to the office staff that a new regime and changing demands necessitate a change in working practices, and that they needed to review as a team how to meet the new demands.

Strategies for improving performance

- Making the office staff log all their activities for a week could help to bring it home to them how much/little they do or achieve.
- Datestamping letters etc as they arrive so that you can monitor how long it takes to deal with them.
- Limiting personal telephone calls to one per person per day.
- Buying an answerphone for use when the office is under pressure.
- If punctuality is an issue, getting the office personnel to clock in and out.
- Setting weekly or daily targets. This will necessitate prioritising work and time for unexpected but urgent tasks must be included. This will also involve allocating work to particular members of the office staff with and giving them a timescale.
- Looking at how the office is arranged. Are they working too closely together? Can the secretary answers the phone be relocated so that she causes minimal disturbance?
- Having a job appraisal interview with each member of the office staff, which could also be an opportunity for making observations on how they work. Monitoring individual performance will help you analyse where the main problems are and through appraisal you can give each member of staff written personal targets. It also allows you to review development needs and arrange training to improve skills or general performance. The fact that non-teaching staff appraisal is linked to pay will give it bite.
- Reviewing the management structure of the office. Would the secretary respond to being given responsibility for managing her team, or is she so far into bad habits that this could not work? An alternative strategy could be to make the bursar, who was extremely efficient, responsible for supervising the office.
- Unrelenting supervision is clearly the key to this problem and a weekly review of progress is essential. Making a fuss about

mistakes will convey the message that such a high level of errors is unacceptable. Make quite clear to the office who is boss and what standard is expected.

- Praising improvement when it occurs could help build loyalty.

CASE STUDY 11.8. FOR ACTION

As part of her efforts to improve the office the headteacher brought in management consultants. One of the things they uncovered was that the staff had different titles and status, for example head's secretary, secretary or assistant, but, although their hours and pay might vary considerably, their job descriptions indicated that they were performing identical tasks. This made some of the office staff very angry and for the second time in a few weeks the head found herself faced with a deputation of furious support staff.

For action:

What are the management issues raised by this case study?
What advice would you give this headteacher and why?

The comments made by the management consultants about the various posts held by the clerical staff made the senior management team (SMT) think more clearly about the nomenclature and workload of other posts held by associate staff or by volunteers.

CASE STUDY 11.9. FOR ACTION

The school had always had a part-time librarian. She was not a teacher, not actually a qualified librarian, but an enthusiast who loved the library, worked well beyond the hours stated in her contract and regularly took work home. Under the new head's direction the library was becoming a study/resources area. New technology was being introduced, and to provide the librarian with much needed help the head had appealed in the parents' newsletter for volunteers to help run the library and provide assistance for the pupils throughout the school week. There was a good response, with the result that there was someone working in the school library at all times during the school day. The librarian found, however, she had a department of staff to manage in an area where she was actually an amateur. Her lack of experience as a manager worried her, and she was concerned that this group of staff were unpaid volunteers – how can you manage volunteers? There was also the issue that she was called 'the librarian' and paid a salary, her assistants were called 'library helpers' and not paid, yet they all seemed to do much the same work.

For action:

What are the issues raised by this case study?
What are the advantages to the school of the change to the system?
What problems does it bring?
What advice would you give the headteacher in dealing with the problems?

The management consultants also reviewed the role of the bursar in the school.

CASE STUDY 11.10. FOR ACTION

The bursar had been appointed by the previous headteacher and her role and job description were historic. The management consultants suggested that Mrs Gatlin should review the bursar's role and use a highly efficient and proactive worker more effectively. A part time assistant bursar already existed. The consultants suggested her hours could be extended to include the routine tasks of the bursar's work, while Sarah Adams assumed more of the financial management which took up much of the head's time. As part of her new role Sarah began to attend SMT meetings. Although the head had explained to the SMT why she had asked Sarah to attend, to her surprise they reacted negatively. When she asked her deputy why the SMT was so hostile Mrs Perkins said bluntly:

Haven't you been reading your *Times Educational Supplement* over the past few weeks? There are descriptions in every edition of how schools have found it more cost effective to employ a bursar than a second deputy head. You know that Fred is due to retire this summer and the senior teachers will all apply for his job. You're sending them messages that there might not be a job to apply for, as you're thinking of not replacing Fred and putting Sarah into the SMT instead of having a second deputy. It's not surprising that they don't like the idea. I've been wanting to ask you if it's true.

For action:

What are the management issues raised in this case study?
What mistakes has the headteacher made in handling the matter?
What advice would you give to the headteacher and why?

For action/discussion:
What are the issues raised by this case study?
Managing change is always a test of a headteacher's skill. How would you introduce and manage the kind of exercise suggested above?

Case study 11.10 raises a fundamental issue for you as a manager. Cost effective use of support or associate staff could save a school time and money and Mrs Gatlin may well want to continue to use the consultants or create a task group to review whether some of the tasks currently undertaken by the SMT would be better done by an administrative officer. It could be argued that 'senior managers (on relatively high salaries) should be freed from much of the financial and administrative minutiae so as to be able to devote more of their time to their leadership role' (Mortimore and Mortimore with Thomas, 1994).

Similarly, in a climate of constantly increasing demands upon teachers' time, and inadequate budgets, schools may have to take a hard look at which of the tasks teachers currently carry out don't need to be done by teachers, and think about what effects increasing administrative or technician time would have, both on the number of teachers employed and on contact time. Whatever decisions are taken, this exercise could be very threatening for the different groups of staff and would need sensitive handling.

Schools are staffed mostly and managed exclusively by teachers. There is a tendency for teacher-led management to choose to have smaller classes (and more teachers) than other more innovative ways of organising the school. Teachers are bound to remain as core staff because their role is so fundamental to the work of a school. But what the delegated powers of LMS have allowed and what the case studies have shown is that it is possible to consider anew who should carry out all those tasks not directly related to pedagogy, but currently use up teachers' time. (Mortimore and Mortimore with Thomas, 1994).

Case study 11.11 highlighted the issue of associate staff as managers and how threatening this development could be to the school's SMT. Unlike the bursar, the caretaker is rarely invited to SMT meetings as yet, but his/her role is a pivotal one, as good caretaking is crucial to the appearance of the school. The caretaker interacts with visitors and contract staff, and is the school's representative on site when everyone else has gone home. His manner can affect the public's image of the school, as the case study below illustrates.

CASE STUDY 11.11. FOR ACTION

When the local play group asked if it could book a room for several weeks in the summer holiday with the option of using it again at Easter Brenda Gatlin, was delighted. It would bring in much needed income and at the same time would give help out to the local community by providing facilities. Jim Spicer, the caretaker, was however far from pleased with the news. Intensely loyal to the school, Jim had been caretaker for as long as anyone could remember. He was extremely hardworking and liked the school to look spick and span at all times. He used the holidays to get the school into good order and the thought of a multitude of small children creating havoc all round the place appalled him. But Brenda insisted, and although Jim grumbled non-stop for the rest of term, he seemed to have accepted that he had to make the best of things. The play group duly came, but rang up after the holiday to say that they would not be taking up their option on further bookings as the facilities didn't quite meet their needs. Brenda suspected that Jim had been so disobliging and put so many difficulties in their way that the play group had decided to look for another venue.

For action:

What are the issues raised in this case study?
The caretaker's attitude to his job had cost the school dearly both in terms of cash and goodwill. How do you get the caretaker to understand and apply the mission statement spelt out in your development plan?

What advice would you give the headteacher and why?

Perhaps the lesson of this case study is the need for a forum in which representatives of the associate staff meet regularly with a member of senior management to discuss matters affecting the development of the school. This could help them understand why incidents which seem unimportant to them reduce you to incoherent fury. For example, it might make the cleaners (a contract firm) more anxious to conform to the non-smoking policy operated by everyone else in the school. You may also find it useful to invite the relevant representative of the associate staff to senior management meetings whenever an item directly connected with them arises.

Skills and techniques in managing associate staff

The case studies described in this chapter highlight some of the problems and issues which may arise in managing the associate staff and include discussion of their roles, job descriptions, status and pay, and their relationship with the teachers.

Employing associate staff presents you with both a challenge and an opportunity as a manager. It is an opportunity because it allows you to be innovative in how you use and deploy staff, and gives worthwhile employment to some people who might previously have had very limited career choice. It could facilitate learning because it brings additional skills and expertise into the school and, if used efficiently, should free teachers from tasks other than teaching and allow them to spend more time on their professional role. It is a challenge for you as a manager to use the opportunity effectively and because you have to work towards creating one staff from two disparate groups.

What kind of skills and techniques do you need in order to manage these problems successfully? Almost all the case studies concerned aspects of *managing people* and to deal with most of the problems discussed you would certainly need to draw on your interpersonal and conflict management skills (see Chapters 5 and 8).

Much however has been about *managing change and development*. If you want to introduce innovative ideas in respect of staffing, you do not want to encounter wholesale resistance because they are incompletely understood or communicated and because people feel threatened by them. I have written fully about this topic elsewhere (Nathan, 1991, especially Chapter 3), and suggest that if you need detailed guidance, you should peruse a work of this kind. A quick checklist however can be a very useful means of focusing our thoughts.

Factors affecting successful change in schools

- change requires support and pressure
- each change has two components – content and process
- headteachers have the most important role in managing change
- change needs to be communicated fully to those involved
- staff need to be convinced of the need for change
- individuals need to take ownership of change
- effective change needs clear plans and procedures
- moving towards small concrete goals works better than setting vast targets, no matter how desirable the latter
- each stage needs to be assimilated for the next to succeed
- past experience of successful/unsuccessful change influences attitudes and expectations
- change works best in an organisation which has been trained to accept change.

We have also discussed creating the attitudes in which change can take place successfully, for example how formal or informally the school was organised, whether it was customary for members of the associate staff to attend staff or senior management meetings and how difficult it would be to change people's feelings about their presence. With this in mind it could be useful for you to spend some time with your middle and senior managers in reviewing your organisational structures because clarity helps motivate and support staff and in some of the more innovative posts the boundaries have not been clearly drawn. It could also be a worthwhile exercise to look again at any organisational analysis you have done (eg staff questionnaires for Investors in People) and think about what these surveys revealed. All too frequently one hears headteachers say, 'It wasn't until I did the gap analysis for Investors in People that I realised that I was answering a lot of the questions with "Yes, except for the support staff!" '

Providing appropriate training and staff development for those involved is also an important factor in managing change. In the past restrictions on how you spent the school's Grants for Education Support and Training (GEST) budget made it difficult to include associate staff in the staff development programme. Now more flexibility exists and the Inset coordinator's plans should take account of their needs. Remember that many of the associate staff are part timers and that the Inset sessions may not fit their working schedule, in much the same way as departmental meetings were not always convenient. The advice here is always to *offer* the opportunity and to stress the value of the training. Part time teachers often attend Inservice days in proportion to the amount of time they work (and according to their level of interest in or involvement in a particular initiative) and this could serve as a guide for associate staff.

The appraisal programme for associate staff is also extremely useful in managing staff development because it enables you to discuss an individual's development needs both in relation to whole school development and their personal career development, and to home in on where the individual fits into the scheme of things. In a primary school the headteacher is most likely to conduct these appraisals personally, but in a secondary school the appraiser is more likely to be the line manager. It is important therefore that associate staff appraisal does not just get by on the nod but plays a central role in their development. To ensure this some training may need to be provided for the appraisers. In case study 11.9 the librarian suddenly found herself a manager with responsibility for her team of helpers – she too may need some management training if she is to carry out her new role effectively.

Bibliography

Adair, J (1973) *Action Centred Leadership*, MacGraw Hill, Maidenhead.

Audit Commission (1986) *Towards Better Management of Secondary Education*, HMSO, London.

Back, Ken and Back, Kate with Bates, Terry (1982) *Assertiveness at Work*, London.

Balchin, R (1993) *Governors and Heads in Grant Maintained Schools*, Longman, Harlow.

Belbin, R M (1981) *Management Teams: Why they Succeed or Fail*, Heinemann, London.

Bennis, W G (1985) 'Leadership in the 21st Century', *Journal of Organisational Change Management*, **2**, 1.

Blake, R and Moulton, J (1978) *The New Managerial Grid*, Gulf Publishing Co, Houston, Texas.

Bolam, R (1986) 'The first two years of the NDC: A progress report', *School Organisation*, **6**, 1, 1–16.

Bramson, R M (1981) *Coping with Difficult People*, Bantam Doubleday Dell, New York.

Bridges, E (1992) *The Incompetent Teacher*, Stanford Series on Education and Public Policy, revised edn, Falmer Press, Brighton.

Davies, B, Ellison, L, Osborne, A and Westburnham, J (1991) *Education Management for the 1990s*, Longman, Harlow.

Dean, J (1985) *Managing The Secondary School*, Croom Helm, Beckenham.

Department for Education (DfE) (1995) *Governing Bodies and Effective Schools*, DfE, Ofsted and Banking Information Service, London.

Donelly, J (1992) *The School Management Handbook*, Kogan Page, London.

Drucker, P F (1968) *The Practice of Management*, Pan, London.

Drucker, P F (1990) *The Effective Executive*, Pan, London.

Drummond, H (1990) *Managing Difficult Staff: Effective Procedures and the Law*, Kogan Page, London.

Elliott Kemp, J and Williams, G L (1980) *The DION Handbook*, Sheffield City Polytechnic, Sheffield.

Everard, B (1986) *Developing Management in Schools*, Blackwell, Oxford.

Everard, B and Morris, G (1985) *Effective School Management*, Harper & Row, London.

Fiddler, B and Cooper, R (1992) *Staff Appraisal in Schools and Colleges*, Longman, Harlow.

Firth, D (ed) (1985) *School Management in Practice*, Longman, Harlow.

Galtter, R, Preedy, M, Riches, C and Masterson, M (1988) *Understanding School Management*, Open University Press, Buckingham.

Handy, C (1976) *Understanding Organizations*, Penguin, Harmondsworth.

Handy, C (1989) *The Age of Unreason*, Hutchinson, London.

Handy, C (1994) *The Empty Raincoat*, Hutchinson, London.

Handy, C and Aiken, R (1986) *Understanding Schools as Organizations*, Penguin, Harmondsworth.

Hersy, P and Blanchard, K (1982) *Management of Organizational Behaviour: Utilizing Human Resources*, Prentice Hall, Englewood Cliffs, New Jersey.

Herzberg, F (1974) *Work and the Nature of Man*, Granada, London.

Hoyle, E and Macmahon, A (eds) (1986) *The Management of Schools*, Kogan Page, London.

Hughes, M (1973) *Secondary School Administration: A Management Approach*, 2nd edn, Pergamon Press, Oxford.

Hume, C (1991) *Grievance and Discipline in Schools*, Agit School Governor Training Series, Longman, Harlow.

Hume, C (1993) *Effective Staff Selection in Schools*, Agit School Governor Training Series, Longman, Harlow.

Hunt, J W (1986) *Managing People at Work: A Manager's Guide to Behaviour in Organisations*, revised edn, McGraw Hill, Maidenhead.

Jenkins, H O (1991) *Getting It Right*, Blackwell, Oxford.

Jones, A (1987) *Leadership for Tomorrow's Schools*, Blackwell, Oxford.

Kyriaxou, C and Sutcliff, J (1978) 'A Model of Teacher Stress', *Educational Studies*, **4**, 1.

Maslow, A H (1954) *Motivation and Personality*, Harper & Row, New York.

Mortimore, P (forthcoming) *Innovative Staffing Policies in City Technology Colleges*, Economic and Social Research Council (ESRC), London.

Mortimore, P and Mortimore, J with Thomas, H (1994) *Managing Associate Staff: Non-teaching staff in primary and seconday schools*, Management in Education Series, Paul Chapman, London.

Murgatroyd, S (1986) 'Management teams and the promotion of staff well-being', *School Organisation*, **6**, 1.

Nathan, M (1991) *Senior Management in Schools: A Survival Guide*, Blackwell, Oxford.

Nathan, M and Kemp, R (1989) *Middle Management in Schools: A Survival Guide*, Blackwell, Oxford.

National Foundation for Education Research (NFER) (1987) *Secondary Headship: The First Years*, NFER/Wilson, Windsor.

Nias, J (1980) 'Leadership styles and job satisfaction in primary schools', in *Approaches to School Management*, T Bush *et al* (eds), Harper & Row, London.

Nicholson, R (1989) *School Management: The Role of the Secondary Headteacher*, Kogan Page, London.

Office for Standards in Education (Ofsted) (1994) *Handbook for the Inspection of Schools*, HMSO, London.

Peters, T J (1987) *Thriving on Chaos*, Harper & Row, London.

Peters, T J and Waterman, R H (1982) *In Search of Excellence*, Harper & Row, London.

Rogers, K (1963) *Managers' Personality and Performance*, Tavistock, London.

Rutter, P, Maughan, B, Mortimore, P and Ouston, J (1979) *Fifteen Thousand Hours*, Open Books, London.

Secondary Heads' Association (SHA) (1989) *If it Moves: A Study of the Role of the Deputy Head*, Secondary Heads' Association Press, Leicester.

Stevens, D B (1991) *Under New Management*, Secondary Heads' Association, Longman, Harlow.

Stewart, V and Stewart, A (1983) *Managing the Poor Performer*, Gower Press, London.

Sutton, J (1985) *School Management in Practice*, Longman, Harlow.

Todd, R and Dennison, W (1978) 'The changing role of the deputy headteacher in English secondary schools', *Educational Review*, 1978.

Torrington, D and Weightman, J (1985) *The Business of Management*, Prentice Hall, Hemel Hempstead.

Torrington, D and Weightman, J (1989) *Management and Organisation in Secondary Schools: A Training Handbook*, Blackwell, Oxford.

Trethowan, D (1985) *Target Setting*, Management in Schools Series Pamphlet, Industrial Society Press, London.

Trethowan, D (1985) *Teamwork in Schools*, Management in Schools Series Pamphlet, Industrial Society Press, London.

Trethowan, D (1991) *Managing with Appraisal*, Management in Education Series, Paul Chapman, London.

Warwick, D (1982) *Effective Meetings*, Management in Schools Series Pamphlet, Industrial Society Press, London.

Weindling, D and Earley, P (1987) *Secondary Headship: The First Years*, National Foundation for Educational Research, NFER/ Nelson, Windsor.

Westburnham, J (1991) 'Human resource mangement in schools', in *Education Management for the 1990s*, B Davies *et al* (eds), Longman, Harlow.

Wheeler, G E (1971) 'Organization stress' in *College Management Readings and Cases*, D D Simmons (ed), The Further Education Staff College, Bristol.

White, P (1983) Foreword to *Delegation Industrial Society*, D Trethowan, Management in Schools Series Pamphlet, Industrial Society Press, London.

White, P (1984) Foreword to *The Leadership of Schools*, D Trethowan, Management in Schools Series Pamphlet, Industrial Society Press, London.

Working Partners, Hawkshead/DFE, distributed by Educational Distribution Services, Peterborough, Cambridge.

Index